Physical Education, Sport and Schooling
Studies in the Sociology of Physical Education

Edited by
John Evans

 The Falmer Press

(A member of the Taylor & Francis Group)
London, New York and Philadephia

UK   The Falmer Press, Falmer House, Barcombe, Lewes, East Sussex, BN8 5DL

USA   The Falmer Press, Taylor & Francis Inc., 242 Cherry Street, Philadelphia, PA 19106-1906

First published 1986

Library of Congress Cataloging in Publication Data

Physical education, sport, and schooling.

1. Physical education and training—Social aspects.
I. Evans, John.
GV342.27.P49   1986   613.7   86-13372
ISBN 1-85000-116-2
ISBN 1-85000-117-0 (pbk.)

Typeset in 10/12 Bembo by
Imago Publishing Ltd, Thame, Oxon

Printed in Great Britain by Taylor & Francis (Printers) Ltd, Basingstoke

Physical Education, Sport and Schooling

For Rhianedd and Ceryn

Contents

Contents

Figures and Tables

1 Introduction: 'Personal Troubles and Public Issues'. Studies in the Sociology of Physical Education

John Evans

In Britain today, the physical education curriculum is in a state of flux. For many PE teachers, as for their academic counterparts, the practices of decades have suddenly become quite problematic rather than acceptable features of their teaching and curriculum. For example, the way in which the curriculum is and has conventionally been organized and differentiated for boys and girls, the principles upon which pupils are grouped for teaching purposes, the content of the curriculum and the attitudes so often expressed in the course of teaching the subject are now the subjects of critical scrutiny. The reasons for this are of course as varied as they are complex. Since the mid 1970s education has occupied a changing world. Teachers have been forced to contend with the effects of a falling birth rate which has often had dramatic effect on the levels of resource and curriculum organization and content inside secondary schools and the British economy has entered a deep and prolonged recession. Unemployment especially amongst young people has accelerated dramatically, its level both in the narrow age band 16–19 and in the broader age band 16–24 category being disproportionately high. In mid-1985 the UK figure stood at 1.2 million and well over 20 per cent of the age group not still in full-time education. For the foreseeable future the rate of reduction in unemployment in general is likely to be low, with youth unemployment in particular remaining higher even as general employment levels improve (Marsland, 1985).

Against this background, dissatisfaction among pupils, parents, employers and politicians has steadily grown in recent years and the task of teaching has become increasingly problematic. As Davies has argued,

> dumping 10 per cent or more of the work force into unemployment designed to cure inflation and put the lower orders back in their pre-Keynsian place has inevitably reacted rather powerfully on the way children, about to be disproportionately unemployed, think

about proper classroom performance and educational participation. (1984, p. 167)

The educational honeymoon inaugurated in the sixties is over. Neither an expansionist education policy nor a change in the overall organization of schooling in the direction of comprehensive forms has greatly improved the quality of the educational experience, or the levels of educational opportunity made available to the majority of the secondary school population. Nor indeed, has it seemed to have much influence on the attitudes of children towards PE and post-school sport and leisure (see Hendry chapter 3). Indeed as we and others have argued (see Ball, 1984, Davies and Evans, 1984, Evans, 1985) it would have been more surprising if it had. Despite surface changes in the organization of schools, little has happened in terms of educational change within them. The majority of schools called comprehensive are pursuing educational policies as meritocratic and selective as ever they were in the days prior to re-organization (see Ball, 1982, 1984; Evans, 1985). The PE curriculum is no exception in this respect. As Hendry reminds us in chapter 3, Whitehead and Hendry reported in 1976 that 'overall much of the content of secondary boys' PE programmes is such that one might have seen in the schools over 20 years ago' (1976, p. 38), while for girls, much also remained the same but for a bit more 'educational gymnastics'. They concluded that 'the content of the secondary school curriculum seems not to have changed as radically as many have believed'. (*ibid*, p. 41)

However, against the background of economic, social and technological change, schools in Britain have begun to face a threefold challenge from the DES, an expansionist Manpower Services Commission (MSC) and popular demands for a more 'relevant' curriculum. A second re-structuring of the education system (Ranson, 1984) has begun to take place inside schools, which has brought into focus the relationships between education and the world of work, non-work and, to a lesser degree, to post-school 'leisure'. Inside schools teachers have become increasingly preoccupied with their own standing in the organization and for physical education teachers this has often meant in addition, a concern not only for their own status within the school community but also for their very survival in the curriculum, a concern often most immediately felt in the form of a 'threat' to (PE) provision for the upper secondary age range. Physical education teachers as those in all areas of the school curriculum have been faced with the problem of how best to respond to a growing number of indifferent learners, how to provide for the less 'able' or those who lag behind, how much to yield to public pressures for relatively greater emphasis on basic skills, or for more sporting success, curricular relevance and vocational training. Meanwhile inside the professional group, from a number of quarters, appeals have emerged for new forms of curricula, for example, more health related fitness, new forms of games teaching, and better curriculum planning (Arnold, 1985).

The PE curriculum and its context are then in volatile states. Yet PE teachers have hardly been provided with the kind of support in the form of qualitative research evidence which might help them address the problems of curricular change or to assess the merits or otherwise of extant, or innovatory practices. Sociological research as Evans and Davies argue in chapter 2, has badly neglected the physical area of the school curriculum. This volume represents one small attempt to begin to redress this imbalance.

Our central focus is upon the curricular activities, games and sports which make up the Physical Education curriculum in schools and other 'Outdoor' educational institutions. We relate it to the culture, interpretive activity and the meanings which people (teachers and pupils) attach to and derive from the social world which constitutes the context of PE teaching. At the broadest level the contributions to this book are together concerned to raise questions about the origins and purpose of Physical Education in contemporary British society. They explore the nature of current, traditional, and innovatory practices and consider their implications for the perspectives and identities of teachers and their pupils. The theoretical starting positions represented in each of the chapters are quite varied but they are intentionally not allowed to dominate the discussion. The purpose of this book is not to provide a detailed introduction to the variety of theoretical positions within sociology which might be brought to bear on the study of Physical Education and sport (see, Hargreaves J., 1982) although it is of course our hope that the chapters will leave the reader wanting to know more about them. Most of the studies contained in this book can be located broadly within what might be termed an interpretive paradigm (see Dawes, 1970 and Wilson, 1971). The term interpretive sociology in fact refers to a variety of sociologies, to the symbolic interactionist position of G.H. Mead; the phenomenology of A. Schutz and the ethnomethodology of H. Garfinkel and A. Cicourel.[1] Although these positions have many marked dissimilarities (see Denzin, 1971) they have common themes and share similar concerns, at the heart of which is a common desire to understand how people interpret, negotiate, attach meaning to and construct the social and cultural worlds which they occupy. They insist that human beings play an *active* role in the social world. They are not as Garfinkel (1967) so colourfully put it, simply 'cultural dopes' programmed to behave in standard ways by socializing agencies, whether of family, school or peers. In recent years a growing number of studies of classrooms have been inspired by interpretive sociologies, sometimes combined with a variety of Marxisms (see Hargreaves and Woods, 1985). The major method of research utilized by sociologists adopting an interpretive perspective (see chapters by Bell, Kirk, Humberstone, Embrey, and Sparkes) is ethnography, and we will say a little more about this method of research in chapter 2.

Focussing on meaning and activity through observation as they do, the studies in this book touch upon and illuminate some of the problems and dilemmas which many Physical Education teachers and pupils in Britain's schools now routinely experience. The chapters by Hendry, Bell, Embrey, Kirk and Almond vividly point out that the context of Physical Education teaching in Britain today is one which is often highly problematic for both teachers *and* pupils. This can be especially the case for those teachers involved in curriculum innovations which are often as nebulous in definition as they are unpredictable in outcome (see Kirk, chapter 9) and which may require significant shifts in the thinking of teachers and their methods of teaching. Here, as in the situation of acute marginality, which Bell portrays in chapter 5, teaching PE can mean experiencing tensions or 'trouble' felt at both the personal and the professional level. It is clear that the pressures to which teachers are subject, are typically experienced in very particular, always local school circumstances. But they also index issues concerning the very nature of schooling, the process and purpose of Physical Education within it, and the kind of society for which children are being prepared. In this respect the investigations presented in this book span a distinction which C.W. Mills made, many years ago, between personal 'troubles' and public 'issues', a distinction which is an essential tool of the sociological imagination (Mills, C.W., 1959) and which it is hoped will lead the reader into consideration of such broader issues via more immediate concerns with 'problems' which may confront them routinely in their PE teaching.

In these terms the apparently private or personal 'troubles' confronting teachers of Physical Education in schools today may stem from how best to effect changes in teaching methods, or how to implement innovations in curriculum organization or content. In daily practice they may well be most acutely experienced as problems of how to motivate pupils, confront dissent or accommodate in oneself and others the changes in attitude or value which new forms of curricular or grouping policy might inevitably demand. Clearly these 'troubles', which ultimately have to be either 'lived with' or resolved by teachers in the departmental and school circumstances, relate to much broader 'public' issues that transcend local environments of the individual and the range of his or her inner life.

> An issue is a public matter, debate is often without form if only because it is the very nature of an issue, unlike even widespread trouble, that it cannot very well be defined in terms of the immediate and everyday environment of ordinary men. An issue, in fact, often involves a crisis in institutional arrangements, and often too it involves what Marxists call 'contradictions' or 'antagonisms'. (Mills, C.W., 1959, p. 15)

This distinction, between personal 'troubles' and public issues offers a useful reminder (voiced in many of the chapters in this book) that there are unlikely to be any simple solutions at the individual teacher level to widespread social and economic problems, whether these 'solutions' are framed in terms of 'leisure education', or new forms of grouping or curricular practice. The issues addressed in this book, via a focus on substantive topics, have to do with the state of secondary schooling (see Bell, chapter 5), unemployment and its impact upon schools and Physical Education in particular, inequalities in society and the differential treatment afforded to people because of their class (see Hendry, chapter 3) gender (see Scraton, chapter 4 and Humberstone, chapter 11) or colour (see Carrington and Leaman, chapter 12), and at the broadest level, the kind of society and values which schools in general and the Physical Education curriculum in particular may be helping to reinforce, reproduce or challenge.

In the next chapter the discussion will try to trace some of the changes towards the study of schooling which have occurred within the sociology of education in recent years. Our intention, it should be stressed, is not to provide a detailed overview either of the sociology of education (see CCCS, 1981, or Davies, 1984) or of the sociology of PE and sport. This has been more than adequately done elsewhere (see Jenkins, 1982, Hargreaves, 1982, Tomlinson, 1982). Our aim is much more modestly to offer a framework in relation to which the rest of studies presented in this book might reasonably be viewed. In so doing we will also try to illustrate how some of the approaches adopted and the questions raised within the sociology of education in recent years might usefully be applied to the study of the PE curriculum and emphasize how great is the need for further *qualitative* sociological research if we are to achieve a better professional understanding of the nature and purpose of this subject in contemporary British schools and society.

The contributions to this book are then organized into two sections. The first deals with features of the contemporary 'conventional' physical education scene and the second with innovatory or 'alternative' practices. Although the majority of the chapters deal with physical education, mostly as it is experienced by pupils and teachers in secondary school, it is hoped that the issues raised concerning sex differentiation, labelling, departmental management, the nature and quality of teaching, innovation etc., will hopefully span the boundaries of the educational subjects and stages.

The chapter by Hendry (chapter 3) goes some way towards setting the contemporary scene of PE in Britain today, and provides an empirical backdrop against which the rest of the studies in this book can be viewed. Drawing upon a substantial amount of empirical research into physical education, much of it undertaken by himself and his co-workers in recent years, the chapter provides an overview of physical education teaching and teachers in secondary schools and considers some of its limitations. The chapter also considers the importance of school sport and leisure to young people in contemporary British schools and society. Hendry locates physical education within a context of social, economic and technological change, to raise questions about the nature of educational practice within a society in which unemployment inescapably looms large in the experience of post-school youth. He explores the leisure interests of young people and the effects of youth unemployment on their leisure patterns. Clearly, for Hendry, the 'solution' to economic and social problems is not to be found solely in a physical education leisure programme. He argues for a form of leisure education, which involves a more substantial re-orientation within the present forms of educational practice and a weakening of the boundaries between schools and the communities they serve. Like Roberts (1984) and Corrigan (1982), Hendry is cautious about prescribing simple solutions to deeply entrenched social and economic problems. Unemployment cannot simply be equated with more free or leisure time. As Corrigan has more poignantly stated, 'the trouble with being unemployed is that you never get a day off' (1982). Schools are no panacea for this economic problem. However, physical education teachers collectively bear a responsibility to address the question of how they might alleviate the traumas of transition into a society where work might feature only occasionally, or for some, hardly at all and Hendry's chapter asks us to begin to seriously question both the nature of contemporary PE and more broadly the organization and content of secondary schooling.

Sheila Scraton (chapter 4) further explores some of the limitations of current practice and addresses the question of how the physical education curriculum got to where it is today in terms of the differentiated grouping policies which feature so prominently, and asks why these organizational practices persist in so many schools. Her analyses combine a discussion of the historical development of girls' physical education with an account of current qualitative research carried out in a large northern LEA. Drawing upon data from extensive interviews with physical education advisors and lecturers and heads of girls physical education as well as detailed observation, the discussion reveals that stereotypical conceptions and attitudes towards boys and girls, are deeply sedimented in the perspectives and practices of PE teachers. From its inception physical education developed on the premise that girls required equal but different opportunities for physical education. The ideologies of physical ability and capacity, motherhood and sexuality, implicit in the development of physical education, have been deeply integrated into its traditions and practices. Scraton goes on to suggest that effecting change in the practices of teachers and the attitudes of girls is likely to require support at levels of policy and practice both within and outside the school system.

Bell (chapter 5) takes us even more deeply into the management of PE departments, exploring some of the problems experienced by physical education departmental heads of two large comprehensive schools. Physical Education in secondary schools, as Bell argues, has conventionally placed a great deal of emphasis upon games and the provision of competitions inside and more importantly, outside the school (an emphasis which others in this book have endeavoured to countervail, see Almond, chapter 8). Their organization has demanded a high degree of commitment and time on the part of physical educational teachers. This commitment has, in turn, been sustained by a degree of job satisfaction and by the expectation of relatively early promotion within physical education departments followed by a career structure into other areas such as pastoral care, thus avoiding the 'age trap' to which physical education teachers are especially susceptible. All of this has, until recently, been possible within an expanding education service. However, this situation is now changing rapidly. Drawing upon his ethnographic research, Bell compares the management problems of physical education teachers in the departments of two comprehensive schools. The discussion focuses on the difficulties and dilemmas which faced these teachers in a context of falling rolls, reduced expenditure and the blocking of usual avenues of promotion. He shows how organizational and social pressures can lead to modifications in the physical education curriculum not for educational or ideological reasons but because of changes in staff commitments. Bell's chapter points to the stark realities of a physical education teacher's world in British schools today. It emphasizes how problematic is the teacher's task and the difficulties of effecting substantial and lasting educational change.

Carroll and Embrey (chapters 6 and 7) also take the reader deeply into the thinking of teachers today, to consider how the perspectives of teachers and others involved in the sporting scene may influence the identities of children. Carroll examines how pupils are labelled in the physical education curriculum and in particular, how certain pupils are able to achieve 'troublemaker' status in the teacher's perspective. Much of the available research in physical education has, to date, glossed the labelling process. Carroll, by attempting to penetrate teacher consciousness is able to trace in some detail the nature of their typifications or labels, consider when they are used, the behavioural cues which teachers perceive in applying them and how teachers rationalize and explain their behaviour and that of their pupils. Embrey's chapter continues with the theme of labelling, to paint a novel picture of the distinct and separate cultural worlds which constitute school and club football. Clearly football is not a uniform or homogeneous phenomena. As the content of Embrey's chapter suggests, it may constitute one game but it operates within two cultures. This can present severe problems not only for the pupils/players who routinely have to try to interpret and make sense of the different rule systems, values and expectations operating within club and school, but also for teachers who are forced to contend with levels of dissent and deviancy which are often inextricably connected to their own attitudes and practice and the massive cultural divide between community and school.

In the second section of the book the first three chapters concentrate attention on attempts made by teachers and lecturers in higher education to effect changes in the curriculum and teaching of physical education in schools. As the earlier chapters may have indicated, while much may be in need of change, the possibilities of achieving innovation in the present conditions of work are very often severely limited. While the chapters in this section vividly endorse this view they also go on to stress that some change is both possible and highly desirable. The chapters by Almond, Kirk, Sparkes and Humberstone in this section all draw upon detailed research work carried out either with teachers, or on teachers in their places of work. Indeed much of the challenge to the PE curriculum in Britain today has emanated not from the discipline of sociology applied to education but from the multidisciplinary field of curriculum studies. At Loughborough, Len Almond has been instrumental in stimulating debate of this nature. In chapter 8 he outlines a research project on games teaching, in which teachers were involved in translating the notion of 'teaching for understanding' into practice while also monitoring their own performances. This chapter along with those of Kirk and Sparkes demonstrate only too clearly how difficult it is for teachers to accommodate new ideas into their conventional thinking and practice, how severe are the restrictions on a teacher's time to engage in research and evaluation and how little support is available to sustain and carry through an innovative idea, particularly when teacher research is considered an essential part of the evaluation process. Kirk, like Sparkes, draws on lengthy periods of observation, to reveal that the problems of implementing a health related fitness programme, can have as much to do with the inherent ambiguity of 'new ideas' as with the 'conservative' attitudes of those in the broader school context. Unsurprisingly, teachers tend to know more clearly what they are changing from, than changing to and Sparkes (chapter 10) reveals in some detail the difficult stages of transition in the thinking of teachers confronted with a 'stranger' (a new head of department) and ideas which can not easily be accommodated into existing departmental structures or practice. The possibilities for educational change within mainstream schools are then, in the perspectives of each of these authors, limited but possible. Humberstone (chapter 11), however, steps outside of the school situation to consider the nature of teaching in an outdoor education centre. Teaching at Shotmoor, she argues, evidences some marked dissimilarities with that very often found in mainstream schools. Physical education here, not only offers children greater opportunities for success than they usually experience at school, but also, it takes a 'form' which challenges conventional stereotypical conceptions of boys' and girls' behaviour and capabilities. Like many of the contributors to the book, Humberstone exercises caution when drawing out policy implications from her research. Mixed sex grouping, and outdoor education may be 'different' and important, but alone it offers no solution to inequalities which may be deeply rooted in the structures of society. The final chapter by Carrington and Leaman endorses this viewpoint. Together these authors take a critical view of some of the innovations now being proposed within the physical education profession. They demand a rigorous consideration of what is meant by 'equal opportunities' in physical education and of practices which they argue may well serve to exacerbate rather than dissipate differences between children.

The problems of formulating and effecting curriculum change in physical education as in other areas of the school curriculum are then, as each of these chapters will reveal, both substantial and varied. And they are problems which are barely understood by academic researchers or indeed by teachers themselves. Together the authors in this collection emphasize how great is the need for further research into the process and problems of physical education teaching and of curriculum reform, investigations which are far more appreciative and sensitive to the perspectives and problems of teachers and pupils and of the social, organizational and political contexts in which they are located than has previously been the case. Without this form of enquiry, endeavours to effect improvement in the curricula of Physical Education may indeed be as insubstantial as they are short lived and they may result in forms of curriculum change which tamper only with the surface features of teaching, in how it publicly appears, leaving the deep structure of intention, assumption, process and consequently the outcomes of actions largely untouched (Evans, 1984). At a time when prescriptions about curriculum reform abound in the physical education profession, innovation without the support of evaluation or research, whether carried out by teachers or with the support of academic researchers, may indeed give rise to situations in which one form of curricular or pedagogical elitism is merely substituted for another. The changes invoked may consequently have an effect as deleterious to the task of inducing pupil involvement in physical activity as the practices they replaced.

Note

1   For an introduction to these sociologies, see CUFF and PAYNE., *et al*, (1979).

Bibliography

ARNOLD, P. J. (1985) 'Rational planning by objectives of the movement curriculum,' in *Physical Education Review*, Vol. 8, No. 1, Summer pp. 50–62.

BALL, S. (1981) *Beachside Comprehensive: A Case Study of Secondary Schooling*, Cambridge, Cambridge University Press.

BALL. S. (1984) *Comprehensive Schooling: A Reader*, Lewes, The Falmer Press.

CCCS (1981) *Unpopular Education*, Hutchinson Group in association with The Centre for Contemporary Cultural Studies, University of Birmingham..

CORRIGAN, P. (1982) 'The trouble with being unemployed is that you never get a day off,' in *Physical Education, Sport and Leisure: Sociological Perspectives*, NATFHE Conference Report, pp. 27–33.

CUFF, E.C. and PAYNE G.C.F. with FRANCIS D. W., HUSTLER D.E. and SHARROCK W.W. (1979) *Perspectives In Sociology*, London, George Allen and Unwin.

DAVIES, B. (1984) 'The sociology of education', in HIRST, P.H. (Ed.), Educational Theory and its Foundation Disciplines, London, Routledge and Kegan Paul, pp. 100–45.

DAVIES, B. and EVANS J. (1984) 'Mixed ability and the comprehensive school,' in BALL S. (Ed.) pp. 155–77.

DAWES, A. (1970) 'The two sociologies', *British Journal of Sociology*, XXI, 2.

DENZIN, N.K. (1971) 'Symbolic interactionism and ethnomethodology', in DOUGLAS, J.D. (Ed.) pp. 259–85.

DOUGLAS, J.D. (Ed.) (1971) *Understanding Everyday Life*, London, Routledge and Kegan Paul.

EVANS, J. (1984) '"Muscle, sweat and showers.'" Girls' conceptions of PE and sport', in *Physical Education Review*, Vol. 7, No. 1, pp. 12–19.

EVANS, J. (1985) *'Teaching In Transition: The Challenge of Mixed Ability Grouping*, Milton Keynes, Open University Press.

GARFINKEL, H. (1967) *Studies In Ethnomethodology*, Englewood Cliffs, Prentice-Hall.

HARGREAVES, A. and WOODS, P. (Eds.) (1984) *Classrooms and Staffrooms*, Milton Keynes, Open University Press.

HARGREAVES, J. (1982) 'Theorizing sport: an introduction', in HARGREAVES, J. (Ed.) *Sport, Culture and Ideology*, London, Routledge and Kegan Paul, pp. 1–30.

HARGREAVES, J. (1982) 'Sport, culture and ideology', in HARGREAVES, J. (Ed.) pp. 30–62.

JENKINS, C. (1982) 'Sociology and physical education,' in HARTNETT, A. (Ed.) *The Social Sciences in Educational Studies: A Selective Guide to the Literature*, Heinemann, pp. 275–283.

MARSLAND, D. (1985) 'Youth workers and unemployment: talk or action?' Paper Presented to the International Sociology of Education Conference, Westhill Birmingham, January.

MILLS, C.W. (1959) *The Sociological Imagination*, Penguin Books.

RANSON, S. (1984) 'Towards a tertiary tripartism: new codes of social control and the 17+,' in BROADFOOT, P. (Ed.) *Selection, Certification and Control*, Lewes, Falmer Press, pp. 221–45.

ROBERTS, K. (1984) *School Leavers and Their Prospects*, Milton Keynes, Open University Press.

SAUNDERS, E. (1976) 'Towards a sociology of physical education', in *Momentum*, Dunfermline College of Education, pp. 46–61.

TOMLINSON, A. (1982) 'Physical education, sport and sociology: the current state and the way forward,' in *Physical Education, Sport and Leisure: Sociological Perspectives*, NATFHE Conference Report, pp. 44–54.

WHITEHEAD, N. and HENDRY L.B. (1976) *Teaching Physical Education in England*, Lepus Books.

WILSON, T.P. (1971) 'Normative and interpretive paradigms in sociology', in DOUGLAS, J.D. (Ed.) pp. 57–80.

2   Sociology, Schooling and Physical Education

John Evans and Brian Davies

Schooling and Physical Education

If the sociology of education in Britain has achieved anything in recent years, it is to have made much more complex our understanding of what goes on inside schools and classrooms. Sociological researchers of all theoretical persuasions have variously set about the tasks of monitoring teacher talk, describing interactions, revealing the expectations of pupils and teachers and making the content of the curriculum (so taken for granted in the sociology of the fifties and sixties) the subject of critical scrutiny. Yet despite the plethora of research activity inside schools, with very few notable exceptions (see Hendry in chapter 3), the physical and the aesthetic areas of the school curriculum have largely been neglected, especially by qualitative sociological research. Even in the more all embracing perspectives of cultural and leisure studies which often have so productively spanned the domains of a pupil's cultural life both inside and outside school (see Willis, 1977, Corrigan, 1979), research has for the most part concentrated its attention on the social and cultural significance of sport and leisure in people's *post*, rather than their *intra* school life styles. The reasons for this relative paucity of sociological research are of course complex and varied and have been outlined in some detail elsewhere (see Jenny Hargreaves, 1982, John Hargreaves, 1982, Saunders, 1973, Tomlinson, 1982). The status imputed to Physical Education and Sport by sociologists and funding bodies alike, along with the difficulties of doing research in the open[1] contexts (as in open classrooms [see Cook, 1985]) in which most Physical Education takes place undoubtedly have together combined to make this area of schooling a marginal, difficult and therefore unattractive area of study. The British educational system has 'traditionally' been dominated by academic curricula which involve assumptions that some study and areas of knowledge are much more worthwhile than others. Researchers, like teachers and children have been deeply socialized within institutionalized structures which legitimate such assumptions. It is hardly surprising therefore that for them as for teachers, high status (and rewards) may well have been associated with areas of the curriculum that are also high status. In the contemporary British educational system, Physical Education has not been accredited such a position (see Hendry, 1975). It would not be unfair to say that to date our knowledge of children within the PE context is largely confined to findings of large scale surveys of participation, along with 'practitioner' news to be found in the professional PE journals. Consequently our conceptions of who participates, when and why are rather unsophisticated and generalized. The PE profession itself, as Jenny Hargreaves (1982) has properly argued, has largely failed to take a reflexive attitude towards its own practices and the rationales which sustain them. As she goes on to comment

> The theoretical treatment of sport in Britain has in the past been almost exclusively the preserve of the PE profession which has given minimal reference to the way in which sport or PE is socially constructed. The traditional influence of the subject has been the entrenched scientific and positivistic bias of much sports theory[2]. (1982, p. 1)

Eric Saunders has put it more charitably:

> PE has by tradition based its knowledge upon the physical, biological and behavioural sciences. As a result, research endeavours have focused upon areas such as physiological, biomechanical and psychological aspects of skill performance and where these have focused upon skilled behaviour of school age and school based children, they have provided a valuable source of information to the physical educator. Because these research activities centre upon the concreteness of human performance, that is upon action which can be readily identified, classified, analyzed and assessed in laboratory situations, they have proved attractive to physical educationalists who have by tradition focused upon the physical dimensions of the subject. This has produced a rich store of research techniques at the expense of other areas of study which have not received such systematic treatment. (1976, pp. 49–50)

As a result of the emphasis placed upon the measurable, the observable and the quantifiable, we know very little indeed about the processes of teaching in physical education or of their consequences for children's social and physical identities. Until very recently, the majority of studies conducted in physical education settings, both in this country and in the USA (see Anderson and Barrette, 1978), have focused on Physical Education *teaching* (see Lawson, 1983), using observational schedules as the main method of describing and analyzing what actually happens in PE classrooms (see Mawer and Brown 1983 and Bailey, 1981). In this form of research, teaching behaviours and classroom experiences are observed and quantified for establishing and describing observable differences in teacher 'styles' and putatively, teacher *effectiveness.* For this reason they long had great appeal amongst those involved in teacher education, even though with hindsight we can now see that their function was rhetorical rather than reasonable. In this form of research, usually referred to as interaction analysis or systematic observation, a manageable record of what is said or done depends on extracting the essential features from an otherwise overwhelming stream of talk or/and behaviour. This is usually done by coding talk but much more rarely even the simplest action into a number of categories which are claimed to abstract these essentials from the surrounding noise. 'The interaction can then be tallied and plotted on a matrix to present an objective picture of their verbal patterns' (Edwards and Furlong, 1978, p. 39). However, while the use of various classification systems has undoubtedly provided convenient data on the more visible aspects and patterns of activity in PE classrooms, their application to the study of teaching and their capacity to generate, *alone*, an understanding of its nature and purpose, remain quite limited and highly problematic (see Delamont and Hamilton, 1984 and Metzler, 1983 for critiques). For example, in this kind of research it has to be assumed that there is a consensus between how the researcher and the teacher perceives and classifies various behaviours, talk or action, in the classroom. The classification criteria do not usually refer to the intentions of those observed, but to the unstated criteria adopted by the researcher. Consequently, while

> The reliability of the most widely used category systems is not in doubt, that is, they allow any trained person who follows stated procedures to observe, record and analyze interactions with the assurance that others viewing the same situation would agree to a great extent with his recorded sequence of behaviour. The observer knows what he is looking for, and he produces precise and quanti- fiable data relevant to his purposes. But the larger question is obviously that of validity. Similarly trained observers may agree with each other, but *are* they seeing what really occurred? (Edwards and Furlong, 1978, p. 39)

The question of validity, as Edwards and Furlong go on to point out, draws attention to the theories underlying systematic observation, because the categories represent preconceived ideas about what is really important in classroom interaction. The value positions inherent within them are not usually deeply hidden (see Delamont, 1976) though they are often inexplicit. Studies of this nature claim objectivity of what can usually be described as a broadly *behavourist* kind. 'The criteria for classification refer to observable effects and not to the intentions of the actors, the basic model of interaction is one of stimulus and response' (Edwards and Furlong, 1978, p. 39). And there are other limitations. It is also usually assumed that it is teachers' behaviour which is of paramount importance in the process of learning and that it is their overt behaviour which directly contributes to the effectivity of teaching. Other factors, which may mediate between teacher and taught, for example resources of time, materials, space and, human motivations and aptitudes, pupil peer group pressures, remain largely unaccounted for. The upshot of all this is that PE teaching which is essentially a social, intentional and interpersonal activity tends to be reduced to a psychological phenomenon and portrayed rather mechanistically as an uncomplicated series of relationships between stimulus and response. Research is limited to factors which can be quantified, frequencies are measured, history and intentionality are sadly overlooked (see Anderson and Barrett, 1978).

Any reconstruction in a more intimate direction of the task of knowing what goes on inside physical education classrooms would be, of course, one of considerable difficulty, not least because what we tend to see as researchers or as teachers so often reflects our more or less hidden and coherently held conceptions of what teaching, pupils, or society more generally ought to be. Observations and consequently descriptions of classroom events are always selective, regardless of whether the method of data collection is by systematic observational schedule or impressionistic note taking, as are our interpretations of the data collected. Theoretical positions whether functionalist or interpretative, can and do determine what is to be looked at, how data are to be collected and how they are to be explained. Unfortunately, this has all too often meant that the questions raised by one position and the methods used to answer them are ignored by another. Things can and should be otherwise if our understanding of the nature and purpose of PE is to progress, and if we are to avoid producing accounts which claim not only to have discovered the truth and the whole truth but also the knowledge that this can only be seen from but one, privileged, particular position. Understanding the complexity of teaching and learning in PE will require at least a willingness to juxtapose methods and the data which they generate within theoretical perspectives, and to listen to the stories yielded by differing perspectival tongues, forbidding any one for the moment to drown out the others (Davies *et al*, 1985; see also Lawson, 1983).

To our rather behaviouristic and measurement oriented understanding of PE classrooms and practices, we should now add the strengths of recent theoretical and methodological developments in sociology. The flurry of research activity inside schools and classrooms by sociological researchers employing more qualitative or 'ethnographic' techniques has undoubtedly torn open the 'black box' of schooling to reveal colourfully how complex are the processes of teaching and learning, socialization, differentiation and selection which occur within it. Whether the theoretical inclination of these researchers has been toward interactionist (sometimes confusingly called 'phenomenological') or structural (usually 'Marxist') explanations, we argue that they all annotate the most significant single notion produced to date within the sociology of education, namely that the *form* and *content* of educational practice *both* matter greatly. This relatively recent discovery of the sheer complexity of educational transmission and the importance of the '*hidden curriculum*' within it by sociologists of all theoretical persuasions, has emphasized that there is no conceivable "content only" transmission' (Davies and

Evans, 1983). What children learn from the school curriculum in general and Physical Education in particular, derives not only from what teachers hope to make available to them in terms of the content of the curriculum but also from the manner or mode (see Hendry, 1981, 1981a; Evans, 1985) in which it is organized and actually provided. To grasp this is to challenge the most powerful of educational rhetorics — that 'education does you good' (Davies and Evans, 1983). And nowhere has this ideal been more endearingly coveted or readily propagated — usually in the form that the more you have of 'it' (fitness or physical activity), then the more good it's doing you — than within the Physical Education community. We should not be surprised to find that this view has also extended into the research communities both within and outside of Physical Education. As John Hargreaves has argued

> On the one hand, sport is easily taken for granted as by definition either an enjoyable, unserious activity, which it would be unbearably pretentious, even self-defeating to subject to analysis (the attitude is often the same to the analysis of jokes), or, on the other hand, as an activity which is unquestionably good for the individual and society. (1982, p. 32)

The views expressed in this book neither challenge nor run counter to the sentiment that Physical Education like any other part of the school curriculum can 'do you good'. It would be absurd if it were otherwise, for most of the contributors have their feet firmly located in Physical Education and teacher education within it. But while they are committed at all levels to the teaching of their subject within schools they would also seek to confront vigorously conventional assumptions about its status and position in the curriculum hierarchy. What passes for Physical Education in the school curriculum is neither arbitrary nor immutable. It is a social and cultural construct, laden with values which not all would adhere to or want to share. Physical Education as with the educational process more generally, consequently makes both friends and enemies of those subjected to it, it inspires and it alienates, it conditions and reconditions class and power structures (see Scraton, chapter 4). This is nice for some (as Hendry's research has revealed, usually disproportionally the middle class, male pupil), and nasty for others. As we have elsewhere argued the price which has to be paid by many for their meagre receipt of knowledge (and we use this concept here to refer not only to the cognitive but also physical skills, abilities and competences) is the heavy cost of knowing more sharply one's lowly place (Davies and Evans, 1983). Even if success is defined only in terms of equipping pupils with the knowledge, skills *and* the motivations to want to take part in post-school physical activity as one form of leisure, then the PE profession has singularly failed in its mission (see Hendry, chapter 3).

But children *do* learn all sorts of things in the PE curriculum. Its share of fifteen thousand hours, after all is not an insignificant amount of time to spend being subject to the intentions and curricular activities of specialist teachers, or perhaps to be told that you are not particularly good or suitable for certain forms of physical activity. Schools do leave children with something, if only in some the strongest aversion to wanting any more education or anything even remotely associated with it. The most that many pupils may have learnt in today's Physical Education curriculum is that they have neither ability, status nor value and that the most judicious course of action to be taken in protection of their fragile educational and physical identities is to adopt a plague-like avoidance of its damaging activities. Much of this of course, is no secret to many Physical Education teachers who (as with those in other subject areas) are abundantly aware of the gross inadequacies of their curricular practices, of what they both say and do to provide a very limited form of instruction, or to those pupils who perhaps routinely experience the feeling that they have been 'taught' Physical Education but yet again have failed to learn anything of significance. Pupils who may begin by explaining such failure disparagingly with reference to the teacher or the 'subject' can then more damagingly go on to complete the explanation with reference to their ability, physical or social selves (Evans, 1985).

This however, is not meant as an indictment of PE teachers. We are simply recording that a great deal of recent classroom research has suggested (see Westbury, 1973; Denscombe, 1980; Lundgren, 1977; Woods, 1977; Evans, 1985) that teaching is not always as it seems. It is not an unproblematic or simple process effecting *learning* in the conventional, knowledge acquisition sense of the word. The limitations of teaching can often occur because teachers and pupils are so often found in a position of having to 'cope the best they can' with limited resources and support (see Bell, chapter 5 and Almond and Kirk, chapters 8 and 9). Coping strategies result which are, as Hargreaves (1978, p. 77) argues, 'creatively articulated solutions to recurring daily problems'. They are not preferred ways of teaching but the 'best on offer', given the pressures which teachers face, with difficult pupils, limited resources, time and expertise or an unsupportive hierarchy. Faced with such pressures, ways of teaching (for example, whole class method) or grouping (for example, setting) can emerge which become so embedded as to appear as not only legitimate but inevitable ways of acting. Teachers using these strategies may resist demands for innovation whether generated by 'old' constraints or 'new' ideas, reluctant to have the *status quo* threatened by the uncertainties of innovation, angry at the stress they may experience when change is thrust upon them.

To date however, very little research has been conducted which is small scale enough to tease out the dynamic interplay between teacher intentions and the organizational context (including the curricular) in which they are located, within Physical Education settings. Thus our understanding of the rationales which may underpin certain teaching strategies, of why certain practices or methods or particular forms of talk persist, despite the contrary messages of professional training and availability of research evidence which has announced their limitations (see Anderson and Barrett, 1978) remains very limited. Conservatism thus sometimes appears as inherent in the Physical Education profession.

Although many of the chapters (Almond, Kirk, Humberstone, Embrey) emphasize that the conventional, traditional diet of games and sports is (and should be) a problematic feature of a teacher's work, the concerns of this volume are not then, only about the content of the Physical Education curriculum. The object of analyses in this book, Physical Education, requires a definition which extends well beyond the subject matter (the goals and intentions, aims and objectives) explicitly contained in Physical Education syllabi. For Jenkins (1982) Physical Education refers to

> All teaching, learning and participation (compulsory or voluntary) in physical education which is planned, guided or encouraged by educational institutions, whether carried out inside a formal timetable or outside a formal timetable. It includes all extra-curricular physical activities, intra- or inter-mural competitions, all representative sport and other involvements in physical activities to the extent that these enjoy at least 'moral' support in serving educational ends in education-al settings. (p. 275)

Now this can be no more than a starting point for our sociological analysis of Physical Education. It usefully sets parameters which are broad enough to encompass the range of curricular activities such as educational gymnastics, sports and games which are contained in the Physical Education curriculum and which often (as implied in the definition) extend well beyond the boundaries of the school. However, so far as this definition emphasizes a focus on the intended and the intentional aspects of Physical Education, it also remains too limited in focus and overly conservative in its implications for research and the explanations brought to bear in the study of PE. Children, as the chapters in this reader will reveal, may learn much more from the PE curriculum than is either intended or indeed desired by teachers. Acknowledging this, it becomes clear that any 'sociology applied to PE' worth its salt would be concerned not only with what is intended (and perhaps embodied in official syllabi) but also with *pedagogy* (how this is made available), the system of *evaluation*; and the social relations engendered by the structured and informal activities and influences of peers *and* adults.

Within the sociology of education, the literature's attempt to objectify this complexity has been traded for twenty years in the concept of 'hidden curriculum'. This concept, however, is particularly problematic when applied in the context of Physical Education, and some clarification of its status is essential. The term 'hidden curriculum', has been used to refer to the social and cultural beliefs, information, values and ways of behaving which children may be exposed to and learn or, we would stress (see Evans, 1985), are required of children in order to learn, within the educational process, but which are not publicly set out in official statements of schools or department philosophy or in course descriptions or syllabi. It has a long history in educational debate and is often portrayed (evaluatively) as a powerful con-servative and 'detrimental force that undermines the professional commitment of the schools to foster intellectual development and a democratic community'

(Cornbleth, 1984, p. 29). Part of the 'hidden curriculum' has been held to be the transmission and inculcation of values supportive of the societal *status quo* which teachers, subjects and schools would not willingly avow. But unlike in other subject areas, where it may well be claimed that aims are only concerned with formal education — 'the transmission of specialized skills, logical operations and abstract system' (Mehan, 1979) — and that these are 'value free', 'objective', uncontaminated by any socializing functions — the Physical Education profession has both historically and contemporaneously paraded its social objectives and socializing functions publicly amongst its professional aims. Competitive sport for example, as McIntosh (1979) so clearly revealed, has historically been seen as an instrument of PE and as a mechanism of social education through which children are taught social accomplishments, modes of behaviour and traits of character, held to be of value in the wider society. More recently, surveys by both Kane (1974) and Underwood (1983) have demonstrated that social objectives still rank highly in the teachers' priorities. If we are, then, to use the term 'hidden curriculum' at all, then we should accept the conceptual distinction between the hidden and the implicit curriculum, and contain both under the rubrics of socialization and schooling.[3] We can then think of the hidden curriculum as those influences or requirements of the curriculum of which neither the promoters nor the participants are fully aware; and the implicit curriculum as the process (influences) of socialization which are intended by teachers, which may be documented in official syllabi etc, and which are often felt to be 'caught' rather than taught in the curricular process (but which are not always made explicit to the recipients of this curriculum). Both focus attention on the messages imparted in 'classrooms', departments and schools through the 'form as well as the content' of instruction. The medium or mode may be a large part of the teacher's/school's message. It might indeed complement, contradict, or parallel the formal, (manifest) goals and content of the implicit curriculum. More importantly, there is no curriculum to be received save through some means, medium or mode. The concept of schooling entails a grasp of the indissolubility of form and content. It demands that we examine the constraints and opportunities as well as the contradictory messages that are communicated within the social milieu of Physical Education, and how they are received by students.

Any conventional distinction between socialization and formal education then tends to collapse even more quickly in the Physical Education curriculum than elsewhere, for socialization as well as education is manifestly intended by its practitioners. *Pace* Hendry, Scraton, Humberstone we must consider such questions as, 'into what and whose values and attributes are pupils being socialized?' What social, emotional (as well as physical) pre-dispositions are required of pupils in order to take part in and succeed at 'learning' in programmes of Physical Education? What is the relationship between the cultural values which children bring to Physical Education and those which teachers require and transmit in the Physical Education curriculum (see Saunders 1982)? Do schools, and Physical Education within them, reproduce existing inequalities in societies, or does Physical Education offer a medium for lessening the inequalities of opportunity, power and knowledge in our society? Is Physical Education strongly determined by wider ideological economic and cultural forces (Brohm, 1977) or does it have a significant degree of autonomy? What actually happens within the Physical Education curriculum and classroom, in the social relations of teaching and learning?

Simply posing these questions should insinuate both that the cultural worlds of classrooms are not contexts which are simply constructed for pupils by teachers and that an understanding of them is fundamental to our insight upon all the above questions. In classrooms, teachers and pupils enter into a complex process of negotiation to define the parameters of acceptable teacher-pupil interaction and to determine what is required by way of skills, understandings and social competencies if a successful performance as a pupil or a teacher is to be achieved. *Both* teachers and pupils enter classroom life with attitudes, interests, expectations and abilities which form the basis for action and interpretation, of what constitutes a 'proper' PE lesson, a good teacher, 'real' learning. There is rarely any straightforward imposition of a teacher's curriculum intentions. As recent research has indicated (Pollard 1979), even though pupils do not have the power or the authority of teachers they can deploy subtle strategies to negotiate an acceptable existence. Teachers, like pupils, have only varying degrees of control over the teaching process, over what they do, how and when they do it. It is important to consider how teachers like pupils are socialized into specific ways of thinking and acting in the process of schooling, for they too are subject to a hidden and implicit curriculum. To date, where sociology has been applied to the content of physical education, attention has predominantly and indeed productively focused on the way in which broader school values and expectations create tensions, even contradictions in the actions or philosophy of PE teachers (see Hendry, chapter 3, Kirk, chapter 9). Recent sociology of education has however increasingly turned its attention to the study of teacher identity and the processes of socialization inside school communities and subject sub-cultures. As Denscombe has argued, neither professional training nor official membership (of a school or department) provides

A guarantee of competence because it is, after all, only an official status. Competent membership on the other hand is something accomplished not through qualification, office or tenure, but through action. It is continually accomplished by the kind of routine activity undertaken by members. (1980, p. 23)

As Denscombe goes on to argue

Two things follow immediately from the premise that competence resides in action not status. First because competent membership is all about action the framework directs attention towards the ordinary and the mundane aspects of work which are the cornerstone of most occupations and to the routine practical activity through which competence is both accomplished and demonstrated. To this end there is a need for a description of the work situation, members' activity and their accounts of the dilemmas, imperatives and possibilities they encounter. Some ethnography of the work situation becomes essential. Secondly, organization and activity is viewed as the product of a particular mode of understanding which characterizes the competent member. It is how competent members interpret situations, how they use rules, bend, neglect or invoke the official prescriptions which explain the activity of members rather than the official prescriptions themselves and this directs research towards the teachers' understandings of the activities in which they engage and is concerned with intentionality rather than the observable indices of behaviour. (*ibid* p. 283.)

There is little doubt that an understanding of the socialization of PE teachers both within professional training and in their departmental sub-cultural communities hardly yet developed as a line of enquiry, is essential to our grasp of PE practices. Physical Educators are not a homogeneous community of teachers. Indeed, some have come close to suggesting that although PE is one subject, two 'gender' sub-cultures operate within it (Fletcher, 1984). It may well be productive to consider, for example, how the training of male and female Physical Education teachers either separately or together produces particular sub-cultures and how these might now limit or facilitate the possibilities of achieving innovation within the school PE curriculum. However, it is the culture of the school to which Denscombe (see also Ball and Lacey 1980) draws our attention. Within the school situation we need to examine how PE departments give rise to particular subject or 'work cultures'. These

Constitute a somewhat covert and tacit level of agreement amongst those in the occupation about the nature of the task they face and the appropriate methods to deal with them and explain, for instance, how it is possible that teachers with differing views about pedagogy can express disagreement about the relative benefits of particular styles of teaching yet still recognize the other's activity as not incompetent. (Denscombe, 1980, p. 283)

To engage in this kind of enquiry is not simply a matter of academic interest or curiosity. The study of teacher socialization and of definitions of competence within PE departments, as Sparkes in this reader (and Evans *et al*, 1985) so clearly evidence, is crucial to our understanding of the limits and possibilities of educational change within physical education, and of what, psychologically, socially and pedagogically is required of teachers when new ideas enter into a department's existing structures and practices. However, answers to this type of question and to many of those raised above are hardly to be found in the sociological literature on physical education and, as we have suggested, they are unlikely to be forthcoming using the methods which have traditionally featured in the study of physical education.

Form and Function in Physical Education

We are conscious that we are making a case for a pitch and concentration of work in the study of PE without any firm basis of accumulated knowledge gained from the application of earlier stages of our developing post war sociological insights. The predominant concern of the sociology of education in Britain and in the USA in the early fifties and sixties was whether the educational system met the changing needs of an expanding industrial society. Within this framework of sociological and socio-economic thought, education was conceived as an important commodity, as 'A consumer good, a mark of status, a means of social personal mobility. The problem with education lay not so much with what it was or what it did but how it was distributed' (CCCS, p. 172). Tacitly it held that the traditional curriculum was unproblematically worthwhile and educational policy was to maximize access to it (Reynolds and Sullivan, 1980).

Theoretically the body of this work was loosely (see Bernstein, 1975) structural functionalist in orientation. Feeding on ideas from Durkheim to Parsons, the school was seen as a complex social system functioning to service the parts (which other sub-systems like the family and the church also reached) and the needs of the broader society. Schools functioned to *socialize* children into values and norms necessary for the effective performance of their roles in wider society; *differentiate* their academic achievements and *allocate* their human resources to the adult role system. The person in this perspective often seemed to be little more (or less) than a complex amalgam of the expectations, values and attitudes handed down to them by one of a variety of socializing agencies. Deviance, though necessary was too easily explicated as individual or sectional pathology.

Textbook introductions to the sociology· of education now find it convenient to refer to this sociological approach as the 'old' sociology and as a sociology of 'order' (see Dawe, 1970) because it concentrates attention on how societies hold together, rather than on conflict and how they might potentially fall apart. However in many ways this characterization is all too easily distortive of a tradition of sociological research which had by the sixties very largely taken on board the softening influence of symbolic interactionism where at least it was clearly recognized that roles were made and not just given, that the powerful prescribed the parameters of position. Such a dilute and modified functionalism, more paternalist (in more than one sense) than penetrative continues to influence educational debate and certainly continues to influence thinking, research and policy within physical education, sport and leisure. As Tomlinson (1982) has argued, the social problems approach is really the Sports Council type of approach, it is concerned with mapping inequalities in participation in sport and in access to sport and leisure provision. Much of the American sociological literature and research on physical education and sport remains albeit rather loosely located within a functionalist position and few (see Coakley, 1983, Earls, 1985, Harris and Park, 1983, McPherson, 1982, Templin, 1978) have attempted to bring even a more interpretative approach to this field. In Britain also, early incursions into the field of sociology applied to PE were, at their heart, functionalist in orienta-tion; concerned with the structure and function of social groups (Mangan, 1973, p. 3) and with the integrative role of physical education within the school and broader social system. Physical Education in this perspective is seen to play a crucial part in the socializing process; it is a 'useful means of producing commitment to school goals and values' (Mangan, 1973, p. 31). It provides an important safety valve providing a 'cultural substitute' (p. 32), and makes,

> a valuable contribution to the smooth functioning of the school — as a means of reducing the interest of the conflict between the academic system and certain types of low academic achiever. It helps to minimize the intensity of the conflict by ensuring by its existence an alternative area in which to achieve status and recognition. (*ibid* p. 32)

It is all too easy having crudely characterized a particular approach or position to engage in the pursuit of 'witch hunting and heresy spotting' (Bernstein, 1975, p. 158) and to forget how the questions which we are now able to raise about schools and PE are dependent on the news created by earlier paradigms and approaches. The form of social science technology, the large scale survey used in earlier (and current Sports Council) studies, served well as a scientific tool to describe and announce patterns of educational achievement and leisure and of sporting opportunities; and a theoretical functionalism has at least drawn attention to the complex process of socialization occurring inside schools and the role of PE within it. However, the functionalism of British and American sociology of PE may well have left the profession sadly uncritical of its curriculum and with very little understanding of the processes of teaching and learning in PE, of cultural production as well as reproduction and of the ways in which the patterns which large scale surveys so regularly describe are together produced by teachers and pupils within the PE curriculum.

Indeed it is not uninteresting to note that Mangan's *Physical Education and Sport, Sociological and Cultural Perspectives* was published two years after M.F.D. Young's *Knowledge and Control*. While the latter asked the sociological and professional educational communities to make problematic the content of the school curriculum, much in the former (as the statements by Mangan above suggest) extolled the virtues of PE's socializing functions, leaving its content largely untouched.

It is also all too easy to see how in the school situation, as in the broader context of leisure research as Tomlinson (1982) has argued, the social problem approach can turn into a form of administrative and social control. Once we accept that societies are not composed of distinct groups of people who share common norms and values, then we have to consider that the 'goals' inside the schools and of PE teachers and their pupils may not always coincide and that there is a potential for conflict. As Levitas states, in writing about functions and integrative mechanisms 'the vital interests inherent in these purposes, the identities of the creators and executors and the social class intentions behind them are effectively hidden. When a sociologist talks about goals anyone may ask whose goals.' (Levitas, quoted in Reid, 1978, p. 39)

Organization Matters

In the mid–1960s the focus of educational and political debate in Britain and in the USA changed quite dramatically. Attention now centred less on the overall school-society link than upon how pupils were grouped for teaching purposes within them or labelled as individual educands, though it still focused very imperfectly on how and what they should be taught. Sociological and educational research largely reflected these concerns. In the early sixties and seventies the research of Hargreaves and Lacey, with its roots searching deeply into anthropology and the Chicago School of Sociology (see Hargreaves and Woods, 1985), turned attention to organizational processes within schools and in particular to the way in which pupils were differentiated by streaming and then because of the different treatments accorded each group of pupils by their teachers, subsequently polarized into separate sub-cultures with opposing values. These studies, as Hargreaves and Woods (1985) have argued, un-doubtedly played a major role in persuading both the sociological and teaching communities that the internal processes of schooling were worth further investigation. And to a degree, Leo Hendry in Britain took up this invitation to turn attention to the content of PE teaching. Though the focus and the methods of these studies (by Hargreaves, Lacey and Hendry) differed marked-ly from the earlier demographic surveys (Hargreaves and Lacey provided detailed case studies of two secondary schools, while Hendry combined both survey and case study techniques), in retrospect we may say that they were asking similar questions about the secondary school that had been framed in the earlier, sociological studies (CCCS, 1981). Their main endeavour was to demonstrate how certain associations between family background, usually thought of in terms of social class (and in Hendry's (1978) work, also per-sonality and physical ability), and school performance were secured. School performance in Hargreaves and Lacey's work is defined in terms of academic achievements, while Hendry's problematic was the under-involvement of pupils in school sport — the bedevilment of the notion of education for leisure. Like Lacey and Hargreaves, Hendry suggested that the formation of a school based sub-culture, anti-sport and anti-school, was as a reflex of failure at school, induced in large measure by the tendency of teachers to label, typify, grade and select pupils in their own middle class image.

> A conflict can be proposed which suggests that school sport, especially in their competitive form reinforces certain values of commitment, conformity and dedication which are rewarded by the school. In this way pupils of relatively high academic ability and of middle class background receive further inducements to support the school values. At the same time the same processes may alienate a large number of pupils who value qualities of physical ability and prowess but without asking for the social trappings and processes necessarily involved in representing the school. (Hendry, 1978, p. 36)

The work of Hargreaves, Lacey and Hendry together provide an invaluable framework for raising much broader questions about the nature and purpose of schooling and of Physical Education within it, and for more penetrating and detailed analyses of the social and cultural processes (of socialization, differentiation and selection) internal to the school system. They also provide a useful reminder that the practices of PE and the behaviours of children within them, cannot be divorced from the broader school context of decision making relating to the organization of pupils and the content of the curriculum. As Ball (1981) has more recently shown, less able pupils taught in mixed ability groups are more committed to schools and Physical Education than their counterparts taught in 'set' groups. Hendry's work also provided a powerful challenge to the functionalist view that PE (as an integrative force) could provide an alternative source of success and status for the academically less able. However, while these studies had much to say about teachers, they had little to say about the content of the curriculum, teaching methods, pupil and teacher interaction and how these factors interact within particular school and departmental circumstances at certain levels of resource, to produce the outcomes reported. They tell us little of how pupils participate or of the motivations which underpin their actions; or of the conditions under which all would/could take part. Indeed PE has more or less missed out even on the 'grouping' debate. We know little (see Hendry, 1978) of how pupils are grouped for teaching purposes in programmes of PE, of the part PE plays in differentiation and selection of how teachers teach when pupils are placed, for example, in set or mixed ability groups, or the principles which underpin a department's or teacher's grouping policies.

It is easy enough to specify a concerted agenda. Accepting the importance of the interplay of class and teacher expectations, we must give rather more emphasis to the content of the curriculum, and how the process of teaching and learning produces the outcomes described, in terms of patterns of success and failure, involvement and under-involvement which persist despite the liberal intentions so often expressed by teachers. Building on the 'streaming' studies, we must consider how or whether the processes described are evident in all schools, irrespective of their organizational context and the content of the curriculum, or the nature (ethnicity, class or gender) of their clientele. Is the same alienation (of less able pupils from schools and Physical Education) to be observed in middle class schools? What about the social relations that cut across and complicate class or status hierarchies such as sex and gender and race? As Carrington (1982) has shown, school sport does not uniformly alienate all working class pupils. Where it has a particular cultural significance for West Indian youth, ethnicity can operate to exclude white working class pupils from involvement in sport. Studies such as those of Hargreaves, Hendry and Lacey, then, provided complex *descriptions* of the outcomes of schooling, they raised questions about the nature of society being reproduced through the process of schooling and sport, about the cultural origins of PE teachers, about class interests, power and control. However, the plethora of more detailed classroom observational studies engendered in their wake once more hardly touched the PE scene. We must still pose the questions and seek the answers of other school subjects yesteryear.

The 'New Sociology' and Physical Education

In the context of the radicalism of the late sixties and early seventies and a rapidly expanding initial teacher education, what came to be known as the 'new sociology of education', commonly identified with the publication of M.F.D. Young's *Knowledge and Control*, firmly influenced and increased the flow of over-theorized and technically imperfect small scale research. Although this book contained a hugely disparate array of papers, it opened approaches to the study of schooling which concentrated attention on the curriculum content of schooling and rejected the rather passive over-socialized conception of 'man' discerned in the functionalist literature. Instead, as Barton and Walker note, it laid stress on the person as an

> active participant in the creation and construction of social reality. (This approach) emphasizes an investigation of the processes by which those involved in the educational enterprise construct, manage and define their everyday world. The nature of school knowledge, the organization of the school, the ideologies of teachers, indeed any educational issues all became relative — and the central task for the sociology of education becomes to reveal what constitutes reality for the participant in a given situation, to explain how those participants come to view reality in this way and to determine what are the social consequences of their interaction. (1978, p. 274)

Theoretically, as Hargreaves and Woods have pointed out, the new sociology of education was a curious mixture of humanistic Marxism and interpretative sociologies. Keddie's paper drew heavily on Howard Becker's notion of the ideal pupil and Alfred Schutz's concept of typification, while the papers by Young and Esland cited Schutz along with Marx, Mead and Weber. However the key point of phenomenology as it entered this sociology was its denial of a 'fixed' reality (a position which often took it quickly and inescapably into a crude relativism [Demaine, 1981]). All educational realities, subjects, categories of children, stood in need of explanation. Hence 'the curriculum', a taken-for-granted category in all earlier sociological work was itself up for consideration, and the task was one of uncovering the way in which 'common sense' notions of the good or bright child, the athlete or the troublemaker (see Carroll, chapter 7) come to organize and constrain social reality. As filtered through into the new sociology, the interpretative sociology of Alfred Schutz asked practitioners and sociologists to consider the conventions of curricular hierarchies — to ask why certain subjects (and indeed, pupils) are given more status than others and to explore the rationale which lay beneath them (see Esland, 1971). Arguably it is not inherent in the nature of things that science gets a higher ranking than PE or that boys' games receive more attention or status than girls' dance. 'Men' make their own knowledge and some have greater power in the social construction and legitimation of knowledge than others. The task becomes to explore through which persons, groups and processes certain forms of knowledge and organization become established in schools.

Despite Hoyles' (1977) valiant efforts to bring this news to the PE profession, the ideas of 'new directions' hardly seemed to capture the imagination of the PE fraternity, or find expression in appropriate interpretative empirical research. There is little doubt that the social organization of schooling and PE in particular should be a focus for sociological analysis and considered as one crucial locus of the attitudes and actions of children towards others, teacher and subjects, their post-school involvement in PE and leisure (see Hendry, 1983). By making problematic how we teach and what we teach, the new sociology of education demands that we begin to explore, or at least treat with caution, our organizing concepts of intelligence, physical ability, skill, educability, the slow learner, and the social ranking of subjects which might routinely be employed in PE contexts.

We should not be surprised at the lack of interest in or even hostility toward questioning these categories within PE. The sanctity, 'naturalness' of many of them stems already from natural science origins. We are all victim of the tendency of the invidiously ranked social category — whether in relation to ability, gender, class, etc. in whatever combination — to become constitutive of our view as to how it 'has to be'. Even among the questors of 'new directions', the fruitlessness of just 'rendering problematic' led many quite simply to seek anchorage in structural limits — usually Marxist — or social possibility (see Whitty, 1977).

Even if we do not choose to follow this new directionist path to more structural Marxisms, we need not see it as requiring us to dive blindly into a solipsistic quagmire. It doesn't have to follow that these concepts (or hierarchical categories of knowledge) are *pure* power or ideological constructs, having no reference (points of contact) in the real world. However elusive the concept intelligence or ability may be, it doesn't follow that there is no differential distribution of genetic talent or physical ability. To consider that the curricular or ability hierarchies are socially constructed, does not mean that there are no principled grounds on which we differentially rank subjects or children.[4] The embracing requirement of the 'new' sociology of education is that we examine the social bases of our conventional practices, that we explore the decision making process, the criteria which underpin curricula selections, the rationales which are used to justify and legitimize them, and locate these not only within epistemic communities but also the particular school organizational, social and political contexts of which they are part. It also commands an incursion into the origins of school subjects, into their social and cultural histories. It implores us to examine how over a particular historical period (subjects) have become legitimated as of high status by those in positions of power. As M.F.D. Young put it,

> One crucial way of reformulating and transcending the limits within which we work is to see ... how such limits are not given as fixed, but produced through the conflicting actions and interests of 'man' in history. (pp. 248–9)

There is little doubt that the historical analysis of the PE curriculum in Britain has been one of the more penetrating and revealing lines of enquiry within the academic study of PE. It has begun (see for example McIntosh, 1979, Fletcher, 1984, Mangan, 1981, Griggs, 1981) focusing upon the social and political origins of the subject, and its 'evolution' within the educational system. However, while much has been revealed about the class and culture origins and functions of PE and sport there remains a good deal of scope for further studies to examine how the PE profession has emerged as a 'loose amalgam of segments pursuing different objectives in different manners and more or less delicately held together under a common name at particular periods in history' (Bucher and Strauss, 1971). Adopting this perspective it is very difficult to sustain a conception of PE as a subject or profession which has evolved, single-line from a stage of drill to the liberal, all embracing, professional programmes of today. As Goodson has forcefully argued, 'subject communities'

> should not be viewed as a homogeneous group whose members show similar values and definitions of role, common interests and identity. Rather the subject community should be seen as comprising a range of conflicting groups, segments or factions (referred to as subject subgroups). The importance of these groups might vary considerably over time. (Goodson, p. 1984: 40)

The agenda for research outlined by Goodson need not and cannot be detailed here (see Goodson, 1984) but it does provide a way of looking at the

PE curriculum which is likely to lead into unchartered areas of enquiry. Adopting Bucher and Strauss' conception of profession, commands that we raise questions not only about how certain activities have evolved and become established and legitimized in the PE curriculum but also to consider (and discover) those that were left out and the social, political and pedagogical reasons for their omission. Currently, histories of sport and PE may well leave the reader with a notion that the profession has developed via the influence of the values of a few but significant middle class males, or through a conflict between their ideas, and those alternatives expressed by a similar handful of middle class females (Fletcher, 1984). But 'great person' views of history tend to offer little advance on that of 'great men'. Conflict and disagreement within the ideas and attitudes (towards physical activity, the 'body' and sport) of middle class males or females, and between their aspirations and other social or ethnic groups, remain largely unexplored. Social histories of PE as Tomlinson (1982) points out, contribute not only to our understanding of PE but also to our sense of how particular kinds of dominant ideologies, cultural relations get produced and reproduced. Like Goodson and Ball (1984) we would want to argue that the techniques of history and ethnography together provide us with good tools to examine and interrogate PE empirically, and to also lay the groundwork for the development of theories which capture and explain the process of change (or absence of change) in PE. In the school

> A twin focused analysis, using histories and ethnographies, allows full account to be taken of the socially and politically constructed nature of school subjects and tends towards a view of the structure and contents of the school curriculum as the products of previous and ongoing struggles within and between subject communities. In this way the 'taken-for-grantedness' of the curriculum and its subject components is challenged. Historical work concentrating on the emergence and establishment (or decline) of school subjects highlights the contested nature of school knowledge, indicating the role played by various, vested interest groups in the selection and definition of appropriate contents. Ethnographic inquiry provides insights into these factors which *mediate* between the espoused and the enacted curriculum as well as emphasizing the realization and experience of the different contents and forms of subject knowledge in the classroom (or laboratory, or workshop). In both cases, conflict, compromise, and negotiation are key concepts. (Ball and Goodson, 1984, pp. 4–5)

However, despite the pleas of new direction sociologists for the study of the organization, selection and content of school knowledge, sociology did not until recently (see Hammersley and Hargreaves, 1981) produce any regular stream of empirical research into the content or organization of the school curriculum or PE in particular. While the scholars of PE pursued their subradical historical analyses, on the wider scene,

Empirical work settled down not to the study of curriculum organization and content but to classroom analysis of teachers as agents of
differentiation and of the hidden forms of control that underlay
versions of teaching which were, so it was claimed, only *ostensibly*
progressive and democratic. (Hargreaves and Woods, 1984, p. 7)

In practice this has meant the study of academic classrooms. Although
Knowledge and Control called on the sociological community to make problematic its conceptions, very few indeed found either time or inclination to
make it to PE lessons or departments.

Towards a Qualitative Understanding

Since the publication of *Knowledge and Control*, the sociology of education in
Britain has proliferated a bewildering array of theoretical approaches. The
discipline is now more divided, but perhaps more methodologically adept and
attuned to the 'sociological imagination' (see Hargreaves, 1980) than ever
before. In the seventies, as Hargreaves and Woods (1984) note, empirical
research settled down to classroom analyses of teachers as agents of *class* and —
as a Feminist critique bit hard into educational practice and sociology — *gender*
differentiation. But the 'new' sociology left debate and empirical research
oscillating wildly between an emphasis on teachers as either 'cultural dopes'
determined by the economic needs of capitalism, or living in 'splendid
isolation' (Hargreaves, 1980) 'unaffected by the economic demands, political
pressures and social influence of wider society' (Hargreaves and Woods, 1984).
Neither approach proved very helpful to teachers who were increasingly being
subjected to public and political pressures to improve standards and effect
greater relevance and control over pupils, within institutional conditions which
provided little opportunity or support for curriculum innovation and change.
The adequacies of both interpretative and Marxian studies of schooling thus
were subjected to heavy criticism, the former for paying too little attention to
the contexts and structures in which teachers worked, and which set limits to
the possibilities for educational change, and the latter for under-playing the
potency of human agency, resource and intention and for replacing these
qualities with structural explanations drawn from various Marxian theoretical
starting positions.

The upshot of all this has been appeals for some form of reproachment
(Hammersley, 1980) or a synthesis in theory (Giddens, 1979) or method
(Silverman, 1985) capable of making the connections between consciousness,
human agency, cultures and social structure. In the study of schooling this has
meant that attention has been drawn to the complexities of teachers' cultures
and actions and intentions and their relationships with forms of curricular
organization and content, the organizational contexts of schools and the

societies in which they are located (Denscombe, 1980; Hargreaves, 1978; Evans, 1985). The agenda for research created by this sensitivity toward structure and process cannot be detailed here (see Hargreaves, 1980). But briefly, if we are to stimulate the sociological imagination in the study of PE, if we are to try and connect the personal experiences — the troubles of teachers and pupils within a particular milieux to public issues and conceptions of structure (Mills, 1959); if we are to begin to understand the nature and quality of teaching in the physical education curriculum and its impact upon the identities of both children and teachers, then we now need research which is sensitive not only to the patterned activities of classroom life, but also to the intentions, interpretations and actions of teachers and pupils *and* to features of the social and organizational contexts in which they are located (see Evans and Cook, 1985, Evans, 1985, Denscombe, 1980, Hargreaves, 1980). This 'level-conscious' analysis of teaching, would crucially attempt to link the teaching process in PE with decision-making outside and above the classroom in the department and broader school and administrative contexts. This quest is likely to require not only a juxtaposition of research methods (see Bell and Newby, 1977), but also a willingness to assume that even with the most sophisticated of combinations, the accounts which we provide about life in PE classrooms will always and inevitably be partial and incomplete. Teaching is a complex, intentional and interpersonal activity, strongly influenced by the social, cultural, and organizational contexts in which it takes place. To study it in this light would mean widening the basis of sociological research within PE, not least by informing it with an ethnographic or anthropological approach. This is not to deny the place or the use of other approaches or techniques such as systematic observation with its precoded instrumentation. There is nothing wrong, in principle, in using this or any other research technique in an ethnographic study although (MacIntyre, 1980) it may not be logically possible to use observational schedules in studies which initially set out to *explore* and describe what happens to teachers, teaching and pupils, innovations and innovation in the normal conditions of their place of work. The concern of interpretative approaches is to describe and explain human agency, and the social construction of the cultural worlds that people occupy. There is a rejection of the view that but for distortion, error or ideology, the world *is*, as it appears, that one simply has to find appropriate means of measuring it (see Hammersley and Atkinson, 1983). The meanings attached to any social world have to be both discovered and understood, a project which entails getting beneath the merely observable, and into the perspectives and thinking of those observed. Taking an ethnographic stance means treating classroom 'scenes' not as familiar phenomena where what is seen is already a large part known and understood but precisely as though they were part of a strange culture. The object is to examine the 'cultural modes of existence, the values, beliefs, rituals, rules, strategies — in short the whole way of life — of a particular group' (Woods, 1985, p. 53). This may be a department, a group of children or an institutional context. The focus may be on the mundane issues that make up the teacher's day, or on the unexpected and innovatory. The attitudes, predispositions, feelings and values of the researcher are very much part of the research process. As data they are necessarily subjected to critical reflection and scrutiny. Research inevitably involves imposition or exchange of meanings and none simply aims at describing the world just as it is. All research however exploratory, involves selections and interpretations.

Ethnographers try to accept the fully social task of trying to understand, explain and communicate to others the cultures (ways of seeing and behaving) of members of a group or society.[5] This kind of approach may seem very unfamiliar to many in PE more used to reports based on surveys or experimental methods. The principles and practice of ethnography have been more than adequately outlined elsewhere (see Hammersley and Atkinson, 1983, Spradley, 1979, 1979a, or Harris and Park, 1983), but a brief note of some of its features, neatly summarized by Harris and Park may prove useful in respect of the studies which follow.

> Ethnographers typically spend a relatively long time — from several months to several years — closely involved with the culture which they are studying. During that period of time they use a variety of research methods, and they frequently find it necessary to create methods for particular purposes after having arrived in the culture. This is done to allow the research methods to conform more closely to the culture in an effort to avoid the application of a set of preconceived methods that might lead to alterations in the very cultural phenomena which the researchers have to study. Because of the length of time over which studies take place and the plethora of research methods employed during that time, detailed descriptions of research methods are impractical in most ethnographic research reports. A complete description of research methods for any one ethnographic study would probably fill an entire book. Thus, in ethnographies one typically finds very abbreviated discussions of methods, and these are frequently interwoven with the findings — the cultural descriptions. The cultural descriptions are usually presented in narrative form, with occasional use of diagrams, photographs, and appropriate quotations from members of the culture. (1983, p. 10)

The term ethnography then represents just one, and a particular way of looking at activities inside schools and PE classrooms; it covers a range of methodological activities, although the two methods most commonly used are interviewing and some form of observation (see Harris and Park, 1983; Spradley, 1979a, 1979b). It lends itself to the application of a variety of theoretical positions for the purpose of both guiding the direction of study and the interpretations of the data generated. It is employed (whether well or badly) by Marxists as well as interactionists.

Not all of the studies reported in this book are ethnographic though most are qualitative in nature. In Britain, interpretative research has also developed in the field of curriculum studies. Case study, or illuminative evaluation as it is sometimes termed, shares most of the features of ethnography, with the emphasis on teacher as researcher and upon the processes of facilitating his or her understanding of the social processes for which they are responsible, rather than with the act of producing accounts *for* teachers. The principles of this method are well documented elsewhere (see Hopkins, 1985) and Almond in chapter 8 illustrates their application in the context of PE.

Detailed studies of Physical Education whether carried out by researchers or teachers, are now badly needed to advance our understanding of what PE teaching is, of what it does to pupils, and of how departments and teachers work and change across all levels of curriculum decision making. But descriptive accounts of what goes on in PE *classrooms* (whether provided by observation schedule or impressionistic techniques, case-study or ethnography) will alone do little to advance our understanding unless there is alongside such description a great deal of further data. If we are to understand PE teaching and learning we need a great deal of contextual information about organizational and social relationships, levels of resource (human and physical), patterns of decision making and control within the department and broader, institutional and social settings in which PE teachers and their pupils work (see Evans, 1985, Denscombe, 1980). Interpretative studies of teaching have too often rather myopically located individual teachers as the central and most influential figures in the teaching process neglecting the context in which they try to work. On the one hand such a focus invites the satisfying but misleading notion that any educational change is possible *and* ultimately determined by the individual teacher; on the other, that it is the teacher who is solely to blame if the anticipated change or learning outcome is not readily forthcoming. As Hargreaves has elsewhere noted, the preference for 'splendid isolation' — treating the classroom as if it existed in a social or cultural vacuum, unaffected by the economic demands, political pressures and social influences of the wider society — leads not only to incomplete accounts of school processes but to distorted ones too (Hargreaves, 1980).

No single theoretical position or methodological technique will capture life in PE classrooms just as it is, in all its complexity, let alone begin to explain it. But if we are to begin to achieve a better understanding of PE, to answer some of the theoretical questions posed by the sociology of education and to respond to the practical concerns of the profession, then we must adopt an attitude of mind which is at least initially as open about the direction of study and the theoretical problems to be addressed as it is about the methodological techniques to be employed.

To talk of the sociology of physical education teaching is ultimately to talk of a sociology applied to physical education. It means taking the concerns and the methodologies of the parent discipline and applying them towards an understanding of the nature, process and purpose of physical education in school and society (*cf.* Hendry, 1983). It means a concern for the questions of social change, order, disorder and conflict and the processes by which these conditions of society are achieved or sustained through the processes of schooling and of physical education within it. It means spending time teasing out how we got to where we are, the relationships between past accretions and present structures. In this spirit we need to consider that the organization of pupils, teaching methods, systems of evaluation etc., may be as historically determined as the content of the curriculum and that teachers only partly choose either of these features. Moreover, any socio-history of PE would only be a sub-quest alongside explanations of school and departmental organization, classrooms, curriculum, pupils and so on. Its central feature would be a focus via classroom transmission on the origins, meaning and consequences of pupil teacher interaction. Our central idea (see Davies and Evans, 1983) is that we may only arrive at a satisfactory view of the activities of PE teachers and teaching as determined and determining, if we locate them historically, organizationally, institutionally and intentionally. And we are a long way from achieving this in the study of physical education.

Acknowledgements

We would like to thank Alan Tomlinson (Brighton Polytechnic Chelsea School of Human Movement) and Leo B. Hendry for reading an earlier draft of this chapter. Unfortunately the limits of space have not allowed us to accommodate all of their suggestions.

Notes

1 This is an elusive concept. We use it here to refer essentially to the physical settings in which much PE occurs (playing fields, gymnasia, etc.,). However, it may also describe contexts in which teacher talk is 'allusive, fragmented and personalized'. This form of talk, as Edward and Furlong (1978, p. 44) point out, isn't easily captured by observers armed with observation schedules. Whether this form of communication prevails in PE classrooms is a matter for investigation.
2 This perhaps is a rather crude characterization of a profession which has long had a humanistic streak. However, whilst its humanistic voice has been heard in a professional debate about curriculum content and method it has hardly found expression in academic research in PE.
3 Although CORNBLETH makes this distinction she simply replaces the concept of 'hidden curriculum' with that of the 'implicit curriculum' and ultimately favours forgoing both in order to 'directly examine the constraints and opportunities as well as the seemingly contradictory messages that are communicated by the school milieu and how they are mediated by students (1980, p. 30). This dissolution, we feel, is unlikely to help clarify the focus of research, especially when the subject of study is PE.
4 A point argued by O'KEEFE, D. in lectures delivered to higher degree students at the Institute of Education, University of London, 1981.
5 We cannot here elaborate on the principles of interpretive sociologies which often inform and direct ethnographic research. However, an excellent introduction to an interpretive theoretical framework is to be found in DOUGLAS, J. (1971).

Bibliography

ANDERSON, W.G. and BARRETTE, G.T. (1978) *What's Going On In Gym: Descriptive Studies of P.E. Classes*, Monograph and Motor Skills: Theory into Practice, 24 Taunton Lake Drive, Newtown, CT0670.

BAILEY, L. (1981) 'Systematic observation of activities in physical education: the need for research', in *Physical Education Review*, Autumn Vol. 4, No. 2, pp. 96–103.

BALL, S. (1981) *Beachside Comprehensive: A Case Study of Secondary Schooling*, Cambridge, Cambridge University Press.

BALL, S. (Ed.) (1984) *Comprehensive Schooling: A Reader*, Lewes, The Falmer Press.

BALL S. and LACEY, C. (1981) 'Subject disciplines as the opportunity for group action: a measured critique of subject sub-culture, in WOODS, P. (Ed.) *Teacher Strategies*, Croom Helm, pp. 157–77.

BALL, S. and GOODSON, I (1984) 'Introduction, defining the curriculum, histories and ethnographies', in GOODSON and BALL (Eds.), *Defining the Curriculum*, Lewes, Falmer Press, pp. 1–15.

BARTON, L, and WALKER, S. (1978) 'Sociology of education at the crossroads', *Educational Review*, Vol. 30, No. 3, pp. 269–83.

BELL, C. and NEWBY, H. (1977) 'The rise of methodological pluralism', in BELL C. and NEWBY, H. *Doing Sociological Research*, George Allen and Unwin, pp. 9–31.

BERNSTEIN, B. (1975) 'The sociology of education: a brief account,' in BERNSTEIN, B. *Class Codes and Control*, Routledge and Kegan Paul, pp. 157–74.

BROHM, J.M. (1977) *Sport — A Prison of Measured Time*, Ink Links.

BUCHER, R. and STRAUSS, A. (1976) 'Professions in process', in HAMMERSLEY, M. and WOODS, P. (Eds.) *The Process of Schooling*, London, Routledge and Kegan Paul.

CARRINGTON, B. (1982) 'Sport as a sidetrack', in BARTON, L. and WALKER, S. (Eds.) (1983) *Race, Class and Education*, Croom Helm, pp. 40–65.

CCCS (1981) *Unpopular Education*, Hutchinson in association with The Centre for Contemporary Cultural Studies, University of Birmingham.

COAKLEY, J.J. (1983) 'Play, games and sport: developmental implications for young people' in HARRIS, J.C. and PARK, R.J. (Eds.) pp. 431–451.

COOK, S. (1985) 'Teaching and learning in physical education: an ethnographic study,' Unpublished MA (Ed.) thesis, University of Southampton.

CORRIGAN, P. (1979) *Schooling The Smash Street Kids*, MacMillan.

CORNBLETH, C. (1984) 'Beyond hidden curriculum', in *Journal of Curriculum Studies*, Vol. 16, No. 1, pp. 29–36.

DAVIES, B. (1977) 'Meanings and motives in going mixed ability', in DAVIES, B. and CAVE, R.G. (Eds.) *Mixed Ability Teaching In The Secondary School*, London, Ward Lock, pp. 18–41.

DAVIES, B. and EVANS, J. (1983) *Bringing Teachers Back In: Toward a Repositioning of the Second Person on the Log*. Paper presented to Teachers' Career and Life Histories Conference at St. Hilda's College, Oxford, September.

DAVIES, B., CORBISHLEY, P., EVANS, J. and KENRICK, C. (1985) 'Integrating methodologies. If the intellectual relations don't get you then the social will', in BURGESS, R. (Ed.) *Strategies of Educational Research*, Lewes, Falmer Press p. 321.

DAWE, A. (1970) 'The two sociologies', *British Journal of Sociology*, XXI (2).

DELAMONT, S. (1976) *Interaction In The Classroom*, Methuen.

DELAMONT, S. and HAMILTON, D. (1984) 'Revisiting classroom research: a continuing cautionary tale', in DELAMONT, S. (Ed.) *Readings on Interaction in The Classroom*, London, Methuen, pp. 3–39.

DEMAINE, J. (1981) *Contemporary Theories in the Sociology of Education*, London, Macmillan.

DENSCOMBE, M. (1980) 'The work context of teaching: an analytic framework for the study of teachers in classrooms', in *British Journal of Sociology of Education*, Vol. 1, No. 3, pp. 279–93.

DOUGLAS, J. (1971) *Understanding Everyday Life*, London, Routledge and Kegan Paul.

EARLS, N. (1985) 'Criteria for Disciplined Naturalistic Inquiry in Physical Education'. Paper presented to the Fourth Conference on Curriculum Theory in PE, Athens, GA, USA.

EDWARDS, A.D. and FURLONG, V.J. (1978) *The Language of Teaching*, London, Heinemann.

ESLAND, G. (1971) 'Teaching and learning as the organization of knowledge', in YOUNG, M.F.D. (Ed.) pp. 70–117.

EVANS, J. (1985) *Teaching In Transition. The Challenge of Mixed Ability Grouping*, Open University Press.

EVANS, J. and COOK, S. (1985) *Teaching and Learning in Physical Education: Towards a Qualitative Understanding*, Paper presented to the ICPHER World Congress, West London Institute of Higher Education, August.

EVANS, J., DUNCAN, M., LOPEZ, S. and EVANS, M. (1985) *Innovation and Evaluation in the Physical Education Curriculum Involving Mixed Sex Grouping*, Paper presented to the ICPHER Conference, West London Institute of Higher Education, August.

FLETCHER, S. (1984) *Women First*, The Athlone Press.

GIDDENS, A. (1979) *Central Problems in Social Theory*, MacMillan.

GOODSON, I. (1984) 'Subjects for study: towards a social history of curriculum', in GOODSON, I.F., and BALL, S.J. (Eds.) *Defining The Curriculum and Ethnographies*, Lewes, Falmer Press, pp. 25–45.

GOODSON, I.F. and BALL, S. *Defining The Curriculum*, Lewes, Falmer Press.

GRIGGS, C. (1981) 'The attitude of the labour movement towards drill in elementary schools, 1870–1925.' in *Bulletin of Physical Education* Summer, pp. 27–31.

HAMMERSLEY, M. (1980) 'On interactionist empiricism', in WOODS, P. (Ed.) *Pupil Strategies*, London, Croom Helm pp. 198–214.

HAMMERSLEY, M. (1980) 'Classroom Ethnography', in HARGREAVES, D.H. (Ed.) *Classroom Studies, Educational Analysis*, Vol. 2 (2), Winter, pp. 47–74.

HAMMERSLEY, M. and ATKINSON, P. (1983) *Ethnography. Principles In Practice*, Tavistock Publications.

HAMMERSLEY, M. and HARGREAVES, A. (1983) *Curriculum Practice*, Lewes, Falmer Press.

HARGREAVES, A. (1978) 'The significance of classroom coping strategies', in BARTON, L. and MEIGHAN, R. (Eds.) *Sociological Interpretations of Schooling and Classrooms: A Reappraisal*, Driffield, Nafferton, pp. 73–101.

HARGREAVES A. (1980) 'Synthesis and the study of strategies: a project for the sociological imagination', in WOODS, P. (Ed.), *Pupil Strategies*, Croom Helm, London, pp. 162–98.

HARGREAVES, A. and WOODS, P. (1984) *Classroom and Staffrooms*, Open University Press.

HARGREAVES D.H. (1967) *Social Relations in a Secondary School*, London, Routledge and Kegan Paul.

HARGREAVES, J. (1982) 'Sport, culture and ideology', in HARGREAVES, J. *Sport, Culture and Ideology*, Routledge and Kegan Paul, pp. 30–62.

HARGREAVES, J. (1982) 'Theorising sport: an introduction', in HARGREAVES, J. (Ed.) pp. 1–30.

HARRIS, J.C. and PARK, R.J. (1983) *Play, Games and Sports in Cultural Contexts*, Human Kinetics.

HENDRY, L.B. (1975) 'Survival in a marginal role: the professional identity of the physical education teacher', in *British Journal of Sociology*, 26, 4, pp. 465–76.

HENDRY, L.B. (1978) *School, Sport and Leisure*, Lepus Books.

HENDRY L.B. (1981) 'School, sport, leisure: psychological aspects of the hidden curriculum,' in *Proceedings of the World Congress of Sports Psychology*, Ottawa.

HENDRY, L.B. (1981a) 'The family, society and leisure: the hidden curriculum,' *Proceedings of an International Seminar on Leisure and Family*, Brugge, Belgium.

HENDRY, L.B. (1983) *Growing Up and Going Out*, Aberdeen University Press.

HOPKINS, D. (1985) *A Teacher's Guide to Classroom Research*, Open University.

HOYLE, E. (1977) 'New directions in the sociology of education and implications for physical education', in KANE, J.E. (Ed.) *Movement Studies and Physical Education*, Routledge and Kegan Paul, pp. 85–111.

JACKSON, P. (1968) *Life In Classrooms*, New York, Holt, Rinehart and Winston.

JENKINS, C. (1982) 'Sociology and physical education', in HARTNETT, A. (Ed.) *The Social Sciences in Educational Studies: a selective guide to literature*, pp. 275–283.

KANE, J.E. (1974) *Physical Education In The Secondary School*, Schools Council Studies, London, Macmillan.

KEDDIE, N. (1971) 'Classroom knowledge', in YOUNG, M.F.D. (Ed.) pp. 133–61.

LACEY, C. (1970) *Hightown Grammar*, Manchester University Press.

LAWSON, H. (1983) 'Paradigms for research on teaching and teachers', in TEMPLIN, T.J. and OLSON, J.K. (Eds.) *Teaching in Physical Education*, Human Kinetics, pp. 339–59.

LUNDGREN, U.P. (1977) *Model Analysis of Pedagogical Process*, Stockholm, Almquist and Wiksell.

MANGAN, J.A. (1973) 'Some sociological concomitants of secondary school physical education: exploratory suggestions', in MANGAN, J.A. (Ed.) *Physical Education and Sport: Sociological and Cultural Perspectives*, Oxford, Basil Blackwell, pp. 23–35.

MANGAN, J.A. (1981) *Athleticism in the Victorian and Edwardian Public School — the Emergence and Consolidation of an Educational Ideology*, Cambridge University Press.

MARDLE, G. and WALKER, M. (1980) 'Strategies and structure: some cultural notes on teacher socialization', in WOODS P. (Ed.) *Pupil Strategies*, London, Croom Helm, pp. 98–125.

MAWER, M. and BROWN, G. (1983) 'Analyzing teaching in physical education', in Aspects of Education 23, *Trends In Physical Education*, The University of Hull, pp. 71–96.

McINTOSH, P. (1979) *Fair Play*, London, Heineman.

McINTYRE, D.I. (1980) 'Systematic observation of classroom activities' in HARGREAVES, D.H. (Ed.) Classroom Studies *Educational Analysis* Vol. 2, No. 2, pp. 3–30, Lewes, The Falmer Press.

McPERSON (1982) 'The child in competitive sport: influence of the social milieu', in MAGILL A., ASH, M.J., SMALL, F.L. (Ed.) *Children In Sport*, Human Kinetics, pp. 247–68.

MEASOR L. and WOODS, P. (1983) *Changing Schools*, Open University Press.

MEHAN, H. (1979) *Learning Lessons: Social Organization in the Classroom*, Cambridge, Harvard University Press.

METZLER, M.W. (1983) 'On styles', in *Quest*, 1983, 35, pp. 145–54.

MILLS, C.W. (1959) *The Sociological Imagination*, Penguin Books.

PARSONS, C. (1982) 'The new evaluation: a cautionary tale,' in McCORMICK, R. (Ed.) *Calling Education To Account*, Heinemann, pp. 192–211.

POLLARD A. (1979) 'Negotiating deviance and "getting done" in a primary school classroom', in BARTON, L. and MEIGHAN, R. (Eds.) *Schools, Pupils and Deviance*, Driffield, Nafferton, pp. 75–95.

REID, I. (1978) *Sociological Perspectives on School and Education*, Open Books.

REYNOLDS, D. and SULLIVAN, M. (1980) 'Towards a new socialist sociology of education', in BARTON, L., MEIGHAN, R. and WALKER, S. (Eds.) *Schooling Ideology and the Curriculum*, Lewes, The Falmer Press, pp. 169–96.

ROSENTHAL, R. and JACOBSON, L. (1968) *Pygmalion in the Classroom*, New York, Holt Rinehart and Winston.

SAUNDERS, E.D. (1973) 'Sociological orientations to the study of physical education', in

MANGAN J.A. (Ed.) pp. 7–20.

SAUNDERS, E.D. (1976) 'Towards a sociology of physical education', in *Momentum*, Dunfermline College of Education, pp. 46–61.

SAUNDERS, E.D. (1982) 'Sport, culture and physical education', in *Physical Education Review*, Spring 1984, Vol. 5. No. 1.

SILVERMAN, D. (1985) *Qualitative Methodology and Sociology*, Gower

SPRADLEY, J.P. (1979) *Participant Observation*, New York, Holt Rinehart and Winston.

SPRADLEY, J.P. (1979a) *The Ethnographic Interview*, New York, Holt Rinehart and Winston.

TEMPLIN, T.J. (1978) *Understanding Life Within Physical Education*, Paper presented at The Mid American College and University Physical Education Conference, Chicago Illinois, January.

TOMLINSON, A. (1982) 'Physical education, sport and sociology: the current state and the way forward', in *Physical Education, Sport and Leisure*: Sociological Perspectives, NATFHE Conference Report, pp. 44–54.

UNDERWOOD, G.L. (1983) *The Physical Education Curriculum in the Secondary School: Planning and Implementation*, Lewes, The Falmer Press.

WALLER, W. (1932) *The Sociology of Teaching*, New York, Wiley.

WESTBURY, I. (1973) 'Conventional classrooms, open classrooms and the technology of teaching', *Journal of Curriculum Studies*, pp. 280–91.

WILLIS, P. (1977) *Learning To Labour*, Saxon House.

WILSON, T.P. (1971) 'Normative and interpretive paradigms in sociology', in DOUGLAS, J.D. (Ed.) *Understanding Everyday Life*, Routledge and Kegan Paul, pp. 57–80.

WOODS, P. (1977) 'Teaching for survival', in WOODS, P. and HAMMERSLEY, M. (Eds.) *School Experience*, Croom Helm, pp. 271–94.

WOODS, P. (1985) 'Sociology, ethnography and teacher practice', in *Teaching and Teacher Education*, Vol. 1, No. 1, pp. 51–62.

WOODCOTT, L.H. (1980) *Ethnographic Research Methods in Education*, Alternative Education Research Association.

WHITTY, G. (1977) Sociology and the problem of radical educational change: notes towards a reconceptualization of the 'new' sociology of education', in YOUNG, M. and WHITTY, G. (Eds.) *Society, State and Schooling*, Lewes, The Falmer Press, pp. 26–59.

YOUNG, M.F.D. (Ed.) (1971) *Knowledge and Control*, Collier-Macmillan.

YOUNG, M.F.D. (1977) 'Curriculum change: limits and possibilities'; in YOUNG, M. and WHITTY, G. (Eds.) *Society, State and Schooling*, Lewes, Falmer Press.

PART I
Current Practice and Future Possibilities

3 Changing Schools in a Changing Society: The Role of Physical Education

Leo B Hendry

Sport, Leisure and Social Change

It has been suggested by Elias and Dunning (1967) that leisure encompasses four spheres of living: family management and private work; rest and idling; sociability and play. Within leisure, idling and relaxation are important, but so too is our quest for excitement. The mimetic (*i.e.* play) sphere is vitally important in producing opportunities for tension and adventure in games, or gambling or in juvenile crime:

> It is in his 'free' time that a man really develops his sense of identity and purpose ... whether it is in a home centred family or an adolescent peer group, for leisure is at least purportedly non–alienated activity. (Young, 1971)

In this context sport has become a massive theatre of our times, spotlighting achievement and success for the players, providing identification and catharsis for the spectators.

In his book *The Third Wave*, the futurologist Toffler (1981) introduced the notion of 'blip' culture to refer to the way the individual is confronted with the mass media.

> On a personal level, we are all besieged and blitzed by fragments of imagery, contradictory or unrelated, that shake up our old ideas and come shooting at us in the form of broken disembodied 'blips'. (Toffler, 1981)

The new kind of culture, '... with its fractured, transitory images ...', described by Toffler can also be applied to leisure sports. Sport occupies many hours of television time, continually feeding us exposure to its value system in a kaleidescope of pictures. It has been pointed out by Kelly (1982) that there is a pervasiveness in televised sport spectacles, and that while the media provides the most common contact with sport for a society, it may also open vistas of possibilities and awaken the desire for participation in individuals:

The democratization of sport is considered something desirable and durable, the main aim of sports activity is to turn it into a leisure pursuit throughout the life cycle of each individual, irrespective of the fact to which socio-professional category he belongs. Therefore, sport should above all be defined in its capacity as a leisure pursuit. (Dumazadier, 1973)

Intensive promotion of leisure sports, especially in the last fifteen years, has converted leisure participation into an expression of mass culture, and in most European countries leisure sports development has been dominated by the notion of 'Sport for All' (European Sports Charter, 1975). This can be seen as a fairly dramatic and recent change in social behaviour. Leisure participation and wide media coverage of sporting spectacles, are not, however, the only aspects of change in modern societies. Family living patterns and styles are also shifting. Tyrrell (1981) suggested that what many consider the archetypal family — at least in more recent times — of two adults and two children is now presented by only fifteen per cent of all households: this underlines how rapid social change can influence the structure of families.

It is important to stress, therefore, that a number of influences and social forces in modern society may have initiated vital changes in leisure and sports participation. Some of these changes — the growth of one parent families, the rise of feminism, a greater symmetry of roles between husband and wife (Young and Willmott, 1973) and the dramatic increase in the number of working women despite growing unemployment (for example, Walters, 1977) are important to understand. Additionally, the move towards a post-industrial society has also produced a new 'leisured' class: the unemployed. An increasing proportion of the population are faced with increased leisure time whether it be a product of shorter working hours, early retirement or unemployment.

In considering the importance of recent social changes for sport and leisure involvement, Emery and Trist (1973) have provided a model of the processes involved in the transition to post-industrialism. The demise of large scale labour intensive and repetitive work obviously has far reaching consequences in altering the relationship between work and leisure, the time available for each dimension, and the role of schools in preparing young people for a leisure existence. Hargreaves (1982) for instance, has suggested that the secondary curriculum should be built around the twin themes of 'community' and 'leisure', while the Alexander Report (1975) recommended life-long learning, the development of a sense of community, local participation in decision-making, and quality of leisure and living.

One of the most important issues to emerge from research findings concerns the leisure interests of working class groups, and more specifically, the perceived attitudes of the working classes towards the increasing amounts of 'free time' available to them either as a result of a shorter working week or by being unemployed. Westergaard (1972), Bacon (1975) and Hendry (1978) all found regular patterns of social but passive leisure involvement despite an increase in the number of available sport organizations and leisure facilities. Even purpose-built industrial sports clubs — providing sporting, games, and social facilities commensurate with privately run clubs — seem to attract few active participants, most employees preferring to adopt a more passive though socially oriented leisure role (for example, Monington, 1972; Hendry and Gordon, 1981). Thus several British studies have emphasized the important relationships between social class and types of leisure involvement at high school level (for example, Emmett, 1971; Hendry, 1978) in later adolescence (for example, Scarlett, 1975; Emmett, 1977; Saunders, 1979) and in adult life (for example, Sillitoe, 1969). In similar vein, a number of studies (for example, Scarlett, 1975; Fogelman, 1976; Hendry, 1978, 1983) have shown that social activities, pop culture and visiting commercial facilities such as public houses are more popular leisure pursuits with teenagers than playing sports or going to youth clubs (Hendry and Simpson, 1977; Hendry *et al*, 1981). Pop culture, as Murdock and Phelps (1973) have outlined, are in many ways central elements in adolescent leisure — particularly for girls — from which many subsidiary activities flow. Studies of leisure and recreational facilities indicate that young people are the most active sub-population in society, trying out and experimenting with a wide range of activities and experiences (for example, Sillitoe, 1969; Rapoport and Rapoport, 1975). But it would seem that even adolescents are involved in social activities in their leisure time rather than necessarily following active sporting pursuits.

A Shifting Leisure Focus in Adolescence

Leisure activities may be chosen for their personal meaning and for social expression, and these choices are, in turn, coloured by influences such as the family, peers, the educational system, the media, leisure promotion industries, and changes in the general social context such as massive unemployment. A crucial point to stress in all this is the way the interplay of factors determining leisure choices varies as the focus of social interests changes across the adolescent years (Coleman, 1979).

If Figure 1 is examined, the changes and continuities in the adolescent's leisure preferences and behaviour (*i.e.* their focus of leisure interests) can be noted. The main factors influencing leisure pursuits are suggested here to be age, sex and social class. These are hardly surprising elements but, when linked to the shifting focus of relationships postulated by Coleman, the model can provide insights into a changing and differential pattern of leisure focus in the teenage years. It is argued that the focus generally shifts from adult-organized clubs and activities, through casual leisure pursuits to commercially organized leisure, and that these transitions may occur roughly at the ages where the main relationship issues postulated by Coleman (1979) — sex, peers, parents — come into focus.

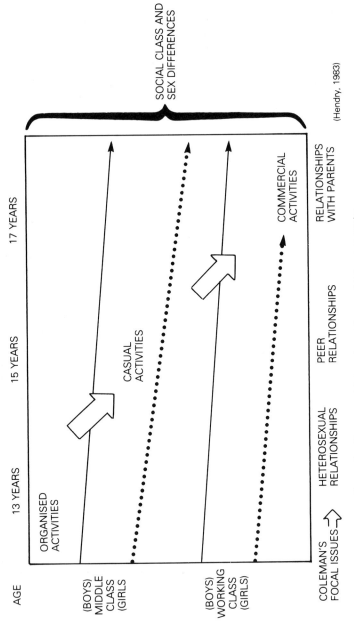

Figure 1. Focuses of interest and types of leisure pursuits

The differential effects of sex and social class on leisure patterns can be explained in relation to a dynamic interplay of factors. The earlier physical and physiological maturity of girls, which underpins their relatively earlier transitions towards peers and casual leisure pursuits, and then towards more exclusive courting dyads and commercial leisure provision may also reflect a more rapid move to social sophistication and may be linked to their perceived 'career' as girl friend and wife.

The continued allegiance of the middle classes, and particularly middle class boys, to games and organized pursuits may be indicative of Sutton-Smith's (1964) conjectures about play-styles and their use as rehearsals for adult life-styles. It may also, of course, reflect the longer dependence on parents (often in conjunction with plans to pursue courses in higher education) which ensures a continuing (and relaxed) relationship with adults, and creates opportunities for further socialization towards particular adult values.

The coincidence of an interest in organized and structured leisure pursuits and clubs, with the focus on heterosexual relationships in early adolescence seems plausible. Conger (1979) has suggested that the increase in the sexual drive that accompanies puberty occurs when close social relationships and leisure activities are largely confined to members of the same sex. It is also a period, Conger pointed out, when the opposite sex can appear rather mysterious and sometimes anxiety-producing. Thus youth clubs and organized adult-led leisure pursuits can provide a 'safe' environment from which to observe and to interact with the opposite sex, but it is a context where the focus of attention is on the action, on the activities, and where the social milieu is less central. Further, the adults present contain the social interactions among members, and the pervading values and norms are directed towards conventional socialization (Eggleston, 1976).

The second leisure focus concerns peer relationships in conjunction with casual pursuits. Because this focal leisure area involves not only peers and casual activities, but also occurs at about the period when the minimal school leaving age is reached, it contains perhaps the stage of greatest diversity of pattern. In part, this conjunction of peer relations and acceptance of sub-cultural values with an interest in casual leisure, may offer some additional insights into the anti-school sub-cultures described by Hargreaves (1967), Murdock and Phelps (1973) and Willis (1977) among others. The lure of the peer group in terms of behaviour is irresistible. Thus, while 'conformist' youths may continue to be more attracted to organizations and adult influence, such structured clubs do not touch many adolescents, who pursue alternative leisure life-styles, which derive identification from attempts to resolve the contradictions of school and work situations. The general feeling among many young people is that official youth clubs are too tame or over-organized to appeal to them and they are too much like school. Organized leisure facilities of necessity require supervision and this fact increases their resemblance to school. Thus, those activities are rejected by those adolescents who reject school, yet are accepted by those who accept school's values (Jephcott, 1967; West, 1967; Hendry, 1978).

At the next focal stage an interest in commercial leisure provision is linked to the peak of conflicts with parents:

> Perhaps, indeed, (adolescents) have been kept in even longer sub-ordination just because they *are* more mature and consequently threatening to the old ... where society does not permit the adolescent to assume a social role compatible with his physical and intellectual development ... adult maturity is come by with more difficulty. (Musgrove, 1964)

Emmett (1977) has reported in a 'follow up' study of over 2000 adolescents three years after leaving school (*i.e.* at nineteen years of age) that factors of gender, social class, occupation, academic attainment and peer group allegiances continued to exert their influence on recreational involvement. For instance, roughly twice as many boys as girls belonged to organized clubs; girls tended to enter (casually) into activities without necessarily joining officially; casual activities which could be undertaken with a friend of the opposite sex (tennis, hill walking, horse riding) were popular with both sexes, yet there was also some 'carry over' beyond school days of traditional school sports. Nevertheless, overall, there was a decline in participation in sport over the three years of post-school life.

Emmett concluded that leisure interests in later adolescence reflect the fact that post-school years are courting years; that young people (and particularly males) at work have more money and greater freedom in selecting their leisure pursuits; and that at eighteen years of age they are legally entitled to drink in public houses. Adolescents in this period of their lives are closer to being perceived as adults, and their leisure-time pursuits will be adult-orientated leisure interests. This fact alone will create a climate for inter-generational disagreements, as Musgrove (1964) described, even although the actual leisure patterns of adolescents may closely match their sub-cultural heritage.

Unemployment Redefines Leisure

Both the cultural framework of Western capitalism and the status and self-esteem of the individual lean heavily, but increasingly precariously, on the concept of work. This helps to explain why, even though work is frequently unpleasant, boring and alienating, it is still firmly held to be preferable to unemployment. Jenkins and Sherman (1979) summed up this paradox:

> Yet, whether skills become outdated or not, whether people start to feel inadequate at work or not, they do feel they have to work — and not just for the money. The work ethic is so deeply engrained in British and other industrialized societies that it has acquired a value in itself even though it is widely regarded as unpleasant.

Education has continued to reflect this emphasis on the value and importance of work. While the modern school may additionally emphasize education for leisure, it is still preparation for leisure within the context of work. Secondary school education has been seen by many pupils, teachers and parents, as being primarily a preparation for work (Morton-Williams and Finch, 1968; Lindsay, 1969; Hendry, 1978). Like government vocational training schemes, this stress helps to reinforce assumptions about the centrality of work in the human life plan, and by implication increases the individual's social and psychological dependence on it.

But as Hargreaves (1981) indicated:

> Very little of our secondary education is strictly vocational: schools are more orientated towards public examinations than towards jobs. Yet for those who leave school at sixteen, a job is the natural next step, one that has been awaited with eagerness for it signifies independence and adult standing.

What is the consequence then when adolescents reach this threshold and there are no jobs waiting? Hargreaves continues:

> ... When employment is then denied to the young school-leaver with his or her scroll of 'qualifications' the reaction is naturally one of shock and disappointment, personal crisis and social dislocation.

A little further thought, however, indicates that this simple assumption is not always justified, and that the relationship between youth unemployment and self-image or self-esteem is a complex one. Closer examination sometimes demonstrates the profound ambivalence exhibited by adolescents towards work. Carter (1971), for instance, argued that many adolescents are not particularly interested in a future job or jobs but rather in 'the status and perquisites of a young worker', and the financial opportunities it offers to develop a rich leisure existence. Recent studies which have examined unemployed school leavers (Roberts *et al*, 1982; Hendry *et al*, 1984) stress both the ability of young people to cope well with unemployment without necessarily enjoying it, and the diversity of responses of adolescents to the experience of unemployment. The heterogeneous nature of youth unemployment suggests that to equate a long period without work with psychological distress is an over-simplification.

The impact of unemployment on adolescence is complex and far-reaching. From the study of one Scottish city carried out by Hendry and Raymond (1983) it was apparent that pupils about to enter the job-market were fully aware of the problems of finding a job, and the school's emphasis on this aspect of unemployment had an indirect effect on working adolescents, creating feelings of insecurity about their jobs and forcing them to remain in jobs they found unpleasant and unsatisfying.

But the major impact of unemployment on adolescents seems to be its ultimate effect on the transition from adolescence to adulthood. Being unable

47

to find work appears to frustrate adolescents' expectations of post-school patterns of work and leisure. Unemployment, even in the short term, redefines the individual's conception of leisure time. Parker (1971), for example, saw leisure as a time of freedom bounded by the constraints of work and non-work commitments. As De Grazia (1962) wrote: 'Work is the antonym of free-time. But not of leisure. Leisure and free-time live in two different worlds ... Anyone can have free-time.'

A study by Hendry and Raymond (1983) seemed to indicate that this relationship determines the attitudes school leavers have towards leisure. 'You can only have leisure when you're working — you'd enjoy yourself more in your free time if you're working.' The unemployed adolescents in their study felt that they were being excluded from the more 'adult' leisure of their employed contemporaries: 'I'm too old for youth clubs now.' 'You can't go out with your mates when they're working, they've got more money than you've got.'

Hendry, Raymond and Stewart (1984) also discovered that a major consequence of unemployment was the adolescents' conception of their workless status as denying them entry into the 'package' of work and leisure which makes up 'adult' lifestyle. In addition, Coffield, Burrill and Marshall (1983) noted how the young unemployed lacked the financial resources to play an active part in the culture of young workers. This isolation from working peers led Roberts (1983) to suggest that the young unemployed are not being socialized into the culture of work. None of the adolescents investigated by Hendry and Raymond (1985) had broken into the 'adult' package of work-related leisure identified by Hendry, Raymond and Stewart (1984). Financial constraints meant that only very few visits could be made to pubs or discos. Cheap, informal, often passive leisure activities were preferred by both boys and girls.

However, the young unemployed were reasonably satisfied with their leisure, though the generally older long-term unemployed were possibly less satisfied because they were more aware of being excluded from adult types of leisure. Although YTS trainees also felt their leisure would improve if they had a 'real' job, their fairly high level of satisfaction with their evening leisure is explained by the fact that they had a purpose to their free time, that is as relaxation from their daily work. Brenner and Bartell (1983) isolated the positive use of free time as being the single most reliable predictor of psychological well-being during unemployment. Hepworth (1980) and Warr and Payne (1983) also stressed the psychological dangers if time is unstructured and directionless.

In Hendry and Raymond's (1983) study some adolescents had made no attempt to structure the large amounts of free time available to them. Others had developed a structure revolving around the fact of being unemployed, using visits to 'sign on' or seek work as the organizing pivots of their week. Girls, they noted, tended to drift into a structure closely related to a traditional domestic role, becoming unpaid housekeepers to their family. While taking on this role imposes a rigid structure on the individual's time (which may be welcome), it also raises important questions. The decline of work should not mean that women find themselves constrained by domestic roles while the possible development of alternative lifestyles is available only to men. Hendry and Raymond's investigation showed that sports and hobbies — the sort of leisure activities encouraged by the schools — were not considered to be important in structuring leisure in the unemployed situation, a fact backed up by the low carry-over effect of school leisure activities among the school leavers. Schools generally do not seem to have done much in terms of helping pupils to develop the skills and attitudes necessary for a 'leisured existence', but then they are caught in a trap where to educate for leisure can be seen as a euphemism for educating for the dole queue. Hargreaves (1981) commented:

> It is quite easy to see special leisure-based courses for pupils destined for the dole queues, or educational grants, or Youth Opportunity Programmes, as modern instruments of social control.

However, many unemployed adolescents in Hendry and Raymond's (1985) study felt that structure emphasized the repetitive nature of their existence. This seems to support Kelvin's (1981) point that structure is not enough to secure a positive response to unemployment. The question of why one adolescent is successful in coping with unemployment while another fails and drifts into despair cannot on the basis of Hendry and Raymond's findings be answered by referring to the length of time spent without work. Nor is it answered by referring to any one of a number of psycho-social factors taken singly. Structure can be supportive or it can be stifling, families can be sympathetic or they can be pressuring, aspirations can be maintained or they can collapse, self-esteem can be kept defensively high during long-term unemployment or it can be low in the apparently supportive atmosphere of YTS course. An understanding of youth unemployment must not only take account how these factors work in combination, but must also understand each one's capacity for positive or negative orientation. The unemployed adolescent will usually experience a mixture of positive and negative factors. It is only when a number of negative factors impinge on the individual concurrently that unemployment becomes an ordeal (like Coleman's (1979) ideas of the 'overlap' of focal issues). Often, the influence of several positive factors can allow the unemployed youth to cope well with the experience.

The period of time unemployed seems to overlay the interaction of other factors. Its influence would appear to be both dependent and independent. Thus, a number of negative factors, for example, low self-image, low aspirations and family pressures would be likely to lengthen a period of unemployment. In other cases time would seem to be independent, a supportive family, enjoyable leisure and good time structure making it fairly easy for an individual to cope with unemployment even after a fairly lengthy period without work.

If, and when, economic recovery allows an escape from the present recession, the gap between the desire for work and the opportunity for actual employment may still not narrow to any great extent. Work-sharing, informal work and changing patterns of leisure are likely to be part of a necessary adjustment to a decline in the net amount of employment available. Although leisure time has increased dramatically in the last century it has consistently remained as being defined by work. As Hargreaves (1981) wrote:

> Within the framework of the work ethic, then, to be denied paid employment is to be rendered not fully human. People complain and grumble about their work, yet they seem willing to spend long hours in its pursuit. Indeed, in preference to working for shorter hours (and so increased leisure time) many people will work longer hours for a higher income and opt for do-it-yourself home repairs and improvements, so permitting the purchase of both labour-saving devices and expensive leisure goods and services, including holidays. These may be understandable instrumental reasons for enduring long hours at work which is distasteful: but surveys indicate surprisingly high levels of work satisfaction, even among manual workers who exercise little skill or responsibility.

Nevertheless, Jahoda (1979) suggested that: 'Human ingenuity could invent new social institutions which could meet the needs normally satisfied by employment ... if current institutions no longer meet these needs, new institutions must be created.'

One such development of our social institutions has been the creation of holistic education. Holistic principles of life-long education have been conceptually and methodologically developed over the last twenty years (OECD, 1975). Within this style of education the emphasis is placed upon an active participation in learning. And, of particular relevance to the present argument, the purpose of holistic education is not only focused on work and employment activities, but also involves learning in leisure, through leisure and for leisure. Educational policy and the development of the Youth Training Scheme may help to buttress adolescents' vocational orientations, but they also reinforce the centrality of work. In the future, education and youth services may have to play a key role in developing alternative attitudes to work and leisure.

> 'Perhaps today we are ready for John Leigh's (1971) insights that the primary skills in which schools must train young people are social organizational ones ... They are skills which relate to groups of people whatever activity they are pursuing ... People become active and responsible when they exert a genuine influence on the decisions which affect them, at home, at work and in all aspects of communal life.' (Hargreaves, 1981)

Perhaps this notion that 'activity' and 'responsibility' should be prime ingredients of an educational skills menu is one that needs to be incorporated into education for leisure. Kelvin (1981) has noted that the 'leisure' activities currently promoted in schools provide only poor structures for social interaction and are poor substitutes for the complex interactions found in work situations. He believes that only activities which demand commitment to, and interdependence with particular (leisure) groups can, to some extent, reproduce this work-like social structure.

Schooling and Preparation for Society

What is the role of the school in helping young people develop the skills — and preoccupations — necessary for a changing society? Is the school's role a successful one?

Some years ago Carter (1972) argued that:

> ... There is this substantial hard core of young people to whom the idea of remaining at school is abhorrent ... and (this is) based in a sub-culture and a social system which rejects school and all it is presumed to stand for.

More recently a study by Hendry and McKenzie (1978) has shown that since the raising of the minimum school leaving age to sixteen years in the 1970s comprehensive schools still contain two groups of pupils, broadly described as being in favour of — and against — raising the school leaving age, each group having sharply different values, attitudes and aspirations. Pupils' pro- and anti-school sub-cultures with their sharply different values, attitudes and aspirations seem as firmly entrenched in comprehensive schools as they were in selective and non-selective schools (*cf.* Hargreaves, 1967; Ball, 1981).

It can be suggested that such a divisive system is no longer appropriate in the changing modern world. There is an increasing awareness of the fact that both for employment and for other aspects of life in the adult world young people of all kinds require many competencies, abilities and qualities other than the cognitive academic skills which are emphasized in schools (see Ryrie, 1981).

The 'inappropriate' nature of what is taught in many secondary schools is well illustrated by the aspirations and awareness of their future displayed by working class pupils in Willis' (1977) case studies. These working class boys saw secondary education as a 'confidence trick' and were totally disengaged from it. They behaved in the school by 'playing the system' in order to gain some personal control over the school organization. Such opposition could appear as an inversion of the values held up by school authority (such as diligence, deference and respect): these behaviour patterns became antithetical as conducted by 'the lads' and their opposition was expressed mainly as a 'style'. Popular criticisms of education are based on the feelings of many pupils and their parents that: 'School by its compulsory nature is a sentence which must be served before the real business of life can begin' (Weir and Nolan, 1977). However, this blanket rejection of the educational diet currently being offered does little to help us construct a system which would be of more use or have more appeal for our young people.

Relatively minor changes can substantially affect pupil attitudes. For instance Rutter *et al* (1979) found that schools with similar pupil-intake varied greatly on outcome measures of school behaviour, attendance, delinquency and academic attainment. The differences were due to the way the schools differed in internal organization. But it seems likely that some more fundamental reorganization of curricular aims is also called for. As was stated earlier Hargreaves (1982) has suggested that the secondary curriculum should be built around the twin themes of 'community' and 'leisure', while the Alexander Report (1975) recommended life-long learning.

Can this broadening of the narrow educational remit to a new theme of education for life increase the aptness of the school experience for our young people? In particular, are leisure education and the physical education component of the leisure programme seen as appropriate for the needs of a generation growing up in a post-industrial society?

Education for Leisure

It can be argued that the importance of leisure has become more apparent in recent years due primarily to shifts in the work-leisure balance in society and to the spectacular increase in unemployment, particular among young people. Unemployment creates a great deal of 'free' time, but the equation of 'free' time with leisure time must be strongly disputed (Hendry *et al*, 1984). It has been suggested by Leigh (1971) that education for leisure attempts: to increase both the true range of choices available and the ability of the individual to make effective and significant choices. The majority of schools attempt to provide leisure education in very similar ways, usually through a mixture of curricular and extra-curricular activities, with the addition of schemes such as the Duke of Edinburgh Award Scheme and community service. Hence the activities which educators often see in terms of the leisure lives of pupils are sports, games, art, music and practical subjects, such as woodwork, metalwork and technical drawing, which, even though they may have a vocational bias in a narrow sense, are useful for 'do it yourself' and recreation (Basini, 1975). Often these subjects are also offered to pupils in extracurricular time.

The restricted appeal of schools in general, and their leisure education programmes in particular, has been commented on by Emmet (1971), Scarlett (1975), Roberts (1983) and Hendry (1978; 1983). Yet in designing leisure education programmes, schools may well reject ways in which adolescents actually spend their leisure time simply because these do not conform to the school's view of how leisure should be 'profitably' used:

> Educationists who plead the new problem of leisure as an urgent
> reason for the development of this or that in the curriculum are

expressing, whether they are frank about it or not, their disappointment with the way that people use their time. (Simpson, 1973)

Thus it has been found that of the range of extra-curricular activities which the vast majority of schools provide in order to substantiate their claim of providing leisure education, most are only actually pursued by a minority of adolescents — mainly middle class, academically able pupils (for example, Hendry, 1983).

It is clear, therefore, that school influences provide important constraints and opportunities for young people's leisure. A recent survey of all secondary schools in one Scottish region and a case study of one school (Hendry and Marr, 1985) has shown that there were few differences between schools in terms of the organization of leisure education despite considerable differences in location and size. Much greater differences emerged however when schools were asked to state the aims of, and their attitudes towards leisure education. All schools reported an extensive range of available extra-curricular activities. Despite this range, the regional survey and the case study both provided evidence (as do other studies) that about one-third of pupils were regularly involved: more than half were completely non-participant. In their leisure time away from school the most popular activities for the mid-adolescent years were socially oriented pursuits, and few of these activities could be directly related to school influences.

Physical Education and Leisure

Attempts to define the objectives of physical education, accepting it as part of education as a whole rather than as a separate discipline, have been made in the past. A Schools' Council paper (1968) presented the view that physical education was concerned with the balanced growth of each individual by developing physical resources, advancing the skilled and efficient use of these resources, the development of a capacity for creative and imaginative work, assisting the development of initiative, moral and social attitudes, and responsible behaviour, providing purposeful and enjoyable experiences in a sufficient range of activities, encouraging increased responsibility in a choice of activities in school, and providing a sense of achievement and positive attitudes towards participation in post-school physical recreation.

A Working Party of the Scottish Education Department (1972) stated:

The aim of physical education could be said to be that of providing young people with opportunities for activities which have intrinsic value in terms of the health and development of the total personality. Some of its contributions are readily recognized, others less so. It is not always recognized, for instance, that physical education assists the social development of individuals.

The idea of social and interpersonal relations (synnoetics) has, in fact, been discussed at length by educationists. There is concern in this realm chiefly with the development of understanding between persons, so that the individual may be enabled to see himself in a less egocentric and self-referential manner. Whitfield (1971) wrote:

> If physical education is to contribute significantly to the synnoetic realm in addition to promoting bodily health, a change of emphasis from the acquisition of particular physical skills to an understanding of others in the context of play and leisure is required.

Such social education within the physical education programme would not detract from aims concerning post-school life: Physical education ... should have helped pupils both directly and indirectly in that they will have had an introduction to the kind of sports they may pursue as young adults (Scottish Education Department, 1972.)

If prescriptions about physical education recommend that this subject has educational potential in developing social awareness and interpersonal understanding, as well as interesting pupils in physical activities during their school days and for their current and post-school leisure, do empirical findings about the influence of the physical education curriculum and about the teaching approaches of physical education teachers paint the same rosy picture?

With regard to the physical education curriculum, Whitehead (1969) found a fairly limited curriculum in operation despite general expansive trends in educational thought and practice at the beginning of the 1970s. Whitehead and Hendry (1976) have further reported that despite the inclusion of more educational gymnastics and modern educational dance than are to be found in boys' schools, girls' secondary school sports programmes are also selected from fairly familiar traditional activities. It could be said therefore that the content of secondary schools' physical education programmes for boys and girls seems not to have changed as radically as many may have believed (Whitehead and Hendry, 1976).

If the prescriptive aims and aspirations outlined for physical education are realized mainly through a rather conservative and traditional programme, then the teachers' approach to the curriculum becomes crucial in attempting to create interest, enjoyment, favourable present and future attitudes to sport on the part of pupils in modern society, and in fostering good interpersonal relationships between teachers and pupils. What is known of teachers' and pupils' perceptions of the physical education programme in British schools? Teachers' perceptions of objectives, content, methodology and teaching strategies were investigated in the mid-seventies by a Schools' Council enquiry (Kane, 1974). There was fairly conventional emphasis on topics within the subject; team games, gymnastics, athletics, swimming, dance (for girls) and outdoor pursuits. Teachers considered pupils interests by lessening compulsion across the years, after a fairly restricted programme in the first two years of the secondary school. With regard to pupil effects, there was a strongly held view that enjoyment and satisfaction were the main effects of participation in physical activities. Other highly ranked items referred to release from tension, physical development, self-confidence and skills acquisition.

Rather similar findings were reported by Hendry (1978), in a study of all the secondary schools in a designated area of Central Scotland. It is possible to suggest, in the light of these studies, that a common ideology runs through the teaching of physical education in Great Britain. Thus, despite variations in the day-to-day encounters between teachers and pupils, in teaching styles among teachers, and in the general 'ethos' of individual schools, general approaches to the sports curriculum, and outcomes in terms of pupil response may show strong commonalities from school to school. Such general findings raise a number of interesting issues about physical education curricula as they exist in schools today.

Major educational outcomes then, as perceived by teachers, were enjoyment, health, skills development and useful preparation for post-school leisure. But in British schools pupils are offered a fairly traditional range of physical activities, though it is a broad menu — especially since it includes compulsory time-tabled lessons and extra-curricular activities — with an emphasis on achievement and competition. Hence, the context of most physical education curricula is rather heavily biased towards selective competitive activities of both team and individual forms, even although potentially there may be a wide sports programme available to pupils.

This suggests that school sports will be most liked by pupils who are highly skilled, competitive and achievement oriented. In the school setting, evidence indicates that it is middle class pupils who 'do well' in school who are by and large the pupils who take part in extra-curricular activities including physical recreation and sports (Start, 1966; Emmett, 1971; Reid, 1972; Hendry, 1978), and non-sporting clubs and pursuits like school choir or debating society (Reid, 1972; Hendry, 1978) and become prefects (Start, 1966; Hargreaves, 1972). These trends have evident implications for post-school sporting and leisure interests (for example, Hendry, 1983).

School sport provides a clear differential effect on pupils — for many there is a decline in interest in sports across the secondary school years as has been noted (Ward *et al*, 1968), and this decline becomes more marked as pupils reach the minimum leaving age (*i.e.* sixteen years of age in Britain), (Monks, 1968; King, 1973; Saunders, 1979). The programme and the ensuing teaching processes create a lessening in pupils' involvement — especially for working class pupils and girls — across the school years (Whitehead and Hendry, 1976; Moir, 1977; Hendry, 1978). It has been argued that this decline in interest in school sports is a reflection of a more general syndrome of 'school rejection' (Hendry and Thorpe, 1977).

What is clear is that school influences provide important constraints and opportunities for young people's leisure. Further, the school's sporting offerings contrast somewhat with many young people's leisure interests where the emphasis can be on informal social activities, often centred on pop culture (Hendry, 1983, Hargreaves, 1967 and Sugarman, 1968). Thus, on the basis of Hendry's (1978) findings a series of dilemmas, contradictions and conflicts can be suggested at various levels. Firstly, in physical activities and sports there appeared to be some expansion of offerings, yet relatively little taken up by pupils: teachers' aims centred on interest and enjoyment, yet competition, status and winning were sought after. This seems to be a deep-seated conflict in the field of physical education. Teachers obviously experienced a reality gap between their stated aims and operational teaching processes, where the under-lying ideology of competitive commitment and achievement as expressed in the implementation of the sports programme clashed with their educational aspirations of satisfaction and success for all pupils and of leisure preparation and education. This is true in the leisure programme generally (Hendry and Marr, 1985). In Eggleston's (1977) terms there are innovatory intentions but a traditional system operating within the physical education curriculum. As Stenhouse (1975) stated: 'I believe that our educational realities seldom conform with our educational intentions'.

Linked to this is a professional dilemma for the teacher of physical education. Teachers were asked by Hendry (1978) to rank the 'ideal' qualities of the successful physical education teacher. The items ranked highest were: knowledge about the subject, ability to win pupils' respect, ability to communicate ideas, capacity to work hard, knowledge of children, a good organizer, and ability to inspire confidence. Yet pupils, whilst considering physical education teachers to be approachable, also saw them as competitive, aggressive and giving greater attention to more highly skilled pupils. While pupils who were involved in school sports stated that physical education teachers gave them confidence and acted as pastoral counsellors, non-participants felt quite the opposite! Here, therefore, is a role conflict of the pupil-centred 'guidance' teacher versus the achievement-orientated coach trying to keep up with the academic Jones's. The idea of the physical education teacher's dilemma caused by conflicting expectations for his role from pupils and staffroom colleagues has been previously outlined (Hendry, 1975).

In Hendry's (1978) study a large number of pupils when questioned indicated feelings of isolation and neglect within the compulsory time-tabled programme. By far the most frequent comments were directed towards physical education teachers' decisions about teaching procedures and choice of activities without any *real* pupil understanding of reasons behind these decisions. Whitfield (1971) has referred to this as 'curricular trade secrets', where pupils are excluded from knowledge of what is happening to them in terms of changes in behaviour. When sports groups were formed teachers appeared to give much of their attention to the more skilful athletes, so that other pupils felt there was a lack of opportunity to be helped in making personal progress. In other words, many felt they were being ignored by teachers and received little coaching as a result. While physical education teachers might well justify their actions in terms of learning strategies, the important point is that from the pupils' perspective, their main concern may be about the social context of learning. An extract of quotations from Hendry (1978) makes this point:

What about school sports and P.E.?

'You do not get taught right ... the teacher tells you to play rounders then just goes away because she has no time for pupils.'
'I don't like changing for PE lessons.'
'Sometimes boring, sometimes OK, but it depends on what you're doing.'
'They're approachable OK, but they've no time for you unless you play for the team.'
'They tell you exactly what to do ... I'd like to choose sometimes.'
'Teachers don't take much interest in individual children ... they concentrate on the "stars" ... they leave us to play on our own.'

The evidence suggested that the differential perceptions of teachers, and the perceived differential treatment of pupils can create a hidden curriculum of school sports potentially every bit as divisive as one operating within classroom subjects (for example, Hargreaves, 1967; Willis, 1977).

Hendry's findings showed that physical education teachers' hold differential views of active and non-participant pupils, with more favourable attitudes towards sports participants. Of the three groups, competitors were seen by teachers to be most enthusiastic, friendly, popular, reliable, and of attractive appearance, and muscular physique, as well as being highly skilled physically.

In rather the same way as classroom teachers, certain personal characteristics may be used by physical education teachers as the basis for differential treatment of pupils. It seems that the interactions between the teacher and pupils, either in the classroom or on the games field, may be crucial in conveying a hidden curriculum of 'messages' of praise or disapproval, and attention or neglect, which subsequently influence different pupils' attitudes, interests and performance in school activities. The physical education teacher is not immune from the 'hidden curriculum' either. The teacher has to create teaching styles and strategies commensurate with the demands and constraints of the organization of the teaching situation and the school and at the same time has to transform various societal influences and expectations into a sports curriculum and a process of physical education teaching.

Further, specialization and professionalism of various types are given status in our society, yet the rapid growth of new sports creates more and more fragmentation (for example, Toffler, 1981) which 'de-skills' the physical education teacher to a greater and greater extent. If the teacher develops real expertise in a limited range of activities (to the neglect of other topics within the sports curriculum) this conflicts with the individual needs and legitimate desires of pupil-choice. Thus given the freedom to plan their teaching approach, should physical education teachers devise a curriculum to match the ideology of classroom colleagues thereby winning their respect and gaining status or attempt to provide a programme of 'sport for all' which might be seen as a paternalistic curriculum for social control, building up 'pupils' motivation to conform'?

Secondly, the present system can lead to a situation where pupils who are active sports participants internalize the 'official values' of competition and achievement in both academic and sporting spheres and receive differential treatment from teachers for this adherence to the dominant ideology in the form of greater attention and verbal reinforcement. They can also gain official social rewards by being given positions of responsibility and minor success roles in the school (such as prefects, team captain) and by being praised at school assemblies for competitive success. Pupils in Hendry's (1978) study were aware of prestige activities and of differential treatment given to those pupils who represented the school in various forms of competitive sports and pursuits. In this way the relational potential of the subject in developing social understanding, relations and social skills (so often cited as a crucial aim for the subject) is ignored so that pupils receive 'messages' of differential prestige and status with consequent effects on their self-esteem particularly in relation to sports participation in both their present and future leisure. Therefore the second conflict relates to the 'appropriate' teaching orientation to adopt based on teachers' curricular decisions and pupils' responses to this approach.

A third dilemma is apparent. Do teachers attempt to maintain their present competitive orientation and continue to risk a high percentage 'drop out' of pupils from voluntary school sport and physical recreation in the face of recent societal shifts like the work-leisure balance, or change their practical teaching approach to encompass a more general source of success and involvement for all pupils, with the possible loss of commitment and dedication by those pupils who are strongly motivated by competitive sports and their resultant rewards which reflects the values of wider society? A reputation for success in school sports may provide greater incentives for continued involvement in post-school life. A series of post-school studies have shown that despite an association between school sport and leisure sport and between past and current involvement in sport, there was a pronounced tendency to reduce the extent of participation or to stop participation in sport on leaving school (for example, Emmett, 1977), but this tendency was less marked among the group who were competitors in school (see Hendry and Douglass, 1975; Hendry, 1976). Thus the link between sport and society — and the conflicts this generates — is in relation to values: sports are reflections of society itself and its various sub-cultures, their relationships with authority, ideologies and other social systems: sport is a reproduction of society, warts and all, so to speak!

Changing School, Changing Society and Physical Education and Sport

If the link between sport and society *is* related to attitudes and values; and if school does act as an important socializing agency for young people in our society, then it is necessary for us to look at future possibilities for schools generally, and, more specifically, within them at the sphere of physical education and sport.

In the 1970s the community school seemed to be both a creative and a convenient response to a wide variety of educational and social movements of the time. It was to respond to the educational needs of all age groups in the spirit of *education permanente*; it was to make a major educational and social contribution to the particular needs of deprived areas; in a world of rapidly changing work patterns it was to rise to the educational challenge of unemployment, redeployment and increased leisure time; and in its management and policy-making structures it was to reflect the growing recognition that everyone, regardless of social background or status, had the right to share in the decisions which affected their lives. The expectations were high; such schools at their best were to be the educational pivot round which a new sense of 'community' would be both reflected and created.

The concept of the community school was widely recognized and accepted in the Western world and, in some countries, the idea attracted considerable capital investment. It resulted in a fever of creativity in which classrooms, staffrooms and school playgrounds found themselves rubbing shoulders with swimming pools, libraries, sports halls, even shops, theatres and clinics in a new physical embodiment of what 'schooling' and its relationship to society — and its local community — might be about. At an economic level, these purpose-built community schools were also a bureaucratic recognition that joint, centralized investment in sports, cultural, social, recreational as well as educational resources could result in a level of provision which would go well beyond the resources of any one department.

The scale of capital investment involved, however, meant that by the late 1970s, within a climate of looming recession, it was unlikely that the purpose-built community school would proliferate on any large scale. What mattered anyway, it was argued, was the spirit of the community school and the philosophy of community education which it generated; that philosophy was in no way dependent on physical plant and was capable of expression in some form in every school.

The Carnegy Report (1977) argued that individual and social objectives were equally important and that:

> The distinctive contribution which the concept of community education may be said to bring ... is its emphasis on the process as one in which the benefits to and the contributions of the individual are matched by those of the groups and communities to which he or she belongs.

Clearly there are close links between 'leisure and recreation' on the one hand and 'community education' on the other. Many of the activities encompassed within both concepts are identical, much of the policy discussion and many of the contemporary problems are similar. At one level it is perhaps easier to see their similarities. First, both are based on the free choice of the individual and how he spends his free time. Second, they encompass many of the same kinds of activities. 'Leisure comprises generally the non-work activities of socializing, amateur sport, tourism, recreation, the arts and some education ...' (Roberts, 1981) Third, they are both committed to participation, recognizing that in areas of their lives where people can exercise complete discretion about whether or how they will become involved they have the right to some say in the decision-making process.

> ... To an increasing number of people an essential ingredient is participation in decision-making; the opportunity to have some say in and control over events. This participation ... can take various forms (and) ... makes the link with leisure particularly appropriate, with its emphasis on discretionary time and choice. Expectations and aspirations for some control over events may be even greater in leisure than in other areas of life. (Haworth, 1979)

Fourth, both claim that participation will improve the quality of life.

> Whatever the views held about leisure, there is general recognition that, for individuals and communities its mode of use is an indicator as well as a powerful determinant of the quality of life they enjoy. (Scottish Standing Consultative Council on Youth and Community Service, 1968)

Fifth, although neither has become institutionalized in the narrow sense, both 'leisure and recreation' and 'community education' have become part of national and local bureaucracy.

Lastly, it is precisely because both 'leisure and recreation' and 'community education' have become part of the bureaucratic structure that both have had to become involved in the bureaucratic procedures of negotiation, planning, monitoring and accountability.

Justifying planning in the context of leisure and recreation, however, Burton (1970) contended: 'The case for planning for recreation is that, if carried through successfully, it will provide a better overall provision of facilities for leisure.' Be that as it may, it remains true that paternalistic planning of leisure provision has failed to attract a wide range of participants or to have much impact on local or national leisure patterns. There are two further anomalies. Firstly, that by far the most popular leisure activities are those which are home-based, watching television, reading, gardening, knitting and so on, and the most important leisure activities outside the home are those which have a social function such as eating out or visiting the local pub. These leisure activities may not measure up to the values which leisure providers wish to emphasize and they may not lend themselves to centrally-based provision in a locality.

Secondly, it is clear that the 15–20 age group is one of the most dependent on out-of-home leisure activities. However, for these young people:

Football apart, preferences would appear to be for activities which could be arranged without having to join an organization, which are not necessarily competitive in a club or team sense, and in which a high degree of technical skill is not necessary in order to gain enjoyment. (Fox, 1977)

Nisbet *et al* (1984) in a study of both rural and urban locales in a Scottish region, found that over 70 per cent of pupils in their last year of compulsory schooling had been members of a sports club or team at some time in the past, but only 47 per cent were members at the time of investigation. With regard to other interests or hobbies clubs 80 per cent had been members in the past, but only 50 per cent were currently involved. The trend was most evident for uniformed organizations like Scouts and Guides where 75 per cent of adolescents had been members but only 16 per cent had maintained membership into their mid-teens.

The educator's task is not to make value judgments on the desirability of one particular leisure activity over another but to stimulate interests and continually assist in the development of skills required to make perceptive choices on leisure issues (Leigh, 1971). Facilities are important but so is the non-directive leisure education in which 'individuals develop an understanding of self-leisure, and the relationship of leisure to their life-styles and the fabric of society' (Mundy and Odum, 1979). These ideas can be generalized more widely to the educational processes available to young people in developing competencies required in modern society. Raven (1982), for example, has made the point that the qualities most urgently required for operating organizations in our society effectively fall into three broad areas:

1   Human resources; value-laden competencies: these include qualities like initiative, leadership, and the willingness to observe the way our organizations and society work and think out the implications for one's own behaviour.
2   Perceptions and expectations relating to the way society works, and one's own role in that structure: under this heading are included such aspects as people's self images, the way they think their organizations work and their own role and that of others in those organizations, their understanding of organizational social climates which make for innovation, responsibility and development.
3   People's understandings of what is meant by a number of terms which describe relationships within organizations — terms like leadership, decision-taking, democracy, responsibility, accountability and delegation.

Raven further argued that the implication for education is that:

Educators need to help people to think through some of the issues . . . they need to help them think about how their organizations should and do operate, and about their own role and the role of others in these organizations and in their society.

There are clear links here with the views of Leigh (1971), Hargreaves (1982) and Hendry (1983) on education through leisure. These ideas raise the vital question of change in education.

New Directions in Leisure Education?

It is possible to argue therefore that approaches and attitudes of schools to sports and leisure have been inclined in the past towards recreation rather than true leisure education. This may be illustrated through reference to the model presented in Figure 2. Many schools appear to conform to a pattern which was described by Mundy and Odum (1979) as 'providing' (*i.e.* Recreational Training) rather than 'enabling' (*i.e.* Leisure Education). Schools have tended

Figure 2. *Diagrammatic representation of comparative approaches to recreational training and leisure education*

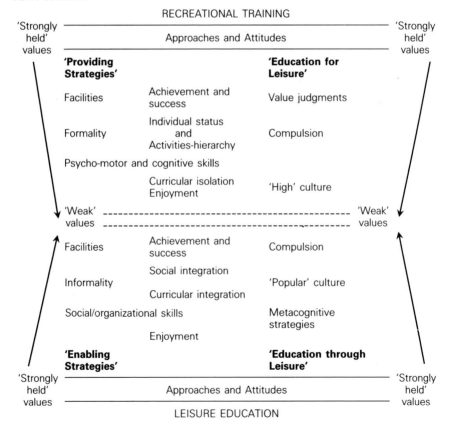

to concentrate on providing short term recreation rather than equipping pupils with the attitudes and skills which will enable them to participate in post-school years. There is a strong bias towards sport, hobbies and aesthetic activities such as art, drama and music and priority has been accorded to the provision of appropriate facilities and activity skills. If schools wish to increase their effectiveness in the area of leisure education, radical changes may have to be made. In terms of our diagrammatic model (see Figure 2) schools must lean towards the 'leisure education' perspective and towards the 'enabling strategies' suggested by Mundy and Odum (1979).

The radical nature of such a shift in emphasis should not be underestimated, for it contains curricular implications which extend far beyond leisure education. It may be desirable that leisure education is no longer seen as a separate entity but should be fully integrated into the curriculum (*cf.* Munn Report, 1977). It could perhaps be argued that such a move may be essential if the curriculum is to retain any relevance for the increasing number of pupils who may leave school to face unemployment. Weir and Nolan (1977) indicated how closely pupils and their parents associated the relevance of education with the ability of school leavers to find employment. The removal of the prospect of employment for many young people could lead increasing numbers of adolescents to reject the purely academic curriculum.

This is not an argument in favour of more recreation and diversion, but one in favour of enabling pupils to perceive aspects of their curriculum which will be relevant to their own development and life-styles. Pupils should be allowed to develop and practice the social skills which may be necessary if they are to possess real freedom of choice in their leisure activities in the post-school years. Such developments and practice may only be possible in informal situations, thus raising the fundamental question of whether the school is an appropriate institution to foster such a radical alternative programme. The evidence contained in research provides few grounds for optimism (for example Nisbet *et al*, 1980; 1984). It would appear that most schools are still displaying approaches and attitudes which could be described as paternalistic, and on occasions, authoritarian. If present approaches and attitudes persist, schools may have to content themselves with providing recreation rather than leisure education, yet it may be an area which the education service in general should not surrender lightly in a future 'leisured' society for as Smith (1973) stated: '. . . to assign a low priority to leisure would leave us in danger of failing to adequately provide for that sphere for life in which man may most fully realize himself, his hopes and his creative abilities.'

By contrast, one body of opinion argues that virtually all the time released from employment by labour-saving technologies must be re-invested in education and training. Stonier (1983) envisages a not-too-distant future when education will occupy 50 per cent of the workforce, as teachers and students. British governments' responses to youth unemployment in the 1980s seek to apply this traditional remedy. They have addressed an alleged mismatch between school-leavers' capabilities and occupational requirements in the service and high-technology sectors which, it is claimed, contain the best hopes for future job creation. Unless the quality of the workforce is improved, the argument runs, economic growth will be retarded, youth unemployment will remain high, and many will face jobless adulthoods. Hence the case for Britain's Technical and Vocational Education Initiative, the Youth Training Scheme, and the 16–18 Action Plan. However, educational solutions to the disappearance of entry jobs are yielding diminishing returns (Bates *et al*, 1984). Young people in Britain are now being given more vocational advice, work experience and generic skills than ever. Arguably they are being prepared more thoroughly than ever before for employment that has become scarcer than ever. These attempts to tighten the bonds between schooling and job requirements, to strengthen young people's vocational orientations and to make them more competitive, lead only to frustration and disillusion when labour markets cannot deliver deferred rewards. The new technologies that are displacing labour may require more highly educated and trained designers, technicians and managers. But the pace at which workers can be discarded seems to be running well-ahead of the need for longer vocational preparation. Most vocational courses contain small elements of a life skills 'package' (*i.e.* social and leisure skills), and recent recommendations for a 'core' curriculum in the last few years of compulsory schooling (for example, Munn Report, 1977) give a reasonably prominent place to physical education. Further, the development of community schools and principles of 'community education' create a climate for more natural school-society links in the process of life-long learning.

Young people need a wide range of sporting and leisure activities and social strategies in conjunction with preparation for a viable working life — skills relevant for handling the work of a highly technological society and crafts and skills unlikely to be replaced by the computer. This combination of approaches would give them a good basis for finding use for a shorter working day or week; or occasional periods of unemployment; or possibly a shorter working life: but to prepare them in the expectation that their lives will simply be 'leisured' (*i.e.* unemployed) or occupied (*i.e.* working) is naive and unjustified as we approach the twenty-first century.

References

ALEXANDER REPORT (1975) *Adult Education: The Challenge of Change*, London, HMSO.
BACON, W. (1975) 'Social caretaking and leisure provision', in PARKER, S. (Ed.) *Sport and Leisure in Contemporary Society*, London, Central Polytechnic.
BALL, S. (1981) *Beachside Comprehensive: A Case Study of Secondary Schooling*, Cambridge University Press.
BASINI, A (1975) 'Education for leisure: a sociological critique', in HAWORTH, J.T. and SMITH, M.A. (Eds.) *Work and Leisure*, London, Lepus, pp. 102–18.
BATES, I, CLARKE, J., COHEN, P. and FINN, D. (1984) *Schooling for the Dole*, London, MacMillan.

BRENNER, S.O. and BARTELL, R. (1983) 'The psychological impact of unemployment: a structural analysis of cross-sectional data', *Journal of Occupational Psychology* 56, 2, pp. 129–36.

BURTON, T.L. (1970) 'Current trends in recreation demands', in BURTON, T.L. (Ed.) *Recreation, Research and Planning*, London, Allen and Unwin.

BUSWELL, C. (1980) 'Pedagogic change and social change', *British Journal of Sociology of Education* 1, 3, pp. 293–306.

CARLISLE, R. (1969) 'The concept of physical education', *Proceedings of the Philosophy of Education Society*, III, London.

CARNEGY REPORT (1977) *Professional Education and Training for Community Education*, Edinburgh, HMSO.

CARROLL, R. (1976) 'Evaluating lessons', *British Journal of Physical Education*, 7, 6, pp. 202–3.

CARTER, M. (1971) *Home, School and Work*, London, Pergamon.

CARTER, M. (1972) 'The world of work and the ROSLA pupil', *Education in the North*, 9, pp. 61–4.

COFFIELD, F., BURRILL, C. and MARSHALL, S. (1983) 'How young people try to survive being unemployed', *New Society*, 2 June.

COLEMAN, J.C. (1979) *The School Years: Current Views on the Adolescent Process*, London, Methuen.

CONGER, J. (1979) *Adolescence: Generation Under Pressure*, London, Harper and Row.

CORLETT, H. (1973) 'Movement analysis', in BROOKE, J.D. and WHITING, H.T.A. (Eds.) *Human Movement — A Field of Study*, London, Kimpton.

CORRIGAN, P. (1976) *The Smash Street Kids*, London, Paladin.

CURL, G.F. (1973) An attempt to justify human movement as a field of study, in BROOKE, J.D. and WHITING, H.T.A. (Eds.). *Human movement — a field of study*, London, Kimpton.

DeGRAZIA S. (1962) *Of Time, Work and Leisure*, New York, Twentieth Century Fund.

DUMAZADIER, J. (1973) 'Sport and sports activities', *International Review of Sports Sociology*, 9.

EGGLESTON, J. (1976) *Adolescence and Community*, London, Arnold.

EGGLESTON, J. (1977) *The Sociology of the School Curriculum*, London, Routledge and Kegan Paul.

ELIAS, N. and DUNNING, E. (1967) 'The quest for excitement in unexciting societies', *British Sociological Association* Conference, London.

EMERY, F. and TRIST, E. (1973) *Towards a Social Ecology*, London, Plenum.

EMMETT, I. (1971) *Youth and Leisure in an Urban Sprawl*, Manchester, University Press.

EMMETT, I. (1977) 'Draft report to the Sports Council on decline in sports participation after leaving school', unpublished, London, Sports Council.

ENGSTORM, L.M. (1979) 'Physical activity during leisure time, a strategy for research', *Scandinavian Journal of Sports Science*, 1, 1, pp. 32–9.

EUROPEAN SPORTS CHARTER (1975) *European 'Sport for All' Charter*, European Sports Ministers Conference, Belgium, Brussels.

FAUNCE, W.A. (1959) 'Automation and leisure', in JACOBSON, J.S. and ROUCEK, J.S. (Eds.), *Automation and Society*, New York, Philosophic Library.

FEATHER, N.T. and BOND, M.J. (1983) 'Time structure and purposeful activity among employed and unemployed university graduates,' *Journal of Occupational Psychology* 56, 3, pp. 241–54.

FINNEMAN, S. (1983) 'Counselling the unemployed help and helplessness', *British Journal of Guide and Counsel*, 11, 1, pp. 1–9.

FLANDERS, N.A. (1970) *Analysing Teaching Behaviour*, Reading, Mass, Addison Wesley.

FLEMING, D. and LAVERCOMBE, S. (1982) 'Talking about unemployment with school leavers.' *British Journal of Guide and Counsel* 10, 1, pp. 22–3.

FOGELMAN, K. (1976) *Britain's Sixteen Year Olds*, London, National Child Bureau.

Fox, W.M. (1977) *Leisure and the Quality of Life*, Vols I and II, London, HMSO.
Glyptis, S. and Riddington, A.C. (1984) *Sport for the Unemployed*, London, Sports Council.
Hargreaves, D.H. (1967) *Social Relations in a Secondary School*, London, Routledge and Kegan Paul.
Hargreaves, D.H. (1972) *Interpersonal Relations and Education*, London, Routledge and Kegan Paul.
Hargreaves, D.H. (1981) 'Unemployment, leisure and education', *Oxford Review of Education* 7, 3, pp. 197–210.
Hargreaves, D.H. (1982) *The challenge for the comprehensive school*, London, Routledge and Kegan Paul.
Hargreaves, D.H., Hester, S.K. and Mellor, F.J. (1975) *Deviance in Classrooms*, London, Routledge and Kegan Paul.
Haworth, J.T. (1979) *Community Involvement and Leisure*, London, Lepus.
Hendry, L.B. (1975) 'Survival in a marginal role: the professional identity of the physical education teacher', *British Journal of Sociology* 26, 4, pp. 465–76.
Hendry, L.B. (1976) 'Early school leavers, sport and leisure', *Scottish Education Studies* 8, 1, pp. 48–51.
Hendry, L.B. (1978) *School, Sport and Leisure*, London, A and C Black.
Hendry, L.B. (1983) *Growing up and going out*, Aberdeen University Press.
Hendry, L.B., Brown, L. and Hutcheon, C. (1981) 'Adolescents in community centres: some urban and rural comparisons', *Scottish Journal of Physical Education* 2, 7, pp. 8–10.
Hendry, L.B. and Douglass, L. (1975) 'University students: attainment and sport', *British Journal Education Psychology* 45, pp. 299–306
Hendry, L.B. and Gordon, A.M.D. (1981) 'Adults and leisure: a case study of a works' sports and social club', *Scottish Journal of Physical Education* 9, 3, pp. 4–14.
Hendry, L.B. and McKenzie, H.F. (1978) 'Advantages and disadvantages of raising the school leaving age: the pupil's viewpoint', *Scottish Educational Review* 10, 2, pp. 53–61.
Hendry, L.B. and Marr, D. (1985) 'Leisure education and young people's leisure, *Scottish Educational Review* 17, 2, pp. 16–27.
Hendry, L.B. and Raymond, M. (1983) 'Youth unemployment and life-styles: some educational considerations', *Scottish Educational Review* 15, 1, pp. 28–40.
Hendry, L.B. and Raymond, M. (1985) 'Coping with unemployment', Unpublished Report to the Scottish Education Department, Edinburgh.
Hendry, L.B., Raymond, M. and Stewart, C. (1984) 'Unemployment, school and leisure: an adolescent study', *Leisure Studies* 3, pp. 175–87.
Hendry, L.B. and Simpson, D.O. (1977) 'One centre: two subcultures,' *Scottish Education Studies* 9, 2, pp. 112–21.
Hendry, L.B. and Singer, F.E. (1981) 'Sport and the adolescent girl: a case study of one comprehensive school', *Scottish Journal of Physical Education* 9, 2, pp. 19–29.
Hendry, L.B. and Thorpe, E. (1977) 'Pupils choice, extracurricular activities: a critique of hierarchical authority?' *International Review of Sporting Sociology*, 12, 4, pp. 39–50.
Hepworth, J.T. (1980) 'Moderating factors of the psychological impace of unemployment', *Journal of Occupational Psychology* 53, pp. 139–45.
Hill, J. (1978) 'The psychological impact of unemployment', *New Society,* 19 January.
Hirst, P.H. and Peters, R.S. (1970) *The Logic of Education*, London, Routledge and Kegan Paul.
Jackson, P.W. (1968) *Life in Classrooms*, New York, Holt, Rinehart and Winston.
Jahoda, M. (1979) 'The impact of unemployment in the 1930s and the 1970s', *Bulletin of British Psychology Sociology* 32, pp. 309–14.
Jenkins, C. and Sherman, B. (1979) *The Collapse of Work*, London, Eyre-Methuen.

JEPHCOTT, P. (1967) *A Time of One's Own*, Edinburgh, Oliver and Boyd.

KANE, J.E. (1974) *Physical Education in Secondary Schools*, London, MacMillan.

KELLY, J. (1982) *Leisure*, Englewood Cliffs, Prentice-Hall.

KELVIN, P. (1981) 'Work as a source of identity: the implications of unemployment', *British Journal Guide and Counsel* 9, 1, pp. 2–11.

KING, R. (1973) *School Organisation and Pupil Involvement: A Study of Secondary Schools*, London, Routledge and Kegan Paul.

KNAPP, B. (1963) *Skill in Sport*, London, Routledge and Kegan Paul.

LAWTON, D. (1973) *Social Change, Educational Theory and Curriculum Planning*, London, University Press.

LAYSON, J. (1973) 'Aesthetics and human movement', in BROOKE, J.D. and WHITING, H.T.A. (Eds.), *Human Movement — A Field of Study*, London, Kingston.

LEIGH, J. (1971) *Young People and Leisure*, London, Routledge and Kegan Paul.

LINDSAY, C. (1969) *School and Community*, London, Pergamon.

MARSDEN, D. and DUFF, E. (1975) *Workless: Some Unemployed Men and Their Families*, London, Penguin.

MOIR, E. (1977) *Female Participation in Physical Activities: A Scottish Study*, Edinburgh, Dunfermline College of PE.

MONINGTON, T. (1972) 'A social historical study of the development and present popularity and viability of industrial sports clubs with particular reference to the Birmingham area', unpublished memorandum, University of Birmingham.

MONKS, T.G. (1968) *Comprehensive Education in England and Wales*. Slough, National Foundation Educational Research.

MORTON-WILLIAMS, R. and FINCH, S. (1968) *Enquiry 1: Young School Leavers*, London, HMSO.

MUNDY, J. and ODUM, L. (1979) *Leisure*, New York, Wiley.

MUNN REPORT (1977) *The structure of the Curriculum in the Third and Fourth Years of the Scottish Secondary School*, Report of Munn Committee, Edinburgh, HMSO.

MURDOCK, G. and PHELPS, G. (1973) *Mass Media and the Secondary School*, London, MacMillan.

MUSGRAVE, P.W. (1968) *The School As An Organisation*, London, MacMillan.

MUSGROVE, F. (1964) *Youth and The Social Order*, London, Routledge and Kegan Paul.

MUSGROVE, F. (1968) 'The contribution of sociology to the study of the curriculum,' in KERR, J.F. (Ed.). *Changing the Curriculum*. London University Press.

NEWSOM REPORT (1963) *Half Our Future*, London, HMSO.

NISBET, J.D., HENDRY, L.B., STEWART, C. and WATT, J. (1980) *Towards Community Education: An Evaluation of Community Schools*, Aberdeen University Press.

NISBET, J.D., HENDRY, L.B., STEWART, C. and WATT, J. (1984) *Participation in Community Groups*, Oxford, Carfax.

NISBET, J.D. and SHUCKSMITH, J. (1984) 'The seventh sense,' *Scottish Educational Review* 16, 2, pp. 75–87.

ORGANISATION FOR ECONOMIC COOPERATION AND DEVELOPMENT (1975) *School and Community*, Paris, OECD.

PARKER, S. (1971) *The Future of Work and Leisure*, London, MacGibbon and Kee.

PATRICK, J. (1973) *A Glasgow Gang Observed*, London, Eyre-Methuen.

PHENIX, P.H. (1964) *Realms of Meaning*, New York, McGraw-Hill.

PIAGET, T. (1952) *The Origins of Intelligence in Children*, New York, International Universities Press.

RAPOPORT, R. (1981) *Unemployment and The Family*, London, Family Welfare Association.

RAPOPORT, R. and RAPOPORT, R.N. (1975) *Leisure and the Family Life-Cycle*. London, Routledge and Kegan Paul.

RAVEN, J. (1982) 'Education and the competencies required in modern society,' *Higher Educational Review* 15, pp. 47–57.

REID, L.A. (1970) 'Movement and meaning', *Laban Art of Movement Guild Magazine*, 45.

REID, M. (1972) 'Comprehensive integration outside the classroom,' *Educational Research* 14, 2, pp. 128–34.

ROBERTS, J. (1981) 'The environment of family leisure', *Proceedings of the Ninth International Seminar 'Sport, Leisure and the Family.'* ICSPE, Brugge, Belgium. September.

ROBERTS, K. (1983) *Youth and Leisure*, London, Allen and Unwin.

ROBERTS, K., DUGGAN, J. and NOBLE, M. (1982) 'Out of school youth in high unemployment areas: an empirical investigation,' *British Journal of Guide and Counsel* 10, 1, pp. 1–12.

RUTTER, M., MAUGHAN, B., MORTIMER, P. and OUSTON, J. (1979) *Fifteen Thousand Hours: Secondary Schools and Their Effects on Children.* London, Open Books.

RYRIE, A.C. (1981) *Routes and Results*, London, Hodder and Stoughton.

SAUNDERS, C. (1979) 'Pupils' involvement in physical activities in comprehensive schools', *Bulletin of Physical Education* 14, 3, pp. 28–37.

SCARLETT, C.L. (1975) *Euroscot: The New European Generation*, The Scottish Standing Conference of Voluntary Youth Organizations, Edinburgh.

SCHOOLS' COUNCIL (1968) 'Objectives of physical education.' *Dialogue*, p. 15.

SCOTTISH CONSULTATIVE COUNCIL ON YOUTH AND COMMUNITY SERVICE (1968) *Youth and Community Service*, Edinburgh, HMSO.

SCOTTISH COUNCIL FOR COMMUNITY EDUCATION (1981) *Community School in Scotland*, SCCE, New St Andrew's House, Edinburgh.

SCOTTISH EDUCATION DEPARTMENT (1972) *Curriculum Paper 12: Physical Education in Secondary Schools*, Edinburgh, HMSO.

SHIPMAN, M. (1968) *The Sociology of The School*, London, Longmans.

SILLITOE, K.K. (1969) *Planning for Leisure*, London, HMSO.

SIMPSON, J. (1973) 'Education for leisure', in SMITH, M.A., PARKER, S. and SMITH, C.S. (Eds.) *Leisure and Society in Britain*, London, Allen Lane.

SKINNER, B.F. (1983) *Science and Human Behaviour*, New York, Free Press.

SMITH, C.S. (1973) 'Adolescence', in SMITH, M.A., PARKER, S. and SMITH, C.S. (Eds.) *Leisure and Society in Britain*, London, Allen Lane.

START, K.B. (1966) 'Substitution of games performance for academic achievement as a means of achieving status among secondary school children,' *British Journal of Sociology* 17, 3, pp. 300–5.

STENHOUSE, L. (1975) *An introduction to Curriculum Research and Development*, London, Heinemann.

STONIER, T. (1983) *The Wealth of Information*, London, Methuen.

SUGARMAN, B. (1968) 'The school as a social system,' *Proceedings from British Sociology Association Annual Conference.*

SUTTON-SMITH, B. and ROBERTS, J.M. (1964) 'Rubrics of competitive behaviour, *Journal of Genetic Psychology* 105, pp. 13–37.

SWINBURNE, P. (1981) 'The psychological impact of unemployment on managers and professional staff,' *Journal of Occupational Psychology* 54, pp. 47–64.

TABA, H. (1962) *Curriculum Development: Theory and Practice*, New York, Harcourt Brace and World.

TALBOT, M. (1979) *Women and Leisure*, London, SSRC/Sports Council.

TOFFLER, A. (1981) *The Third Wave*, New York, Bantam.

TORBERT, M. (1980) *The Secrets to Success in Sport and Play.* Englewood Cliffs, NJ, Prentice-Hall.

TORBERT, M. (1982) *Follow Me*, Englewood Cliffs, NJ, Prentice-Hall.

TYLER, R.W. (1949) *Basic Principles of Curriculum and Instruction*, Chicago, University Press.

TYRRELL, R. (1981) 'Trends in and attitudes to work, leisure and social image,' *Leisure*

Research Seminar, Imperial College, London, June.

WALTERS, M. (1977) 'Women at work: men and children are still put first', *Sunday Times*, 27 February.

WARD, E., HARDMAN, K. and ALMOND, L. (1968) 'Investigation into pattern of participation in physical activity of 11 to 18 year old boys', *Research in Physical Education* 3, pp. 18–25.

WARR, P. (1982) 'Psychological aspects of employment and unemployment', *Psychological Medicine* 12, pp. 7–11.

WARR, P. and PAYNE, R. (1983) 'Social class and reported changes in behaviour after job loss,' *Journal of Application Society Psychology* 13, 3, pp. 206–22.

WEIR, D. and NOLAN, F. (1977) *Glad To Be Out?* Edinburgh, SCRE.

WEST, D.J. (1967) *The Young Offender*, Harmondsworth, Penguin.

WESTERGAARD, J.H. (1972) 'The myth of classlessness,' in BLACKBURN, R. (Ed.) *Ideology in Social Science*, London, Fontana.

WHITEHEAD, N. (1969) 'Physical education in men's colleges of boys' schools,' MEd thesis, University of Leicester.

WHITEHEAD, N. and HENDRY, L.B. (1976) *Teaching Physical Education In England: Description and Analysis*, London, Lepus.

WHITFIELD, R.C. (1971) *Disciplines of the Curriculum*, London, McGraw-Hill.

WHITING, H.T.A. (1969) *Acquiring Ball Skill: A Psychological Interpretation*, London, Bell.

WILLIS, P. (1977) *Learning To Labour*, Farnborough, Saxon House.

YOUNG, J. (1971) *The Drug Takers*, London, Paladin.

YOUNG, M. (1971) *Knowledge and Control*, London, Collier-Macmillan.

YOUNG, M. and WILLMOTT, P. (1973) *The Symmetrical Family*, London, Routledge and Kegan Paul.

4 Images of Femininity and the Teaching of Girls' Physical Education

Sheila J. Scraton

Introduction

Girls' schooling and the political and ideological assumptions, which underpin it has received increased recognition in the UK throughout the 1970s and 1980s. Research in this area includes broad-based studies of gender differentiation (for example, Sutherland, 1982; Whylde, 1983; Weiner, 1985) classroom interaction (for example, Delamont, 1980, Spender and Sarah; 1980, Stanworth; 1983); the relationship of girls' schooling to the sexual division of labour (for example, Wolpe, 1978; Deem, 1980) and work in specialist subject areas (for example, Kelly, 1981; Millman, 1984). Throughout this work PE[1] has received scant attention. It is difficult to identify precisely why this should be the case except to suggest that within many educational circles PE remains low-status academically and is considered relatively unimportant having no obvious relationship to the future world of work and the sexual division of labour. Probably more significant is the lack of understanding and knowledge of PE by those involved in research into girls' schooling. Furthermore Pratt's (1984) work on teachers' attitudes, shows that a large percentage of PE teachers are unsympathetic towards the notion of equality of opportunity in education. Indeed the lack of physical educationalists in the areas of gender differentiation, discrimination, etc. is demonstrated by the fact that it has taken until the mid 1980s for the first major specialist publications in this area to appear (ILEA, 1984; Leaman, 1984). Certainly much of the feminist[2] work on girls' schooling has little direct knowledge of or involvement in PE and few feminist educationalists have a specific background in this area.[3]

    This chapter introduces a feminist analysis of PE by critically examining its relationship to the reinforcement of images of 'femininity' and gender appropriate behaviour. In this, it is important to distinguish between the concepts 'sex' and 'gender'. Both terms are used throughout the literature on girls' schooling, often with no clear distinction, and with a tendency to use them interchangeably.[4] This chapter will rely on the most commonly accepted

71

definition where 'sex' refers to the biological aspects of being female or male and 'gender' to the social/cultural/psychological constructions of 'femininity' and 'masculinity' (Oakley, 1972). Using this definition, it must be acknowledged that 'gender' is not constant and can vary across cultures, throughout history and even during the life-cycle of an individual (Deem, 1984). However, there are certain characteristics associated with a stereotyped view of 'femininity' which strongly reinforce the expectations of what is appropriate for girls and women at different ages.[5] Within state institutions these images are consolidated and reproduced as ideologies which form the basis of the political management of sexual divisions in wider society. Work in this area has focused on the media (for example, Winship, 1978; McRobbie, 1978), the family and home (for example, Belotti, 1975; Sharpe, 1976), schooling (for example Clarricoates, 1978; Spender, 1982; Stanworth, 1983) etc. However it should not be assumed that the existence of gender stereotypes is all pervasive resulting in the conformity of all girls to expected roles, behaviour and attitudes. Clearly many individuals challenge the process of gender stereotyping (not always consciously) and thus the transmission of stereotypes is by no means simplistic, absolute or uncontested. Equally the strength and power of commonsense assumptions about what it means 'to be a girl' or 'to be a boy' cannot be underestimated. Whilst the definitions of 'femininity' and 'masculinity' may vary, there are enough overlapping assumptions to support powerful dominant ideologies which have important consequences for both cultural and institutional practice.

Gender stereotyping exists throughout the policies (for example, Wolpe, 1977) and process of schooling:

> ... in the official curriculum, teaching materials and organization of subject choice, in teacher behaviour both inside and outside the classroom, and in the hidden curriculum of traditional assumptions, unquestioned expectations and codes of behaviour. (Megarry, 1984, p. 22)

This chapter considers whether PE reinforces images of 'femininity' through its structure and teaching. The first section looks at PE in its historical context, considering the 'traditions' of PE and the relationship of PE to ideologies of 'femininity' throughout its development. The second section examines in detail the contemporary situation of PE in one local education authority. It considers present policies and practice concentrating on an examination of commonsense assumptions around femininity, sexuality and physical ability which underpin the curriculum and influence the content, organization and teaching of PE. The final section moves towards a feminist analysis of PE and argues the need to move beyond a 'liberal', 'equal rights' stance (for example, 'girls into soccer' campaigns) by locating PE within sexual divisions in wider society (*i.e.* in relation to the economic, sociopolitical and physical determinants of male power).

Historical Context

> This priority of bodily training is common to both sexes but it is directed to a different object. In the case of boys the object is to develop strength, in the case of girls to bring about their charms ... Women need enough strength to act gracefully, men enough skill to act easily. (Rousseau, quoted in Archer, 1964, p. 221)

The roots of secondary school PE extend from the pioneering schools for middle class girls in the mid and late nineteenth century.[6] Prior to this, girls from the middle classes were educated at home or in small private schools.[7] The curriculum was geared to the acquisition of manners and social skills considered appropriate and necessary for 'ladylike' behaviour. Exercise was restricted to marching for deportment, social dance and, occasionally, calisthenics (Borer, 1976). The demand for the improvement and expansion of female education developed through the pioneering women of the mid nineteenth century (*i.e.* Frances Mary Buss, Dorothea Beale, Emily Davies) who saw education as an urgent feminist cause and a prerequisite to political emancipation (Hargreaves, 1979). For the image of the Victorian 'lady' was that of a weak helpless creature who 'was incapable and ultimately disabled such that she must be protected and prohibited from serious participation in society' (Duffin, 1978, p. 26). It was the myth of 'woman as invalid' (Ehrenrich and English, 1975) which was challenged by the early feminists in order to establish access to schooling, higher education and, ultimately, the social and economic liberation of women.[8] They considered it imperative that in the newly emerging secondary schools physical education was used to counter the arguments from the opponents of women's emancipation that women were not sufficiently physically fit to undertake sustained mental work (Atkinson, 1978). Thus in the new secondary day schools emphasis was placed on exercise for health; a fit body would enhance the development of a fit mind and, consequently, a fit mother.

Within this 'progressive' demand, then, can be identified a reinforcement of dominant patriarchal ideologies around women's role and behaviour in society. Nowhere was this more apparent than within the development of a systematic, comprehensive programme of girls' physical education. On the one hand the development of girls' PE in schools represented a radical and progressive challenge to dominant ideologies and commonsense assumptions which defined the female body as delicate, weak and illness-prone. On the other hand, however, was the development of a subject within the confines of sexist ideologies which delineated clear boundaries for young women's behaviour, attitudes, etc. Whilst PE gave legitimacy to a new, freer development of physical exercise which was paralleled by increased access of women to sport and recreation, it remained within 'the taken-for-granted assumptions about the different innate characteristics and needs of men and women' (Hargreaves, 1979). These assumptions in relation to PE can be identified as dominant ideologies relating to physical ability and capacity, motherhood and sexuality.

Physical Ability and Capacity.

One way of dealing with these disparities between the athletic promise and achievements of men and women is to view women as truncated males. As such they could be permitted to engage in the same sports that men do ... but in foreshortened versions ... So far as excellence of performance depends mainly on the kind of muscles, bones, size, strength that one has, women can be dealt with as fractional men? (Weiss, 1969, pp. 215–16.)

Weiss' statement, made in the late 1960s, reflects a view that is apparent throughout the history and development of sport for women and within the development of a comprehensive system of girls' physical education in formal schooling. From its inception, PE developed on the premise that girls required 'separate' and 'different' opportunities in physical activity. From the early nineteenth century physical exercise for women was concerned with developing beauty and grace befitting a 'lady' (Fletcher, 1984, Hargreaves, 1979). This can be seen in Donald Walker's 1834 treatise 'Exercises for ladies' and is reiterated by Dorothea Beale[9] who, in her evidence to the Schools Inquiry Commission in 1868, suggested that: 'the vigorous exercise which boys get from cricket *must* be supplied in the case of girls by walking and callisthenic exercises.' (School Inquiry Commission, 1868, p. 740, emphasis added.)

The introduction of Swedish gymnastics during the latter part of the nineteenth century soon became an integral part of the physical education programme for girls in secondary schools. While this represented a shift towards a more energetic system of movements than previously promoted by callisthenics it retained a commitment to the ideology of women's 'natural', biologically-determined abilities. Ling, who introduced and developed the Swedish system, emphasized the importance of maintaining the 'natural abilities' of women without inducing undue strain or unwelcome physical changes. Central to his system was the assumption that women's: '... physiological predisposition demands less vigorous treatment. The *law of beauty* is based purely on the conception of life and must not be abused. The *rounded forms* of women must not be transformed into angularity or nodosity such as in man' (quoted in Webb, 1967; emphases added.)

The pre-set, presumably biological, 'law of beauty' together with women's 'natural' predisposition to 'rounded forms' are the taken-for-granted assumptions which lay at the heart of the ideology of biology underpinning the institutionalization of physical education for girls.

Towards the end of the nineteenth century the introduction of team games into girls' public schooling, initiated by the developing public schools (for example, Roedean, Wickham Abbey, St. Leonards), reinforced the 'separate' and 'different' ethos. While moving towards the provision of vigorous physical activity, more closely aligned to that experienced by their public school brothers, the games of the girls' public school remained within the boundaries of acceptable 'feminine' behaviour. That does not deny that changes in the definition of 'femininity' were taking place. The new 'high schools' and the girls' public schools represented a real challenge to the Victorian ideal of the 'feminine' woman. As Penelope Lawrence, head teacher of Roedean reported in 1898: 'The ideal of mental and physical feebleness and helplessness as an attribute of the really admirable woman has disappeared' (Special Reports on Educational Subjects, 1898, p. 145).

Roedean demonstrated the new physical 'freedom' for bourgeois women by including walking, running, swimming, gymnastics, fencing, dancing and games in its curriculum. Furthermore the games introduced included hockey, fives, cricket, tennis and rounders. However, Lawrence stressed that they must 'rigorously exclude games with vulgar and vicious associations'. While challenging the Victorian image of femininity the 'new' woman engaged in games which were foreshortened or adapted. Ultimately there was an acceptance of innate physical differences between men and women thus limiting girls' access to sports which stressed endurance, strength or physical contact (McCrone, 1982). Consequently 'male' sports were adapted to accommodate women's 'innate' abilities or new sports were introduced, such as netball, lacrosse, hockey which 'did not carry the stigma of overt masculinity' (McCrone, *ibid*, p. 28). By the beginning of the twentieth century the principle of 'separate' and 'different' had been firmly established in the physical education of young women. This principle remained throughout the development, progression and changes in PE brought about by increased teacher training and the introduction of secondary schooling for all from 1944. As women from the working classes gained access to secondary schooling the traditions prevalent in the original, elitist secondary establishments were established in the state-provided post-war secondary schools. While the traditional team games continued to be played, Swedish gymnastics gradually lost favour. The work of Laban and 'movement' education [10] emerged as a central influence by the 1950s and 1960s. With its emphasis on co-operation, discovery and the aesthetic, creative experience, this did little to challenge the dominant ideological assumptions of the innate physical inferiority of women. By now these popular assumptions, supported by spurious 'scientific' evidence, both physiological and psychological, were well-established in popular ideas and deeply institutionalized in the policies and practices of schooling.

Motherhood

Eurythmics and gymnastics are of great help in preparing women for maternity ... The object of sport should be to encourage healthy women to become healthier and to prepare their bodies for maternity in the best possible manner ...

Woman does not merely become mother: rather for this end she is born. (Westmann, 1939, p. 73.)

Westmann's text on Sport, Physical Training and Motherhood emphasized the taken-for-granted relationship established and accepted between physical exercise and healthy motherhood. In the late nineteenth century, as secondary schooling developed for the middle class girls, PE was seen as an important counterbalance to the 'strain' of mental concentration recognized as an inherent problem faced by girls' increased access to academic study. During the early years of the twentieth century however, there was an emerging commitment to the preparation of girls for healthy motherhood. This commitment was rooted in the growing concern for national fitness and physique arising out of the disastrous experiences of the Boer War (Dyhouse, 1977; Davin, 1978). The publication of the findings of the Physical Deterioration Committee in 1904 drew attention to the need for healthy motherhood. As Bland (1982, p. 5) comments:

The mother's health was of especial importance, since in addition to contributions genetically, she also carried the foetus. Thus healthy teaching stressed not only a woman's duty to apply rules of hygiene to the raising of her children, but also her obligation to keep her body healthy and gear it for her future childbearing role.

Eugenic arguments[11] about race regeneration were at the forefront of medical and educational thinking. PE, being concerned with physical activity and development, was seen as making an important contribution to the realization of ideal, healthy motherhood. Mm. Bergmann-Osterberg, the pioneer of girls' PE in secondary schools and founder of the first teacher training college for PE students at Dartford, constantly reiterated the eugenic arguments about race regeneration. 'I try to train my girls to help raise their own sex, and so to accelerate the progress of the race; for unless the women are strong, healthy, pure and true, how can the race progress' (Quoted in May, 1969, p. 52.)[12]

Eugenic and Social Darwinistic arguments also emphasized the 'problem' of 'over-strain', being concerned that excessive physical demands on women would sap their maternal energy and thus threaten the 'survival of the race'. PE, developed in this climate and, while challenging the arguments of over strain put forward most strongly by Dr. Henry Maudsley in Britain and Dr. Edward Clarke in the United States, the acceptance of woman's ultimate role in life — motherhood — went unchallenged. Exercises which affected the pelvic region or the chest were carefully regulated and the Board of Education's Syllabus of Physical Training for Schools in 1919[13] recommended certain activities as being more 'suitable' for boys than girls. The Ling system of gymnastics, with its emphasis on remedial and therapeutic work, was recognized as being particularly relevant for promoting qualities of caring and helping others through physical education. These were qualities directly associated with the ideal of perfect 'motherhood'.

Woman as 'mother' became part of the ethos of PE training. The teacher training establishments initiated a system of college 'mothers' whereby a first year teacher training student was allocated a 'mother' from the second year to help her through her first tentative months of training. In many colleges this tradition has continued to this day. The ideological construction of 'motherhood' has prevailed throughout the history of the PE profession. For example in the inauguration of the All England Netball Association (AENA) in 1926 the Journal of Scientific Training reported the 'honour of Miss Edith Thompson as President in being asked to "mother" the new assocation'. The ideology of 'motherhood' influenced not only the physical activities offered but the attitudes and practices which underpinned the development of an emerging PE profession and thus became an important aspect of its tradition.[14]

Sexuality

Women's sexuality, through the Victorian and Edwardian eras, was seen to require regulation. The two concepts central to the definition of female sexuality are identified by Bland (1982) as 'responsibility' and 'protection'. Women were responsible, as the previous section discussed, for providing the future generation — they were the 'Guardians of the Race' (Bland, *ibid*). However, women were seen also as responsible for male sexual behaviour. The belief was that due to their weaker sex-drives women were more able than men to control their sexual behaviour. They were responsible therefore, for morality through their behaviour and appearance. Furthermore, the impetus to protect women was concerned not only with medical protection against sexually transmitted diseases but also the protection of her body due to its vulnerability and fragility. As Bland recognizes such protection can easily 'tip over into a desire for active supervision of women's sexuality'.

The regulation of sexuality can be identified as an integral aspect of physical education from its inception. Diggle (1937) in a text used in girls' secondary schools writes:

> — a *natural* sense of modesty is apparent in most girls and shows in either an unwillingness to do the exercise or an endeavour to keep the legs of their shorts in place. This *innate* modesty should not be ignored nor should any attempt be made to defeat it, it is an important attribute in the development of *desirable* dignity and behaviour. (Diggle, 1937, emphases added.)

The development of 'desirable dignity and behaviour' stressed by Diggle was emphasized throughout the development of PE in secondary schooling. Swedish gymnastics with its emphasis on 'precision and smartness' (Lawrence,

1898) provided the perfect activity to encourage the 'standards' of discipline, neatness, self-control, respect for authority and dedication, which were to become central values in the teaching of PE. They were passed down the generations through the specialist colleges and in secondary school practice. In 1905 the *Anstey College of Physical Training Magazine* reported that the main aims of physical training included:

> Regular attendance, good behaviour throughout the year, and general improvement in all respects. Smart personal appearance shown by general care of the body as regards hair, teeth, skin, nails, clothing and good health. Good posture when standing and sitting and good carriage in walking. Attention to word of command, absence of mistakes and vigorous work in the gymnasium. General forms and style of movement, sense of time, self-control and power of relaxation. (Quoted in Crunden, 1974, p. 19.)

Appearance, specifically dress, neatness and posture, has been emphasized in PE throughout its history. Comments made by PE staff and recorded by past students at Anstey included: How can you keep your children in order if you cannot keep your hair tidy ... if you cannot control your legs, how can you control your class? (Crunden, 1974, p. 20.) Within the new found freedom of physical exercise there existed limitations imposed by assumptions around young women's developing sexuality. Nowhere was this more apparent than in proposals for reforms in women's dress and clothing. PE contributed significantly to innovations in young women's dress at the turn of the century, releasing women from the confining stays, bodices and corsets that had encumbered the female body throughout the Victorian era. Although the gymslip and tunic allowed for far greater freedom of movement than previously had been considered socially acceptable or sexually appropriate, these changes retained an emphasis on modesty and carefully masked any hint of the developing sexuality of young women. As Okeley reports:

> ... our bodies were invisible, anaesthetised and protected for one man's intrusion later. As female flesh and curves, we were concealed by the uniform. Take the traditional gymslip — a barrel shape with deep pleats designed to hide breasts, waist, hips and buttocks, giving freedom of movement without contour. (Okeley, 1979, p. 131.)

Morality and modesty — sexually appropriate behaviour — remained the firm responsibility of girls and young women through their appearance and behaviour. Physical Education, although liberating women from many bodily restrictions and conventions of dress, was careful to protect the sexuality of young women with a reaffirmation of 'feminine' modesty and 'desirable' dignity.

Apart from the uniform the physical activities themselves incorporated this ideology. The team games introduced for girls in secondary schooling allowed for energetic activity but restricted direct contact with other players or the hockey/lacrosse ball. These games were acceptable because there was an implement between the ball and the player. Physical contact was taboo on the playing field and within the gymnasium. Netball, while allowing contact with the ball, was adapted for girls in its restriction of space, reduction in speed and avoidance of physical contact. In all activities 'girls' bodies are extended and constrained in this choreography of their future which they learn unconsciously in legs, arms, hands, feet and torso' (Okely, *ibid*, p. 132). PE contributed to the continuation and development of an ideology of girls sexuality. Women's responsibility for the future generation and sexual morality, and the need to protect them for this function, received little challenge from the development of PE.

From this brief excursion into the history of PE it is apparent that ideologies of physical ability and capacity, motherhood and sexuality were implicit in the development of PE and have become integrated into its traditions and practice. Although only briefly introducing this history, it is important to recognize that the development of PE in secondary schools for girls was not simply a progressive movement which contributed to women's increased access to physical activity and the experience of freedom of movement. The development of PE did not occur in a vacuum but reflected the social, political and economic position of women in the late nineteenth and early twentieth centuries. Ideologies around women's ability, role and behaviour became institutionalized within the PE profession such that secondary school girls experienced a subject which on the one hand contributed to their liberation in terms of dress, opportunities for physical acitivity, and access to a future profession but on the other hand reaffirmed clear physical sex differences, their future role as mother and the boundaries and limitations of women's sexuality. Furthermore working class girls had to wait many years before they could begin to experience similar opportunities of physical activity. It was the legacy from the elitist, middle class schools of the nineteenth century which provided the basis for the comprehensive system of girls' PE which entered the tripartite system of schooling in the post 1944 era.

This history of girls' PE raises fundamental questions about the contemporary situation in secondary schooling. Can similar assumptions around physical activity/capacity, motherhood, sexuality be identified in the teaching and practice of PE in today's secondary schools? Does PE reflect a 'new' liberated image of woman in the 1980s, unfettered by sexist assumptions and practice? The following section will look more closely at these questions and will draw on qualitative research undertaken in the PE departments of a city education authority.

Girls' Physical Education Today

The research project involved structured interviews with all heads of girls' PE departments, advisory staff, peripatetic teaching staff and lecturers in a college of education. This was followed by observation in four schools over a period of approximately half a term in each. The case study schools were selected as representative of the types of schooling available in the city and each offered differing emphases in their approach and practice of PE teaching.

			Pupils
School 'A':	Co-educational Inner city Comprehensive	Multi-racial Working class intake	1400
School 'B':	Co-educational Suburban Comprehensive	Working class and middle class intake	1400
School 'C':	Inner-city Single sex Comprehensive	White working class intake	1200 girls
School 'D':	Single sex Church of England Comprehensive	Middle class intake negot- iated by Diocese	750 girls

Throughout the city there is considerable correspondence between schools in relation to curriculum content, organization and teaching method. In general the curriculum is organized into a core for the first three years which includes gymnastics, team games, athletics, dance and swimming. Team games dominate the curriculum taking up over half the total teaching time with swimming and dance taking up only nine per cent and six per cent respectively. In approximately a third of the schools these latter activities are absent from the curriculum. The team games offered are hockey and/or netball, rounders with the addition of tennis during the summer months. From the fourth year upwards most schools offer a series of 'options' which include more individual-based activities, for example, badminton, keep fit, trampolining. Although termed 'options' PE remains compulsory up to school-leaving age in all the authority schools. In general PE is taught in single-sex groups with isolated exceptions where a particular activity is taught to mixed groups throughout a specific year.[15] The trend is towards mixed groupings for 'options' in later years of schooling, although often this appears to be for economic and organizational convenience rather than any 'educational' justification.[16]

The in-depth interviews with heads of departments and assistant teachers and the class observations provided a thorough insight into the practices of physical education teaching throughout the authority. The transcripts of the interviews also contain clear evidence of the attitudes and ideas commonly held by those both involved in the policy (*i.e.* advisory staff) and the practice of physical education. It is in the often extensive definitions and justifications of 'good practice' given by teachers and advisors that assumptions concerning the ideologies of physical ability/capacity, motherhood and sexuality can be found. It was at this level answers to the questions raised by the historical legacy were sought.

Physical Ability/Capacity

'A lot of people feel that boys can give the girls much more daring, adventure, excitement and of course girls can give grace and 'finish', those things that they are better at.'

'... lets face it boys have far more strength, speed, daring. Women are much more the devious species. We need to play the games to suit our abilities.'

(Taped interview: PE advisor.)

The notion of 'separate' and 'different' physical opportunities and experiences, from which the tradition of separate distinct PE for girls developed remains a central concept in today's schools. The following quotes are representative of the views of physical education teachers around the differences in physical ability between girls and boys.

'Look at gymnastics, boys have no finesse but all little girls are poised. Little boys just throw themselves about.'

'... Boys and girls complement each other. They are different and we shouldn't be trying to make them the same. They can give to each other — girls subtlety and control. Boys can stretch the girls and make them want to try harder.'

'... very few girls are willing to launch themselves out of line — it's a physical difference. They've (boys) got spunk — girls naturally don't launch themselves.'

(Heads of Department — taped interviews.)

The explanations for these accepted physical differences fall into two categories. First, differences in physical ability and capacity are regarded as 'natural' and thus biologically determined:

'Boys have a lot of 'natural' ability 'cos they do things on their own. Girls are a bit more shy and timid. In this school girls don't have a lot of natural ability.

I support the fact that there are *clear* natural differences between boys and girls.'

'There are clear natural differences between boys and girls.'

(Head of Department — taped interviews.)

The second explanation does not rely on a biological explanation but identifies social tradition and cultural determination as significant:

'... it's nothing to do with their ability, it's tradition — just what's always happened.'

'I'm sure it isn't that girls can't do it, it's just that the activities, time and everything else makes it so difficult.'

(Taped interviews.)

It became evident from the full range of interviews with PE heads of department that, whether or not physical sex differences are viewed as biological or cultural, the differences are viewed as being inevitable. This attitude is well illustrated and typified by the following comment: 'I think it is tradition but I'm part of that tradition and convention and I wouldn't want to change it.'

The interviews indicate that there remain powerful attitudes around girls' physical ability and capacity. These attitudes are based on the assumption that girls are physically less capable than boys and, in general, exhibit specific 'female'/'feminine' characteristics, for example, poise, grace, flexibility, control, finesse. Although the interviews show a difference of opinion as to whether these differences are rooted in biology or culture, the emphasis remains on the *acceptance* of physical differences in ability and capacity and the desirability to reproduce these difference through the teaching of PE. This is highlighted in discussions over the issue of girls playing soccer at school. While many teachers agree that girls are capable of the physical skill to play soccer the following quotes represent the strength of attitude against soccer as a *desirable* female activity:-

'I have yet to see an elegant woman footballer. Maybe I'm just prejudiced but they just look horrible. I just don't like seeing women play football, if they did I would definitely want to modify it. The pitch is far too big and the ball too hard. No I certainly wouldn't ever want to see girls playing football.'

'Football! — I have a personal thing about this. I've been to a woman's football match and there's nothing sorer to my feminine eyes than a big bust and a big behind and the attracted crowd and spectators. ... I won't let the girls play because to me it is very, very unfeminine — I associate that with a man. I feel very strongly that I will never let the girls play soccer.'

'I don't think soccer is a girl's sport — physical contact and all that rolling in the mud.'

(Taped interviews.)

Observation in the four case study schools confirmed an unquestioning acceptance of different physical activities for girls and a reliance on 'traditional' sports (for example, netball, hockey, tennis) which have changed little since those pioneering days of the nineteenth century. While girls are seen as being much stronger and more physically able than the stereotype of the frail, weak, Victorian 'lady' the traditions and ideologies which determine girls' opportunities to develop their physical ability and capacity remain largely unchallenged. Even in School 'A', which professes a 'progressive' outlook, offering a slightly wider choice of activity to the girls and mixed option activities in the upper years, stereotypes die hard. Having 'progressively' offered soccer with the boys as an option for the fourth year lesson, the two girls taking up the offer had to handle the following jibe from the female head of department:–
'Football in this weather, you must be mad. You really should have been born a lad.'

Motherhood

If there has to be some difference in the physical education of girls at school, this will need to concern the specifically female functions of their organism and to aim at countering the infirmities brought about by the unnatural life of women in the civilized world.... From this point of view their physical education will need to be supplemented by exercises strengthening them in their specifically female role of childbearing. It should include training for motherhood ... (Pantazopoulou, 1979, p. 1.)

This view of women's future role in motherhood reflects similar arguments presented by the eugenics movement of the early twentieth century. However there is little evidence from the study that similar attitudes are held by today's PE staff. Whereas, historically PE was seen as health related, ensuring the future health of the race, today health objectives tend to be more concerned with 'encouraging and promoting an active life style' and 'making the most of oneself' (Almond, 1983). Most PE teachers see PE as a means of encouraging fitness to counteract the problems and excesses of nutrition, alcohol, smoking and an increasingly sedentary lifestyle. Physical fitness for motherhood is no longer viewed as an essential factor in the education of girls. This does not deny the significance of the ideology of motherhood in determining women's central contemporary role, but medical care, the National Health Service, developments in techniques of childbirth and improved infant health care have diminished the assumed necessity for education to concentrate on this aspect of physical fitness. Having said that, many of the teachers interviewed concentrate on the roles of wife and mother:

'They'll all be married within a couple of years with a couple of kids to look after.'

'In this day and age most of the girls will have kids quite soon. With unemployment there's little alternative really.'

(Taped interviews.)

The strength of ideologies of motherhood and domesticity lie in their inevitability for most girls and young women. In the teaching of PE this has direct consequences both for women PE staff and their young women students. Unique constraints on time are experienced by women, be they daughter, sister, wife or mother. The expectation is that it is the woman who undertakes the 'caring' role and women PE staff recognize the restrictions on their time and the consequences which govern their opportunities to offer comprehensive and detailed extra-curricular programmes. They are well aware from their own experiences that the primary responsibility for collecting children, buying food, cooking dinner, cleaning and organizing the household lies with women. Similarly, young women students are often restricted by similar domestic and childcare 'duties'.[17] Clearly this has consequences for their opportunities to participate:

'Lots of girls would stay but they have to pick up little brothers and sisters from school, get the family allowance etc. Boys don't have the same commitments.'

'Some kids have to pick up younger kids from junior school etc. The girls tend to do the messages don't they?'

'... girls are the one that do the laundry and household tasks. That is so obvious with women if you look at Sunday league football.'

(Taped interviews.)

In an explicit sense, ideologies of motherhood and domesticity no longer appear to influence directly the content and teaching of PE. However, it is the dominance and internalization of these ideological constructions of the 'woman's place' which places indirect but substantial limitations on PE through restrictions on the experiences and opportunities afforded to both women staff and young women students. While PE teachers no longer identify their central objective as being the preparation of physically fit young women for healthy motherhood, neither do they identify any need to challenge directly societal expectations of women's primary roles being those of wife and mother. Indeed many still view this as woman's *natural* function or, if not biologically determined then culturally expected. PE does not reinforce overtly such expectations but they remain on the hidden agenda of attitudes and ethos which underpin the curriculum.

Sexuality

Discipline, good behaviour and appearance, so much a part of the tradition and 'standards' set by PE in the pioneering girls' schools of the late nineteenth century continue to be stressed today.

'I think there must be very high standards.'

'. . . within PE departments girls can't get away with much. Standards are set quite high — we impose standards which other teachers may not impose.'

'I think the standards in all the school need to be high. I think PE people quite often have higher standards than a lot of people . . . we expect a higher standard of behaviour and attitude — loyalty almost.'

(Taped interviews.)

Standards of behaviour and dress for girls are not seen as being the same as those expected for boys. As one teacher commented: 'I think we do stipulate more, trying to make them into 'young ladies'.' In practice this is emphasized in the language used by teachers in talking to or instructing their pupils. The case study schools represented different catchment areas in terms of social class/cultural background and also single sex and co-educational organization. In *all* of the schools one or all of the following expressions, used by women teachers, were commonplace in the everyday teaching situation: 'ladies'; 'madam'; 'dear'; 'dearies'; 'young ladies'; 'lovies'. The following teachers' comments were noted in the four different schools and were used often when returning from lessons to the changing rooms:

'Come on get in line — you'll never make young ladies.' (Case Study A)

'Walk — leave the gymnasium like Miss World.' (Case Study B)

'Walk in properly. Imagine you're in a beauty parade.' (Case Study C)

'Walk in like young ladies.' (Case Study D)

The emphasis on 'young ladies' implies a specific notion of behaviour and discipline traditionally expected of girls and it centres on restraint, quietness and orderliness. Particular emphasis is placed on appearance and posture. For girls the expectations of appearance has strict boundaries:

> 'We don't just teach the girls PE, we always include a lot of other bits and pieces, for example, hygiene, cleanliness, dressing well in PE kit — uniform.'

> 'I teach them to have correct uniform, kit, hair tied back, attention to detail . . .'

(Taped interviews)

Certain standards of appearance are expected of 'young ladies' and although dealing with physical activity, PE teachers are careful to encourage the 'correct' conforming standards. The notion of 'playing like gentlemen whilst behaving like ladies' (Hargreaves 1979) holds true today. Girls are encouraged to be active, energetic and lively in the gymnasium and on the playing fields, but must revert to more 'ladylike' behaviour once the lesson is over. As one head of department neatly expressed the situation in her school:

> 'The whole thing is dictated by the fact that there is a very female atmosphere in PE here and the look of the thing is as important as the doing it. It's not so for the boys — they look as scruffy going onto the rugby pitch as they do coming off it.'

Apart from 'standards' the most important issue identified by women PE teachers relates to the problem they see with physical contact between women participants. This is cited as the prime objection to girls having access to the same physical activities as boys.

> '. . . the game of rugby is all about contact — that would be dreadful.'

> 'I wouldn't teach girls to play rugby. They wouldn't — I can't see these playing it to be honest. I'm not against any sport but I feel you couldn't really.'

> 'I don't mind boys playing rugby but I don't think it's a girls' sport. It's like boxing really. They might enjoy it but I wouldn't enjoy seeing them battering each other.'

(Taped interviews.)

It is not that violent sports should be considered unsuitable for anyone but that 'contact' is not suitable for girls. They are physically capable of playing the games but such behaviour does not befit a 'young lady'. They do not seem to mind, however, the boys 'battering each other'. 'Well it's different for boys, they enjoy it. I just don't think it would be particularly good for girls.'

Physical contact between women remains an issue throughout all sporting activity. Hall suggests:

> For a woman to subdue another woman through physical force and bodily contact is categorically unacceptable, the innuendo sexual, and the act considered unnatural. There exists an age old prohibition against aggressive, physical contact between women; indeed, there is no acceptable female equivalent to the Brutbruderschaft, the mental, spiritual and physical male alliance. (Hall, 1979, pp. 25–6)

The acceptance of *aggressive* and *violent* physical contact, be it between men or women, is questionable. Yet there remains a double standard whereby only women's behaviour and activity is seen to require regulation. Ideologies of femininity and masculinity demarcate clear boundaries which are reinforced by separate and different opportunities afforded to girls and boys. They reflect and reinforce cultures of femininity and masculinity and the message to girls in relation to their sexuality remains articulated clearly through PE. Women's bodies are physically developed in order to look good and presentable, particularly to men, but they must be protected from 'overdevelopment' or physical contact in order to avoid 'unnatural' and 'unhealthy' touch and danger to their more 'delicate' parts. As this statement from the PE advisor concludes:

> 'In fact I am very concerned about any sport involving physical contact. I believe in feminine charms and hard contact sport just isn't right. Also there is a physiological point. If we put adolescent girls into that situation I am very concerned about the damage they might do to their breasts with hard knocks. After all hockey, although a tough game, there is an implement between yourself and the ball. You can protect yourself, it isn't bust to bust.' (Taped interview — PE Advisor)

The need for protection of the female body relates specifically to the damage that might be caused to their reproductive capacity. Recent research (see Dyer, 1982; Mees Hardman, 1979) debunks many of the myths surrounding women's supposed physical vulnerability and as Hall succinctly states:

> We see man the protector raging against contact sports for females on the grounds that they will irreparably damage, among other things, their *naturally* protected reproductive organs, whereas the fact that the exposed male genitals *have* to be protected is never considered problematic! (Hall, 1979, p. 28)

From this brief introduction to the evidence collected from the research project it is clear that the dominant ideologies, and their associated 'common-sense assumptions', of women's physical ability/capacity, motherhood/domesticity and sexuality remain intact in women's PE. Although these images of 'femininity' by no means have remained static they have remained deeply rooted and institutionalized as ideologies which continue to underpin the teaching of PE and have direct consequences for practices in the gymnasium and on the playing fields. Furthermore they place limitations on the participation and performance of young women. Whilst not suggesting that the evidence from one local education authority would necessarily be replicated throughout every PE department nationwide, it is clear that the contemporary teaching of PE remains underpinned by a tradition and an ethos informed by sexist ideologies. Women's PE remains caught in a double bind. On the one hand it challenges many traditional images of femininity by encouraging physical activity and increased participation in physical leisure pursuits. On the other hand it remains locked within the traditions and assumptions which differentiate between girls and boys, women and men. The *image* of the 'new' woman of the 1980s is portrayed as being advanced socially, politically and economically on the *image* of her late nineteenth century sisters. Yet fundamental issues around women's behaviour, role and abilities remain unmoved and sites of future feminist struggle. PE in our secondary schools continues to reinforce gender differences both overtly, in the activities offered, and covertly, through the attitudes and reactions of those involved in the policy and practice of PE teaching. Can PE challenge images of 'femininity' and assumptions around female behaviour, role and abilities? This leads to a discussion of possible moves towards a feminist analysis of PE and the implications of such an analysis for policy and 'classroom' practice.

Towards a Feminist Critique of PE

> Expanding equal opportunities is not just a question of juggling resources or rearranging option choices ... To liberalize access to an inadequate system might be acceptable in the short term but for more permanent change a major restructuring of all social institutions, including schools is needed. (Weiner, 1985, p. 10)

Weiner identifies two main approaches which have emerged as challenges to sexism and sex differentiation in schools: an *equal opportunities* approach, concentrating on equality of access to all educational benefits and an *anti-sexist* approach, concentrating on girl centred education with its central consideration' the 'relationship between patriarchy, power and women's subordination'. The 'equal opportunities' approach encompasses physical education initiatives such as mixed PE and equal access to facilities, activities and curricular/extracurricular time. As the evidence from the research project demonstrates, however, the assumptions and stereotyped notions about women's role, abilities and behaviour have persisted. A study in ILEA (1984) concluded that 'for historical reasons, boys and girls are still generally treated according to their sex rather than their potential in all phases of physical education' (p. 82). The historical traditions of PE have provided the foundations for differential treatment, access, participation and performance. These foundations remain firm and have survived the many and varied influences on PE teaching. As with any form of schooling, PE is a process and is subject to change. 'Equal Opportunity' initiatives, introduced by dedicated and committed teachers, are an important political response to generations of limitations imposed on young women in a whole range of school and related activities. Increased opportunities relating to participation, however, can offer only cosmetic change, particularly while attitudes and assumptions based on ideological constructions of 'femininity' and 'masculinity' are retained. Analytically there must be consideration of the 'relationship between patriarchy, power and women's subordination' (Weiner, 1985, p. 9) if the gender divisions and their consequences, which persist in PE are to be understood. Physical education should not be viewed in isolation but as part of a broader schooling process which contributes to the reproduction of a sexually-differentiated society (Deem, 1982; Stanworth, 1981; Spender, 1982; Weiner, 1985). Sexual divisions are experienced daily by women at the interpersonal, lived in world of *social* experience. They exist also at the institutionalized, *structural* level of the state's response to work, leisure, health, welfare etc. Schooling, sport and physical activity are all part of the process whereby patriarchal power relations are reproduced and reinforced. In Britain sport remains a male domain definitively linked to images and practices of 'masculinity' (Hargreaves, 1982). 'Equal opportunities' approaches tend to encourage equal access to this 'male domain'. Not only is equal access problematic for girls and women, while stereotypes of masculinity and feminity prevail, but there is a danger that these stereotypes will be reinforced by giving equal access to an unequal situation. For example, opportunities for mixed soccer in schools for adolescent young women are fine in theory but do not allow for the persistent and well established differences in socialization and primary schooling or the limitations imposed by the Football Association and media coverage. Mixed soccer may serve only to prove to many girls/young women that they are physically less capable, unable to play in competitive teams and less suited to what is predominantly a 'male' activity.

If PE is to challenge sexual divisions then it needs to undergo fundamental and radical change. At the basis of an anti-sexist approach there needs to be an effective shift towards the denial of ideologies of femininity and masculinity. This would involve a move towards the challenging of 'physical' power relations. Girls and women should be encouraged to become more confident, assertive, physically and mentally strong with greater control over their own bodies in order to redefine perceptions of women as necessarily submissive, passive, inactive and dependent. Given the extent of limitations on young women's experiences this is by no means a straightforward task but it should be the objective towards which PE must progress. In practice, the difficulties of implementing radical change are acknowledged but the following ideas for change are introduced as a starting point for thought and discussion.

First, the importance of girl-centred organization should be recognized.

While in the long-term mixed activity *may* be a positive step in PE, initially girls need both space and time to develop their physical potential. In some instances this may involve the retention of a single sex programme as the norm throughout the secondary school with selective periods of mixed teaching, if appropriate, for individual activities, for example, trampolining, gymnastics, or for the introduction of 'new' activities, for example, orienteering, rock climbing, handball etc.

Second, change should involve a move away from the dominant, competitive sporting ethos. Willis (1982) suggests:

> Sport could be presented as a form of activity which emphasizes human similarity and not dissimilarity, a form of activity which expresses values which are indeed immeasurable, a form of activity which is concerned with individual well being and satisfaction rather than with comparison. (Willis, 1982, p. 134)

This does not imply that all team games should be abandoned, Indeed the primary concern should not be the *type* of activity but the form, emphasis and philosophy behind the activity. Thus the value of playing team games, for example netball, hockey, soccer, volleyball, should be in the collective experience of shared physical activity and its associated skill — the fundamental enjoyment of working/playing together. Achievement can be measured, as Willis suggests, by 'individual well-being and satisfaction rather than by comparison'. This is of particular importance for young adolescent women where group membership and experience tends to be played down.[18] PE can contribute to giving girls and women a sense of solidarity with other members of their sex and hence a female-based confidence and motivation (Weiner, 1985, p. 11). In many ways the 'movement' approach of girls' PE, prevalent in the 1960s and 1970s and to some extent perpetuated in schools today, has emphasized these qualities. Where it has failed, however, is in its tendency to reinforce gender stereotypes and emphasize sexual divisions while encouraging a level of cooperation and a sense of community. Young women should be encouraged to use these experiences as a real counter to the imposition of 'feminine' stereotypes by developing their strength, muscle potential and, consequently, their physical fitness. It is through such collective physical experiences that women can develop the confidence and assertiveness necessary to challenge the physical, social and psychological limitations imposed by a sexually divided society.

Third, it is necessary for teachers, advisors, parents and pupils to develop an awareness of the significance of these issues. In schools the PE programme can emphasize women's physical potential by the use of photographs and displays and the creation of a positive 'female' atmosphere. In many schools the posters in the changing rooms and in the PE corridors exhibit typical male sporting 'heroes'. In their place should be positive physical images of women which challenge the stereotyped ideas of women in relation to appearance, body image, shape and dress, and which encourage young women's participation in, and enjoyment of, physical ability.

Related to this, is the need to promote active discussion about the main issues of 'physicality' and 'sexuality'. Adolescent young women need to be encouraged to address these issues within a broader political framework. If physical 'education' is to move beyond the rigid, traditions of skill acquisition it needs to address the issues of the politics of sexuality and the structures of sexual divisions within the timetable. This more theoretical component should be reinforced further through informal contact during the teaching of physical activities etc.

These initiatives represent preliminary and, no doubt, controversial ideas for the future development of PE. They are dependent on the commitment of teachers and would require some changes in the general organization of schools. For example, in order to encourage girls to experience and develop cooperative outdoor activities, block timetabling would need to be implemented giving PE extended periods to work on new initiatives both on and off the school premises. Girls' and women's groups need to be established in schools to address the issues of anti-sexist schooling and to provide support for both staff and pupils engaged in such work. As Weiner (1985) acknowledges, it is a long, hard road to successful anti-sexist policy and practice and involves a 'major restructuring of all social institutions, including schools ...'

PE is in a strong position to take up this challenge. It it unfettered by the constraints of examinations and can initiate change through basic policy decisions at school or advisory level. Indeed, for any changes to succeed in school practice they must be supported by increased awareness *and action* at advisory level, in teacher training, in-service training and through research initiatives. Support is required at *all* levels of policy and practice if PE is to emphasize positive girl-centred approaches which deny ideologies of femininity. In the short term reforms in the 'classroom' are of value but for the long term PE needs to question fundamental issues around physicality and sexuality. For 'physical' power relations and, ultimately, the politics of patriarchy to be challenged, girls and young women should be encouraged to enjoy physical movement on *their* terms and develop confidence, assertiveness and control over their own bodies.

Acknowledgements

Many thanks to Pat Craddock, Rosemary Deem and Paul Scraton for their support and helpful comments.

Notes

1 For the purposes of this chapter PE will be used to denote girls' physical education.

2　Sмiтн (1977) stresses three points which help define a 'feminist' position:
　　a)　It takes the standpoint of women.
　　b)　It opposes the oppression of women.
　　c)　It recognizes the importance of sisterhood.
　　Whilst accepting that there are many different feminist positions (*i.e.* radical, Marxist, liberal, socialist) this paper uses 'feminist' in the broad sense as defined by Sмiтн.

3　A further point here is that debates about PE, unlike those about science, language, maths have tended to be directed to specialist audiences only.

4　See Eichler, M. (1980) for further discussion on the definitions of 'sex' and 'gender'.

5　Further research into the relationship of boys' PE and images of masculinity would be useful and interesting.

6　For a detailed account of PE in the late nineteenth century and early twentieth centuries see Hargreaves, J. (1979).

7　See Delamont (1978) and Murray (1984).

8　It must be acknowledged that only middle class girls are considered here. Working class girls had no access to secondary schooling at this time. As Ehrenreich and English (1976) suggest: upper and middle class women were 'sick', working class women were 'sickening'.

9　Dorothea Beale was appointed headmistress of Cheltenham Ladies College in 1858.

10　Rudolf Laban introduced modern educational dance into Britain in the late 1930s/early 1940s. His book *Modern Educational Dance* was published in 1948 and his 'movement' approach inspired several generations of PE teachers.

11　Eugenics was introduced by Francis Galton to describe 'sciences for the management of human heredity in the interests of improving the stock' (Fletcher, 1984, p. 27).

12　See Fletcher (1984), Hargreaves (1979), Murray (1984) for further discussion in this area.

13　Although the 1919 Syllabus for Physical Training primarily dealt with elementary schools, many of the exercises also featured in the Swedish System prevalent in the girls' secondary schools.

14　Ideologies of motherhood and domesticity influenced not only the development of PE but education in general. See Delamont (1978); Dyhouse (1977); Wolpe (1978) for further discussion.

15　An example of this was the successful teaching of mixed dance for the first years in School A. A mixed fifth form option in dance was also offered in this school.

16　See Scraton, S. (1984) 'Losing ground: the implications for girls of mixed physical education', a paper presented to Girl Friendly Schooling Conference, Manchester.

17　See Dorn, N. and South, N. (1983/4).

18　See McRobbie (1978); Nava and McRobbie (1984), Griffin (1985) for work on young women's sub-cultures.

Bibliography

Almond, L. (1983) 'Health related fitness', *British Journal of Physical Education* Vol. 14 No. 2.

Archer (1964) (Ed.) *Emile, Julie and Other Writings*, New York.

Atkinson, P. (1978) 'Fitness, feminism and schooling' in Delamont, S. and Duffin, L.

(Eds.) *The Nineteenth Century Woman: The Cultural and Physical World*, Croom Helm.

BELOTTI, G. (1975) *Little Girls*, Writers and Readers Publishing Cooperative.

BLAND, L. (1982) *'Guardians of the Race' or 'Vampires upon the Nations' Health?': Female Sexuality and its Regulation in Early Twentieth Century Britain*, Paper presented to BSA Conference.

BOARD OF EDUCATION (1919) *Syllabus of Physical Training for Schools*, London, HMSO.

BORER, M. (1976) *Willingly to School. A History of Women's Education*, Butterworth Press.

CLARRICOATES, K. (1978) 'Dinosaurs in the classroom' *Women's Studies International Quarterly,* Vol 1, no. 4.

CRUNDEN, C. (1974) *A History of Anstey College of Physical Education 1897–1972* Anstey CPE.

DAVIN, A. (1978) 'Imperialism and motherhood' *History Workshop*, 5, Spring.

DEEM, R. (Ed.) (1980) *Schooling for Women's Work*, London, Routledge and Kegan Paul.

DEEM, R. (Ed.) (1984) *Co-education Reconsidered*, Milton Keynes, Open University Press.

DELAMONT, S. (1978) 'The domestic ideology and women's education' in DELAMONT and DUFFIN.

DELAMONT, S. (1980) *Sex Roles and the School,* London, Methuen.

DIGGLE, K.A. (1937) *PE for Girls. A Book for Secondary Schools*, London.

DORN, N. and SOUTH, N. (1983/4) 'Youth, the family and the regulation of the informal' *Resources for Feminist Research* XII, 4 Dec/Jan Toronto, OISE.

DUFFIN, L. (1978) 'The Conspicuous Consumptive: Woman as Invalid' in DELAMONT and DUFFIN.

DYER, K.F. (1982) *Catching Up the Men: Women in Sport*, Junction Books.

DYHOUSE, C. (1977) 'Good wives and little mothers: social anxieties and schoolgirls curriculum 1890–1920' *Oxford Review of Education* Vol. 3, No. 1.

EHRENRICH, B. and ENGLISH, D. (1976) *Complaints and Disorders*, Writers and Readers Publishing Cooperative.

EICHLER, M. (1980) *The Double Standard*, London, Croom Helm.

FLETCHER, S. (1984) *Women First*, Athlone Press.

GRIFFIN, C. (1985) *Typical Girls*, Routledge and Kegan Paul.

HALL, A. (1979) 'Women and the Lawrentian wrestle' *Canadian Women's Studies* 1 pp. 39–41

HARGREAVES, J. (1979) 'Playing like gentlemen while behaving like ladies' MA Thesis University of London Institute of Education.

HARGREAVES, J. (Ed.) (1982) *Sport, Culture and Ideology*, Routledge and Kegan Paul.

ILEA (1984) *Providing Equal Opportunities for Girls and Boys in Physical Education Journal of Scientific Training* (1926) Vol, XIX, p. 7.

KELLY, A. (1981) *The Missing Half: Girls and Science,* Manchester University Press.

LEAMAN, O. (1984) *Sit on the sidelines and watch the boys play*, Longman.

MAY, J. (1969) *Madame Bergman Osterberg*, Harrap and Co.

McCRONE, K. (1982) 'Victorian women and sport: playing the game in colleges and public schools' *Canadian Historical Association*

McROBBIE, A. (1978) *Jackie: An ideology of adolescent femininity* , CCCS.

MEES HARDMAN (1979) 'Women in Sport: a review of physiological factors *PE Review*, Vol. 2, No. 1, pp. 44–49.

MEGARRY, J. (1984) 'Introduction: sex, gender and education' in ACKER *et al* (Ed.) *World Yearbook of Education 1984 Women and Education*, Kogan Page.

MILLMAN, V. (1984) *Teaching Technology to Girls; A Workshop Approach*, Coventry LEA.

MURRAY, J. (1984) *Strong-Minded Women*, Harmondsworth, Penguin.

NAVA, M. and McROBBIE, A. (Ed.) (1984) *Gender and Generation*, MacMillan.

OAKLEY, A. (1972) *Sex, Gender and Society* London, Temple Smith.

OKELEY, J. (1979) 'Privileged, schooled and finished: boarding school for girls' in ARDENER, S. (Ed.) *Defining Females* London, Croom Helm.

PANTAZPOULOU, E. (1979) 'The requirements of physical training and sport in female education' *Prospects*, Vol. IX, No. 4.

PRATT (1984) 'The attitudes of teachers' paper, presented to *Girl-Friendly Schooling Conference*, September.

PP 1867–1868 Schools Inquiry Commission Vol 5, Minutes of Evidence, XXVIII, 4.

SHARPE, S. (1976) *Just Like a Girl*, Harmondsworth, Penguin.

SMITH, D. (1977) *Feminism and Marxism — A Place to Begin, A Way To Go*, Vancouver, New Star Books.

Special Reports on Educational Subjects, (1898) Vol. 2.

SPENDER, D. and SARAH (Eds) (1980) *Learning to Lose*, The Women's Press.

SPENDER, D. (1982) *Invisible Women; The Schooling Scandal*, Writers and Readers Publishing Cooperative.

STANWORTH, M. (1983) *Gender and Schooling*, London, Hutchinson.

SUTHERLAND, M. (1982) *Sex Bias in Education*, Oxford, Blackwell.

WALKER, D. (1934) *Exercises for Ladies*, London,

WEBB (1967) *Women's Place in PE in Great Britain 1800–1966*, Unpublished thesis, University of Lancaster.

WEINER, G. (Ed.) (1985) *Just a Bunch of Girls*, Milton Keynes, Open University Press.

WEISS, P. (1969) *Sport — a Philosophic Inquiry*.

WESTMANN, S. (1939) *Sport, PT and Womanhood*, London, Bailliere, Tindall and Cox.

WHYLDE, J. (Ed.) (1983) *Sexism in the Secondary Curriculum*, Harper and Row.

WILLIS, P. (1982) 'Women in sport in ideology' in HARGREAVES, J. (Ed.) *op cit.*

WINSHIP, J. (1978) 'A Woman's World: an ideology of femininity' in CCCS *Women Take Issue*, Hutchinson.

WOLPE, A.M. (1977) *Some Processes in Sexist Education*, London, WRRC.

WOLPE, A.M. (1978) 'Education and the sexual division of labour' in KUHN and WOLPE (Ed.) *Feminism and Materialism*, Routledge and Kegan Paul.

5 Managing to Survive in Secondary School Physical Education

Les Bell

This is the story of two physical education departments in two different schools. One school is a Catholic school for boys on the outskirts of a city in the Midlands. As such it has not been as exposed to the pressures of educational contraction and falling pupil numbers to quite the same extent as other schools within its local education authority. Nevertheless it is about to merge with a nearby girls' school which is also Catholic. The PE Department in that school consists of three men. The most junior member of the department has been at the school five years. The head of department has held his post for fifteen years and his deputy has been at the school for ten years. The other school is set in the heart of a rural county in the East Midlands. It was a new school when the present Head of the PE Department joined the staff in 1979. His deputy head of department came at the same time on a scale two post to accept responsibility for girls' PE and, in 1980 they were joined by a second man who subsequently obtained a scale post for work outside the department. The most junior member of the department has been there two years and shares responsibility for girls' PE throughout the school. The two schools are approximately the same size with about 850 pupils and approximately 45 members of staff. The major difference is that the rural school, School B, achieved that size by growth and expansion while School A has contracted slowly over seven years. This difference assumes considerable significance in the minds of those teachers who work in the two schools and, in particular, in the minds of the members of the two PE Departments.

The research on which this analysis is based is ethnographic. What matters is not the details of the extent to which pupil numbers are declining in a given school, within an LEA, or even nationally but the way in which that information is interpreted by teachers in the schools and how, as a result of those interpretations, judgments are formed, decisions made and actions taken. This is not to attribute some spurious rationality to the participants for, as Rex (1961) has pointed out in his paraphrasing of Weber, human behaviour is often governed by motivation which does not follow the conventional view of means-ends rationality because certain ends may, in some way, be taboo to those involved and may, therefore, be ignored as possible alternatives for action however rational they may appear to an outsider. Other responses may not, for the actors, be thought to produce the desired ends although an observer may disagree with this judgment. It might also be the case that the actor's knowledge of the situation was imperfect and that, while his action might have appeared rational from the basis of imperfect knowledge, it appears irrational from a more informed standpoint. Finally the actor may be well aware of the details of the situation but may follow a logic which is quite different from that of the observer, thus making judgments and producing actions that seem non-rational. All ethnographic research has to take account of the nature of human behaviour since it is tempting, on the basis of participant observation and unstructured interviews, for the researcher to impose meanings and interpretations which are not those of the participants in the action. As Burgess (1985) has pointed out, the research process is not a clear cut sequence of procedures to be followed. Rather it is a messy interaction between the conceptual and the empirical, between deduction and induction, and between description and analysis.

Thus this study is limited to the extent that no attempt has been made to explore all the alternative perceptions and interpretations of the situations related to these two Physical Education Departments. The main concern here is how the department and its work fits into the wider context of the school and how this is perceived by the heads of the two departments.

It will be argued that the work of the department and, in particular, the curriculum which is offered to its pupils is not the result of rational curriculum development over time, nor is it a response to the current trends at the frontiers of physical educational knowledge. Rather, it will be suggested, the curriculum as presented is a product of what have been described as 'coping strategies' (Barton and Meighan, 1978). These strategies are the responses which teachers adopt to the demands of their world as they see it. The strategies will change according to which groups of pupils are being taught, the nature of the different situations in which teachers find themselves and, most important of all, according to how successful the particular strategy appears to be. Thus the more a particular solution is seen to work in a recurring situation then the more that solution will become institutionalized, routinized and, ultimately, taken for granted. These strategies may, to the outsider, appear to be *ad hoc* responses to immediate difficulties or, at best, short term pragmatic stances. To the insider, however, they take on a coherence which is rooted in a logic derived from specific perceptions of the situation. In the case of these two Physical Education Departments the most significant characteristic of both their situations appears to be the need to find a solution to the problem of survival in the face of increasing pressure which emanates from the school itself, from within the departments and from the different attitudes and aspirations of the staff of those departments. Both of the departments, as well as the teachers within them, have to find strategies which enable them to manage to survive. This then is an analysis of what these strategies were, and how they have affected the PE Curriculum within the two schools.

Schools and Departments

The Catholic Boys' School in this study, School A, has experienced a gradual decline in its intake since 1978 while, over the same period of time School B has expanded to its full size. It might be thought that the two situations are entirely different since, as conventional wisdom has it, it is infinitely easier to expand rather than to contract (Holt, 1980), because a convenient way to avoid taking difficult decisions is to opt for the diversity that can be contained within an expanding system. Contraction, on the other hand, tends to leave fewer options open and to require that more increasingly difficult decisions are taken. Diversity in the name of freedom of choice might, under other circumstances, be regarded as a waste of resources. What School B had to face, however, was not expansion in a period of expansion but growth in a period of decline.

As Pettigrew (1983) has argued, an environment in which expansion is the dominant motivating force will generate a different set of values from one in which decline or retrenchment is the most common response to the prevailing circumstances. These values and the change from one set to another, will have as much influence on those who are still growing as they will on those who are contracting. In his 'rich' environment, Pettigrew argues that there is little concern for the setting of priorities or the management of resources. There is little open hostility between conflicting interest groups because the main issues centre around who gets what rather than upon who gets nothing and, in any case, rising aspirations can be met, at least in part, by the inevitable processes of growth and expansion. McQueeney (1984) has argued that during a period characterized by a stability brought about by a steady expansion:

> employee relations in the school were characterized by a high degree of mutual accommodation and trust. Although during the periods of wage restraint teachers, through their associations, expressed discontent about their earnings ... their actions did not affect the day to day running of the school. Staff relations were not an issue at school or LEA level. (McQueeney, 1984, p. 3)

In a 'poor' environment, however, the situation is different. All actions have to be justified in terms of their cost–effectiveness rather than in terms of their educational desirability and, within this process of justification, much more account has to be taken of the overall priorities of the organization. The individual department is subject, therefore, to scrutiny not only in terms of the internal consistency and rationale which underpins its own work but also in terms of where that work fits into the overarching priorities of the school.

This is not to say that either of these two schools had carefully formulated and articulated statements of aims and objectives. They did not. The priorities of the schools became most obvious when they came into conflict with those of the department or, to put it more simply, when the head of the school and the head of the department disagreed over particular issues, especially those concerned with the distribution of scarce resources like staff appointments or the allocation of staff time.

If the shift from a 'rich' to a 'poor' environment generates conflict over resources it also leads to a fundamental reconceptualization of the notion of career within a school. Until recently teachers could realistically expect their career to be a steady progression through various stages on the ladder of promotion. Some even achieved this within a single school where loyalty and seniority brought their own rewards. These attitudes still continue to be held despite all the evidence which exists to show that such aspirations are unrealistic and even unattainable (Fiske, 1979). This can certainly be seen in School A where long service has clearly not reaped its own reward. It can be seen in a different form in School B where teachers tried to develop a range of skills and gain a variety of experiences in order to open up a range of options to them in the future. Both strategies have had an effect on the way in which the PE Departments in those schools have coped. Neither strategy is based entirely on what Pettigrew argues is the rational response. That is to develop a notion of career which is seen in terms of personal survival through a process of moving around the organization at the same level. Horizontal promotion may describe this but, more often, it is called staff development.

Staff development often involves giving an individual the opportunity to gain insight into a different aspect of the work of the school. This frequently requires the individual to participate in the making of decisions. In a fairly orthodox view of school organization, decisions are the product of a hierarchical structure with different people within that structure claiming with varying degrees of success to have the right to take certain decisions. The head, perhaps with the senior management team, might take the decision to offer PE as an option in the fifth year. The Head of PE decides who is to teach the option and makes the resources available and the teacher does the rest. Where all are equal and treated equally this may be an accurate description of the decision–making process but in the two schools in this study that was not the case. As will be seen, the focus of decision-making about the curriculum moves from individual to department to head and back. It could not even be argued, as Burgess's Mr. Goddard, the Head of Archbishop McGregor School, who thought that in spite of the divisions within the school; '. . . McGregor was united by a common purpose which allowed the school to act as a group, where unity could arise out of the different interests, tensions and conflicts that would occur in different subgroups among the staff' (Burgess 1983, p. 40).

What Mr. Goddard did recognize was the dynamic nature of the relations between departments and sub-groups within his school. He saw that processes of adaptation are continually taking place as strategies are formulated, tested, rejected or accepted. He recognized implicity what Schon (1971) made explicit. All organizations are made up of a structure or sets of relationships between individual members; a set of technologies or techniques for performing tasks or extending the capabilities of the members of the organization; and a set of views about the organization itself concerning its operation, purposes, environment and its future. A change in any one of these areas will have an effect on the others and that effect may or may not be predictable or even desirable. Equally the part played by any group within the organization in the activities of the whole is a product of the perceptions held by the members of that sub-group about their place in the structure, their relationship to the technology and their views about the organization. Thus it was with our two PE departments.

Departments and Heads of Departments

Within schools, departments are those groupings of teachers who have general responsibility for teaching a particular subject area to identifiable groups of pupils. Not that we should regard subjects themselves as immutable for, as Goodson has argued; 'Subjects and disciplines are made up of teachers and scholars attracted to differing factions and traditions within their subject's concern; and these factions and traditions develop or decline as the subject evolves' (Goodson, 1983, p. II). PE Departments are an interesting example of the inter-relationship between a subject or discipline, albeit one which is essentially activity based, and the school structure. As Holt (1980), for example, points out, PE is one of the four subjects which make up the core curriculum in almost any school. Yet Whitehead and Hendry (1976) have argued that those teaching PE occupy a marginal role in schools since their activities are peripheral to the main functioning of schools which is taken to be the passing of examinations.

Faced with this problem a head of a PE department can adopt one or both of two different strategies. He can seek to ensure that his department can imitate those behaviours which, in others, brings a high status. In this case that means organizing the work of the PE department in such a way that it is not only less activity based but so that pupils can sit a public examination in the subject. This strategy has been widely adopted in recent years. In 1976 just over 9000 pupils took some form of CSE examination in PE or related subjects in 547 different schools but by 1982 almost 16,000 pupils from 777 schools were examined (Carroll, 1983).

Neither head of department in this study chose to cope with the status problem in this way. The Head of Department B believed that 'Subject disciplines simply narrow childrens' minds' and 'The work of this department should be relevant to the needs of the pupils. That is all of the pupils, not just some of them'. Examinations, however well designed would, in his opinion, detract from his ability to ensure that the department met these needs since, inevitably, resources would have to move towards those forms taking examinations and away from those not to be examined. In Department A the stance was similar but the rationale was different. When a new PE advisor came to the LEA in 1979 she wanted all PE departments to offer CSE in PE. The Head of this department refused on the grounds that it was a bandwagon with very little educational justification. He resisted pressure from the advisor until the Director of Education announced that he did not regard it as a justifiable use of resources to enter pupils for mode 3 CSE examinations. That ended the argument but did nothing to improve relations between the Head of department and his advisor.

The other strategy consists of emphasizing the traditional strengths of physical education within the school in the hope that those strengths will be recognized and will, as a result, bring some status to the department for its activities in those areas. Lashley (1980) has argued that the main arenas for success as far as PE teachers and their departments are concerned is in the gymnasium and on the playing field. Underwood's work confirms this but suggests that the most significant aspect of all, as far as the department's profile within the school goes, is that of extra-curricular work. One of his respondents put the situation clearly when he said; 'We just can't put in enough hours. Lunch hours, after school, week-ends and holidays ...' (Underwood, 1983, p. 49). Many of Underwood's teachers argued that considerable prestige was attached to achieving a satisfactory level of performance in inter-school fixtures to the extent that, as one teacher put it; 'The only way that I can compete with academic subjects is through county representative players rather than the good programme I have in the school' (Underwood 1983, p. 49).

In this instance the total justification of the PE curriculum appeared to depend on the athletic prowess of a very few pupils. The Heads of both the departments were aware of this aspect of their work and the effect that it might have on their department but both discussed the matter at a time when two of the largest LEAs in the country, Birmingham and ILEA, had instructed schools to stop all forms of organized sporting competition between schools and when the dispute over teachers' pay had almost brought all extra-curricular activities to a standstill. This is in marked contrast to the time, in the early 1970s which the Head of Department B described as 'The Golden Age of Physical Education when jobs were in abundance and teachers were interested in the pursuit of excellence'. This is an example of how the shift from 'rich' to 'poor' environments in the wider education system can have a direct influence on the fortunes of small groups of people within that system. In School B, the Head of PE struggled to maintain his fixture list because in a rural county, 'Saturday fixtures are an absolute must and are still pursued very actively', although he conceded that he had to organize an annual sponsored event in order to pay for the costs of transport and staff time. It was no longer a central part of the normal school activity and he recognized that, even in his own relatively favourable environment that,

'The long established traditions of Physical Education Departments are under threat from the DES, from LEAs, HMI and even from the headteachers in the schools'. He believed that this strategy went some way to safeguarding the position of his department within the school. As we shall see in the next section, however, all of the members of that department including the Head of it were heavily engaged in work which had no direct connection with the PE Department although, within departmental meetings for example, it was taboo to suggest that this might have an adverse effect on the overall work of that department or that it might be, in any way, indicative of a lessening of commitment to physical education on the part of the PE staff.

In School A the Head of Department was also struggling to preserve his pattern of extra-curricular activities although he believed that this would do nothing to enhance the status of his department within the school. In 1980 the school had a football team for each year, four basketball teams and five rugby teams. In order to run these the department was heavily dependent on help from interested colleagues outside the department. In 1980 the department lost one member of staff who was not replaced and no extra help was forthcoming from colleagues outside the department in order to sustain the school teams. The Head of PE took the decision to abandon the rugby fixture list, for which there was no outside help. In this he had the active support of his second in department, the rugby specialist in the school, who wanted to use his time pursuing other interests outside the department. Two years later another member of the department left without a replacement. At this point the Head of Department took over the running of two teams which were in the final stages of local cup competitions but refused to continue to do this extra work in the following year. By 1984 he was responsible for three teams and his two colleagues were running two teams each but there was every possibility that this load would be reduced again in the 1986–7 school year.

Reducing the programme of extra-curricular activities was, for this Head of PE, limiting his own scope to show how much he had achieved for the school. He frequently discussed teams in terms of 'their record of achievement'. In order to try to obtain more help for his department he discussed this matter with the headteacher in terms of, 'my record, my personal record. What the teams I had been in charge of had achieved'. The Head of school's cutting response was to say that, 'you are the Head of the department. That is what you are there for.' The Head of PE regarded that remark as symptomatic of the general lack of interest in PE on the part of the headteacher who, he complained, 'Never came to fixtures, not even when we have been in cup finals. You get no thanks, no thanks at all.' He suggested that eventually his department would do what had been done by a PE Department in a neighbouring school which was widely regarded as the best footballing school in the city. 'The department went to the head and told him that they were not going to do football anymore. If you want football you will have to get outside help'.

The Head of this PE department also found that, while help from non-physical education colleagues had been forthcoming prior to the teachers' action, it had been insufficient to meet the needs and that it had declined significantly in the last three years. This was, he argued, because staff realized that the present head was not concerned about this aspect of school work and would not even know if a teacher was running a team. If staff run teams, he suggested, they either do it for the pupils or, 'They do it for themselves, to win.' In more favourable times, when teachers could move relatively easily from one school to another the fact that they had helped with teams might have helped on their application forms. Now that there is little or no movement there is, he argued, not incentive to help at all. He also believed that the teachers' action would make the situation worse even after it was over because, 'People will get used to having their Saturdays at home. Nobody will want to work. Already people in PE departments in this city have stopped working themselves silly because they recognize that however hard you work there is no promotion. You are on a scale three and you are stuck there no matter what you do.'

Why then, it might be asked, does this department continue with extra-curricular activities at all? Three reasons appear to emerge for this. The effect of the long tradition within school PE departments and the expectations which PE teachers have been led to have of themselves through their professional training cannot be discounted. Most PE teachers have excelled at sport in some field and believe that all children should be given the opportunity to do the same, whether they like it or not. As the Head of Department A put it, 'I was surprised to learn that many of the boys did not like football', his own area of expertise,' I only found out by accident when I asked a group of them why they repeatedly failed to bring their kit'. Of such stuff is curriculum planning made. Success in inter-school competition was also an important performance indicator for this Head of department. He not only judged himself in this way but he also judged his colleagues by this standard. Of his second in department he said, 'He has never won anything with a team. It has been an embarrassment really. You get these good non-physical education guys who win things with their teams but my deputy can't win anything.' Finally the struggle to continue the extra-curricular activities by this Head of department, even though he knows that it will not produce the effect within the school that he wants, is evidence of the 'while there is life there is hope' syndrome because, 'since I had my row with the head about not coming to fixtures we do get a mention in the school bulletin now and again'.

The Head of Department A had no illusions about the extent to which his subject and his department had a marginal status within the school. This had not only been brought home to him through the problems with finding help with teams. He had seen his department decline from five to three in a very short time and had also witnessed the protection, if not the expansion, of other departments in the school. When the last member of the department had left to emigrate to Australia where he is now a head of a very large department, an interview was held to replace him. A good candidate was almost offered the job but a moratorium was imposed by the LEA and the school governors on new appointments so no replacement was forthcoming. However, two weeks later an appointment was made to the RE Department. The Head of PE saw this as a clear indication of the status of his own department within the school. He also believed that,

'The head is more interested in Science than in PE but we are not the only department to suffer. Art, Drama and Music, all those sort of things have gone. There has been a shift to the basic subjects, Maths, English and Science. Every member of the Science Department is on an allowance and some of them are manufactured allowances. Young guys have actually come in on scale two and these are completely new to the school. I see a lowering of resources everywhere to pay for the Science people. I am told that because of falling rolls I shouldn't need as much money but equipment is expensive and it still has to be bought.'

In part he blamed himself for this state of affairs. 'I think I brought a lot of the problems on myself due to my failure to get on with the Head and my stupidity in writing down on paper that he was a bumbler, which got into his hands. That hasn't helped the PE Department.' Perhaps this did serve to reinforce the marginality of his department within this particular school, although of far more significance would seem to be the general change in attitude towards certain aspects of the curriculum in a 'poor' environment where resources are limited, promotion is difficult to obtain, and the ways to gain promotion appear, for many teachers, to be clouded in obscurity. As the Head of Department B put it,

' It is not so much that people do not respect what we are trying to do but, both inside and outside the department, teachers have their own priorities. They have to build a career in the best way they can and this may mean that they are not as committed to the department as I would like.'

Teachers and Departments

In neither of the two departments can it be claimed, with any degree of accuracy, that the teachers regarded themselves only as teachers of physical education. In fact, in some cases this was a secondary role to be fitted in with other commitments. Yet it has always been recognized that to teach PE successfully, an extremely high level of commitment to the subject and to the work of the department is necessary. Kane argued that PE teachers are;

dedicated (averaging an additional eight hours of unpaid extra-curricular service each week), have a broad educational commitment, and consider that successful teaching in physical education depends on social concern, wide professional education and an enlightened capacity for sustained hard work. (Kane, 1974, p. 62)

As if to reinforce this point Whitehead has stated that teaching physical education is;

an arduous, challenging, rewarding profession provided that teachers concentrate on their own task and do not compare their 'lot' with that of other teachers .... Boredom, cynicism, low standards, laziness and unprofessionalism are not what you would expect of physical educationalists. (Whitehead, Hilliam and Young, 1983, p. 48)

The heads of both of these departments certainly saw PE that way when they came into the profession but recognized that the hard work rapidly brought its own rewards. The Head of Department A became a Head of Department after three years teaching and expected to stay in that post for about five years. 'I wanted to see one year through.' Fifteen years later he is still there. The same step took the Head of Department B seven years but this was partly because he did not want to move too far from London. Their relative success is typical for, as Hilsum and Start (1974) found, early and rapid promotion was the norm for PE teachers. The average length of time it took for a PE teacher to gain a first promotion was just over two years compared with six years for a Mathematics teacher and eight years for a teacher of General Studies. Although 65 per cent of PE teachers could expect this promotion they were, according to Barnard (1982) likely to be stuck on the careerless scale three post. In the face of lack of opportunities for promotion the situation is likely to remain as it is rather than to improve.

In the past the natural avenue for promotion for PE teachers has been through the pastoral structure of schools. Scott (1982) has argued that PE teachers were in a good position to develop sound relationships with pupils and to understand their sub-cultures in ways which were denied to the classroom teacher. Hendry supported this view when he argued that; 'by virtue of the often informal nature of the role of physical education, teachers may gain insight into pupils' sub-cultures unavailable to academic members of staff' (Hendry, 1975, p. 118). The Head of Department B shared this perception because, 'After taking them on five bus journeys a week you get to know them very well', while the Head of Department A argued that, 'We see them in different ways, in a more relaxed atmosphere so we get to know them better. They see that we are human.' Yet, as the educational service continues its shift from a 'rich' to a 'poor' environment with the accompanying decline in available resources and the probability that schools will become smaller and, therefore, will have fewer scale points available for distribution, this avenue for promotion appears, as Glew (1981) has argued, to be closing rapidly. He goes on to suggest that with the closure of many colleges of education specializing in PE such as Madeley, Chester and Dartford and the reorganization of many advisory services within LEAs so as to diminish the emphasis which had, hitherto, been placed on the subject specialist, other avenues of promotion are closing at the same time.

The Heads of both these departments were aware of this situation as far as their own careers and those of their colleagues within the departments were concerned. The Head of Department A adopted a number of different strategies for himself. He obtained a BEd and the MEd degree, the latter with special papers in Management and in Pastoral Care. He then sought to strengthen his position by running the school's youth club which ended badly because it was closed by the Head who believed that it attracted 'an unruly element from the local estate'. The Head of PE then focused on parents and set up the first PTA that the school has had. Eventually he withdrew from this when he lost his second member of department and could get no extra help with running teams. All of this time he continued to apply for pastoral care posts within his own school and in other schools in the LEA. When he failed to get a larger head of department's post in another school disillusionment set in. Together with his wife he sought planning permission to convert an old house into a private school but was unsuccessful. His view now is that, 'the pupils are not motivated in any lesson. They see that PE does not carry any weight. I have started running a football team for my son and I am not doing any extra here'. He went on to say that, because he was not putting in as much extra work as he had done previously he felt more enthusiastic about his teaching and he had more energy for it. This was not his opinion about his second in the department, however.

The deputy head of this department had recently completed a part-time diploma in pastoral care which he had started immediately after a one year secondment during which time he took a BEd in Education and Community Studies. In the opinion of the Head of Department,

'He's rubbish but he thinks that he is doing a good job. He believes that he deserves promotion and more cash but he does not want any more responsibility within the department. He hasn't ever done anything much anyway but, in truth, he's not much worse than many other staff in the school. I suppose that I have to try to understand his predicament.'

At the moment the second in the department is teaching thirty-four periods of PE out of a forty period week but he sees his future in pastoral care. He is working as a deputy year-head, unpaid. As the Head of Department put it, 'He has been doing it for two years now. It's nothing official and nothing has ever been said but he desperately wants to move away from PE. It's his age.' In 1986–7 it is planned that this man will teach twenty-nine periods of PE, and the two periods of car driving that he has been doing with the sixth form in his free periods will then be timetabled. The rest of his time will be spent teaching Maths. This will place additional pressure on the other two members of the PE Department but the deputy head of the department feels threatened by the impending amalgamation and believes that he may be redeployed so he is, 'trying to get as many strings to his bow as he can so that he can say he is doing this and that. At least that is what he told me but it is a bit belated'. Whether or not the Head of the department has accurately assessed the motives of his colleague in wishing to seek promotion or even security outside PE it is very clear that, in the face of falling rolls and a merger of two schools he has a fairly forlorn hope of being successful. The strategies which he has adopted to survive in what he sees as a hostile and threatening environment have had and will continue to have a profound effect on the PE Department and its curriculum, as will be seen in the next section.

The third member of the department is affected by the strategies adopted by the deputy head of the department in two ways. He enjoys his work in the department, unlike his more senior colleague, and he tackles it with enthusiasm. He has no chance of obtaining the scale two post which he wants until either a new member of staff joins the department or the deputy head of department leaves. Thus he is a little disenchanted because he sees the deputy doing less and less, and not doing it very well but still holding down a scale two post. The opportunities for the type of curriculum development which this man would like to have are blocked because of the additional teaching that has to be done within the department as his colleague gradually withdraws. In the words of his Head of Department,

'He likes working with me and he is good. If he could get a scale two he would be quite happy. He won't do secondment. I've tried to get him to. He has got no academic qualifications but he doesn't want to do a degree. I think he needs to push himself a bit more.'

In the face of blocked promotion and a heavy teaching load this man has evolved his own strategy for coping. He earns almost £3000 each year by doing private car maintenance.

In Department B the problems associated with promotion are less severe since the school is newer and, therefore, teachers have not been in post for the same length of time as those in School A. Thus they can still retain the belief that promotion will come to them either within the school or by moving. They have not, as yet, put this to the test and confronted the realities of a 'poor' environment. Nevertheless the realities of such an environment have confronted them, and especially the Head of the Department. Unlike the Head of Department A who tends to see his role within the department as that of reacting to crisis and confronting those who threaten his own traditional views, the Head of Department B has a more coherent view of his departmental duties. He argues that, 'Our work in this department depends on my ability to create a situation in which PE can flourish. I am basically a facilitator. I must be aware of the backgrounds, cultures and environments of the pupils and the interests and specialisms of my staff.' He suggested that a great many PE teachers, including his own staff, were following a career within a career since, 'after ten or twelve years they will want to switch out of PE into other areas like pastoral care', always, it might be added, assuming that opportunities for such a change still exist in the 1990s. To what extent this Head of Department had considered the implications of a 'poor' environment in the long term for his colleagues and his department it is difficult to judge but he did acknowledge that, as Head of Department, 'I am responsible for the career development of all the members of my department and doing this requires that jobs within the department are clearly known. This is the first step in good delegation which is the start of career development'. It was also necessary to help him cope with the results of his own strategy for career development.

After two years at the school he became Head of First and Second Years in addition to his PE responsibilities. This involved him in working with two teams of six tutors. At the same time he was taking a part-time BEd degree. As the school grew to its full size, 'I began to find the job impossible. I could not manage my time. I realized that time spent on one job was time not spent on the other and I could not be doing both jobs efficiently.' Attempting to do both jobs was a result of recognizing that, 'I am going no further in PE. There are just not the jobs available. I would not find a department bigger than this one, and there is almost no chance of an advisor's job or one in a college.' When the opportunity to diversify into pastoral care came it was taken. In the light of the subsequent difficulties the choice has been justified thus. 'There is no doubt that being a pastoral head has helped me in my teaching and organizing a syllabus as Head of Physical Education.' However, the conflict over priorities remains and is unresolved because, 'I cannot be in two places at once. As a year head I should be around the school and on hand to deal with any problems. As a Head of PE I should be involved in the very necessary work of the department, including extra-curricular activity. I cannot solve this problem'.

Perhaps an obvious step would be to delegate more of the work to other members of the department but they also have evolved strategies for themselves. These strategies make delegation within the department difficult. The Head of Department argued that, 'My main plan for the future must be to look at the department and develop a structure. The problem here is that the man who was appointed in 1980 has now become Head of Fourth and Fifth Year and he faces the same problems that I do'. He too has been confronted with the problems of dual responsibility in a school in which there are insufficient scale points to be able to ensure that all the necessary duties can be covered by different teachers and a pattern of additional responsibility rather than alternative responsibility has developed within the school as its own response to a 'poor' environment. This has severe consequences for some departments especially where, as in this case, the remaining two members of department are also heavily committed.

'The Second in the Department, until recently, carried all the responsibility for girls' PE and games. With the addition of a probationer she had to accept the duty of helping the probationer who, in turn, did provide help with the work of girls' PE. The situation might improve a little as the new member of staff gains experience but, she will want to develop her own specialisms, Dance and Outdoor Pursuits, and she will soon be looking for ways to get promotion. It is a vicious circle.'

The Head of Department is now pressing the Head of School B to do one of two things.

'He should either create a post of Senior Tutor which would relieve year heads of some work or he should appoint another Head of PE. The problem with this is that the other man in the department doesn't want the job. He wants to go pastoral. The second in the department could do the job well if she wanted to, which is doubtful because of her family commitments but we would still need a male member of staff to look after the boys'.

In these two departments, then, it is possible to identify a number of coping strategies which individual teachers have adopted in order to survive in the face of a shift from a 'rich' to a 'poor' environment. These strategies are a result of circumstances well outside the control of most of the individuals involved and, in most cases, outside the control of the schools. Nevertheless the influence of these strategies on the work of the departments within the schools is significant. The development of dual responsibilities within the school and the acceptance of them by members of the PE Department who see no other avenue of promotion had a limiting effect on the work of Department B. The three different strategies adopted by the members of Department A, intense activity, then withdrawal by its Head of Department, moving into Pastoral Care and Mathematics by the second in the department, and the retreat into car maintenance by the third member resulted in the gradual erosion of the PE curriculum in School A, a process which is still continuing.

Curriculum and Curriculum Change

The curriculum of any school might be defined as the totality of learning experiences which that school offers to the pupils for whom it is responsible. As Weston (1979) has pointed out, such a definition stresses the school's intention towards its pupils and leads to the curriculum being seen as a programme planned in advance for the benefit of pupils, taking into account the context of the school and the needs of the pupils. It would be worked out in advance outside the classroom as a plan which teachers would attempt to realize during the school year. An alternative view is to regard the curriculum as a negotiated collection of socially organized knowledge shaped either through the effect of dominant ideologies within society on curricular provision in schools (Young, 1971) or through a process of modification of the intended learning experiences which is brought about by the interaction of teachers and pupils in a specific context (Weston, 1979). Thus the curriculum is a complex and dynamic set of factors which, in any given subject area, will take into account the prevailing views about the content and pedagogy of the subject as mediated, for example, through advisors, professional bodies, and journals.

In a series of articles, Almond (1982, 1983) has argued that there are four aspects to the changing content and pedagogy in Physical Education. There is an increased emphasis on health related fitness including a study of diet and different forms of exercise such as Dance. This stresses the quality of particular activities for the individual. There is a move towards personal improvement in the form of activity which provides success as well as enjoyment. This is linked with the development of understanding rather than the repetitious acquisition of 'correct' techniques. At the same time a wider range of extra-curricular activities beyond the traditional inter-school fixtures is now expected. These trends emphasize a concern for individual pupils rather than with performance and excellence. Within them, however, can be found disagreements about how best to follow these trends. Some PE Departments have turned to formal public examinations while others have developed courses which stress education for leisure or personal and social development. It has been argued, however, that the practical and theoretical insights which come from a CSE course are more likely to prepare pupils for leisure than vague, loosely structured courses based on sampling a wide range of activities in a short space of time, often unsupported by specialist expertise in many areas (Carroll, 1983).

Be that as it may, both of our departments have rejected the CSE approach to their subject in favour of other forms of curricula shaped in different ways. Underwood has argued that the PE curriculum should be characterized by; ... progression in the curriculum ... This should not be a haphazard affair but something that is planned and worked for systematically (Underwood, 1983, p. 50). In neither of these two departments did such systematic planning appear to be particularly influential in shaping the curriculum. The Head of Department B wanted to see 'more activities being placed under the PE umbrella and a school timetable constructed in such a way as to allow time for those things like outdoor pursuits which are being stressed by the DES at the moment'. He also argued that his department ought to give more consideration to the contribution which the subject can make to the personal and social development of pupils. 'It is vital that teachers of PE develop a curriculum which is relevant to the needs of today's school leavers. Doing this requires that we have sensitive, caring and totally committed people with high professional standards' and, he might have added, with no extra responsibilities elsewhere in the school, which was his personal dilemma. He did identify a broader dilemma, however.

'There is an almost total exclusion in these ideas of traditional PE programmes. Hardly any mention of team games, competitive matches and the pursuit of excellence. This is the dilemma facing experienced PE teachers and their departments. Most of us feel that the programmes we have been running for a number of years still have an important part to play, and it is how to integrate the new developments and yet retain the best of the old that is the crucial issue'.

In his own department, however, the crucial issue appeared to be how to staff the programme which was already in existence or, more accurately, how to structure the existing programme so that it could be staffed. He recognized that it was his responsibility to provide, 'a full syllabus for the department and to ensure that it is taught' but he also pointed out that such a syllabus could only be taught as and when staff were available to teach it. Given that both of the men in the department were heavily committed in other aspects of school work, this must put considerable strain on the ability of the department to cover all the boys' team games which were in the syllabus. Football, rugby, cricket and basketball figured largely in all years. 'In the future', argued the Head of Department, 'something will have to go and it will have to be in the specialist area of the person in the department who is most committed elsewhere.' He meant himself. 'We might be able to slip in some Dance or something that the girl can do', he suggests, making reference to the newest member of his department. Already the department had moved away from separate gymnastics teaching for boys and girls in order that the second in the department could teach all of the gymnastics and not, as hitherto, just that provided for girls. This might or might not be educationally sound. Indeed there is evidence to suggest that such a move is to be welcomed (Barnard, 1982). What is at issue here is why such a decision was taken. It was not part of an overall review of the curriculum. Nor was it a conscious and deliberate strategy designed to improve one aspect of the work of the department. Rather it was an *ad hoc* response to pressure on particular members of staff which was being exerted as a result of their work elsewhere in the school. It is evident from the remarks of the Head of this department that other changes which may be made in the future will be of this order and that is a far cry from the planned, systematic progression sought by Underwood. It produces a negotiated curriculum but one which is negotiated in a specific and limited way.

The other department in this study provides evidence of a similar approach to curriculum change. It has been shown already how staff reductions and attempts by teachers to change their career patterns affected extra-curricular activities. The same factors had a similar affect on the PE curriculum within the school, especially in the fourth and fifth years. In the first three years every class had two double periods of PE, one inside and the other outside. In the next two years this was reduced to a double period based on an option system staffed by all the department at the same time in order to provide more activities, smaller groups, and better supervision. When the department lost its first member of staff fewer options could be provided so groups became bigger and when the second teacher left the chioce was reduced still further. Other changes also had to be made. Canoeing was no longer taught at all in the school and it was decided that gymnastics, the specialism of the most recently departed teacher, should be removed from the PE curriculum entirely. The three remaining teachers all, 'had worries about gymnastics, safety particularly, but we didn't teach it very well anyway. What we were doing the children didn't like and they were voting with their feet.' The decision was accepted without question inside the school but the Head of Department, 'knew that we would get serious problems with the advisory service who didn't want us to stop doing gymnastics.' He was right but the change was made anyway.

This was not the only unsuccessful attempt made by the advisor to influence the curriculum in School A. As the Head of the Department put it, referring to the PE Advisor for the school,

'She wants me to change my whole philosophy. She thinks I am very dictatorial, very traditional, and not flexible enough. I think she is wrong but I have to give her some air-time. I like to get the kids doing things quickly. You know! It takes some of them nearly two hours to get started but when I get them I can have them playing in three minutes. The Advisor, she wants me to be more chatty and to be concerned with development and things like that. There is just not the time.'

This view was not shared by the second in the department. 'He is into all that through his pastoral work and he tries to change his PE teaching but it doesn't work. Anyway, most of the time I have to change the timetable to let him do his tutor bit.'

Some changes have taken place in the curriculum, however. As a response to the removal of gymnastics, which needed expert supervision and the concentrated attention of teachers, the Head of Department introduced rollerskating.

'We thought it was the nearest we could get to a gymnastic type personal activity, to an activity where the co-ordination, balance was as near as we could get to gymnastics. It had to be an activity which the children would do, would enjoy doing and was easy on staff time. We have almost 100 per cent participation. It is the one activity where we question all our traditional values.'

That is not quite accurate, however. There is one other area of the curriculum in which the Head of the Department would now accept that his traditional values have been challenged. Again it was introduced in an attempt to minimize the pressure on staff who were heavily committed elsewhere in the school. It also brought the department and the school into conflict with the PE Advisor again. She objected strongly to the introduction of snooker into the curriculum and, more particularly, she objected to the fact that the Head of Department wanted to spend a substantial part of his PE captitation on the necessary equipment. Here, however, the Headteacher came to the rescue.' He bailed me out. I was using my money from the Authority and the Advisor put a stop to it. The Head said he would stand it because he thought snooker was a good activity. He's not all bad.' Snooker is now an integral part of the PE curriculum for the fourth and fifth years.

Some other changes are contemplated. The Head of Department now believes that the department might have been falling short in the health related fitness area. 'I have to accept that. We have always done circuit training, assault courses and work like that. Now we will have to do more of it.' As for personal and social development, the LEA has been leading the way in this field for over a decade and it would be surprising if any PE Department was not under pressure to pay considerable attention to this area. This department certainly was.

> 'I have had two advisors tell me that they don't like my curriculum because it is too traditional but my second in department is doing more social development work anyway, when he is not being a tutor. He is trying to teach in a different way from the other two of us which is putting increasing pressure on the children. There are two different philosophies at work in the department.'

This situation remains unresolved. Very little change has actually taken place and the curriculum is still under review in an attempt to find ways of coping with the reduction in PE time which the second in the department will now have.

In both departments, therefore, the basic approach to curriculum planning seems to be based on attempts to find ways of coping with a reduced commitment by PE staff to their PE teaching, or with an actual reduction in the staff itself. In one sense both departments had a negotiated curriculum. It was the product of achieving a balance between what was desirable and what could be covered. In School A the pupils also were seen to exert some little influence by 'voting with their feet'. The same may have been true in School B but no evidence emerged in this study to suggest that it was so. The curriculum offered to the pupils in both schools, on the whole, appears to be a product of the interplay between the strategies adopted by individual teachers in order to cope with their own career positions as they interpreted them at this particular time and of those managerial coping strategies used by the heads of the departments in order to ensure that the work of the department continued and survived.

Conclusion

How far the factors which have combined to produce the curricula in these two departments are, in any way, typical of other PE departments or of other subject departments in these or other schools remains to be seen. It is clear, however, that the strategies adopted were appropriate and rational strategies for those people who used them. Some possible alternatives to the deliberate reduction of extra-curriculuar activities in School B and the making of concessions to the PE Advisor in School A, for example, were never seriously considered. Perhaps it was felt that neither would produce the desired result in the end. The move into pastoral work by several of the teachers in this study may have been based on a realistic assessment of their promotion prospects in PE and in the pastoral area. Given the extent to which both schools were likely to be affected by demographic changes, however, it can be argued that these moves were based either on imperfect knowledge or on a form of logic that excludes the particular individual from the effects of general changes. Whatever the reasons for coping in the way that they did, the teachers here do demonstrate how right Max Weber was to point out that rationality, where human behaviour is concerned, is far more than a simple relationship between means and ends.

Whatever the reasons for adopting these particular strategies, it is clear that; 'They are not isolated acts, but packages of acts interrelated by intention and structure. The intention is the individual's resolution of the problems thrown up by structure in the achievement of his goals' (Woods, 1980, p. 26). In this case the structure had created the problems as a more general response to the shift from a 'rich' environment in which; 'So deified becomes the value of growth that it rarely needs to be articulated to justify actions taken in its name', (Pettigrew, 1983, p. 3); to a 'poor' environment in which; 'The language of survival becomes the central legitimating force for action, and the pressure for action is to regain control over resource management.' (Pettigrew, 1983, p. 4).

This shift served to emphasize the marginality, not just of PE teachers, but also of the departments within which they work, forcing heads of department in particular to develop strategies for coping with the marginal position of their departments within the school at a time of very scarce resources in order to ensure that they could, at least, minimize the damage which might be done to the departments by a diminution of the resource base, including that of staff time. These changes in the environment are transmitted from the outside world through the school to the department and its staff. They require the department to operate as part of the wider social system in which it is found — that of the school. Changes in one aspect of that social system, even where these are changes in attitudes, priorities and interpretations rather than the more substantial changes in structure, organization and resourcing, will all affect the department and its members in some way or other, although these effects may be different and elicit different responses for different people and at different times. The nature of the changes which were derived from the individual and departmental coping strategies adopted in these two departments in order that their members could manage to survive, may lead to speculation about how far these two PE departments were operating as fully integrated parts of a wider social system. It may be that it would be more accurate to view them as semi-autonomous units within larger, relatively anarchic organizations which had no clear understanding of goals, technologies or members (Bell, 1983), but that is another story.

Bibliography

ALMOND, L. (1982) 'Changing the focus', in *The British Journal of Physical Education*, Vol. 13, No. 5, p. 132.

ALMOND, L. (1983) 'A guide to practice', in *The British Journal of Physical Education*. Vol. 14, No. 5, pp. 134–5.

BARNARD, P. (1982) 'Boys and girls come out to play' in *British Journal of Physical Education*, Vol. 13, No. 2, p. 37.

BARTON, L. and MEIGHAN, R. (Eds.) (1978) *Sociological Interpretations of Schooling and Classrooms; A Reappraisal*, Driffield, Nafferton Books.

BELL, L.A. (1983) 'The sociology of school organisation: a reappraisal', in *The British Journal of Sociology of Education*, Vol. 1, No. 2, pp. 183–92.

BURGESS, R.G. (1983) *Experiencing Comprehensive Education*, London, Methuen.

BURGESS, R.G. (1985) *Field Methods in the Study of Education*, Lewes, The Falmer Press.

CARROLL, R. (1983) 'Developments in CSE and the leisure paradox' in *The British Journal of Physical Education*, Vol. 14, No. 6, pp. 25–7.

FISKE, D. (1979) 'Combating falling rolls', in *Education*, 12 January.

GLEW, P. (1981) 'Physical education as a career for men', in *The British Journal of Physical Education*, Vol. 12, No. 3, p. 57.

GLEW, P. (1982) 'Alternative career structures in PE.' in *The British Journal of Physical Education*. Vol. 13, No. 3, p. 81.

GOODSON, I.F. (1983) *School Subjects and Curriculum Change*, Beckenham, Croom Helm.

HENDRY, L.B. (1975) 'The role of the physical education teacher', in *The British Journal of Physical Education*, Vol. 24, No. 4.

HILSUM, S. and START, K. (1974) *Promotion and Careers in Teaching*, London, NFER.

HOLT, M. (1980) *Schools and curriculum Change*, London, McGraw Hill.

KANE, J.E. (1974) *Physical Education in Secondary Schools*, London, Macmillan.

LASHLEY, H. (1980) 'Lessons to be learned' in *The British Journal of Physical Education*. Vol. 11, No. 1, pp. 5–6.

McQUEENEY, J. (1984) 'The development of secondary school organization and staff management'. Paper presented to *The British Education and Management Association Society Conference*, Cambridge, 14–16 September.

PETTIGREW, A.M. (1983) 'Patterns of managerial response as organizations move from rich to poor environments' in *Educational Management and Administration*, Vol. 1, No. 2, pp. 104–14.

REX, J. (1961) *Key Problems in Sociological Theory*, London, Routledge and Kegan Paul.

SCHON, D. (1971) *Beyond the Stable State*, London, Temple Smith.

SCOTT, A. (1982) 'Preparation beyond PE' in *The British Journal of Physical Education*, Vol. 13, No. 4, p. 114.

UNDERWOOD, G.L. (1983) *The PE Curriculum. Planning and Implementation*, Lewes, Falmer Press.

WESTON, P.B. (1979) *Negotiating the Curriculum: A Study of Secondary Schooling*. London, NFER.

WHITEHEAD, N. and HENDRY, L.B. (1976) *Teaching Physical Education in England*, London, Lepus Books.

WHITEHEAD, N., HILLIAM, S. and YOUNG, D. (1983) *The Physical Education Teacher*, London, Lepus Books.

WOODS, P. (Ed.)(1980) *Teacher Strategies. Explorations in the Sociology of the School*, London, Croom Helm.

YOUNG, M.F.D. (1971) *Knowledge and Control. New Directions in the Sociology of Education*, London, Collier Macmillan.

6 'Troublemakers': Making a Name in Physical Education: A Study of a Label

Bob Carroll

Making a Name

'Casper, You make me sick . . .'
'Every lesson for four years! And in all that time you've made no attempt whatsoever to get any kit, you've skyved and scrounged and borrowed and . . .'
'Casper, shut up lad, what are you trying to do, disrupt the whole school?' (Hines, 1968)

Casper had made a name for himself. He had already been in trouble that day; — in registration, for 'blurting out and making a mess of my register'; in assembly, for 'being an irreverent scoundrel'; in lessons, for 'being awkward' and refusing 'to be interested in anything'; at break-time, for fighting. There was more trouble to come, for later in the PE lesson he was making a nuisance of himself by climbing on the goalposts and refusing to take a shower. As Casper says, 'They're (the teachers) allus sayin I'm a pest or a nuisance, they talk as if I like gettin' into trouble'. Teachers may read *Kes* with uneasy amusement, because they do not find it quite so funny when they are faced with similar, persistent, 'difficult behaviours'. They too, find boys and girls like Casper 'a nuisance', 'irritating' and 'troublesome'. Of course not all pupils are like Casper, many are just the opposite. These pupils do or appear to do as they are told and are rarely in trouble, and teachers refer to these as 'good girls', 'good lads', 'enthusiastic', 'great kids'. They, too, have made a name for themselves.

In the study on which this chapter is based I found teachers willing to discuss the names pupils have made for themselves, and the way they themselves have identified pupils. In effect they have given pupils an educational identity. At the same time, many of the teachers (not all) were reluctant to admit that they were labelling or 'casting a pupil in a particular mould', and they liked to feel that they saw pupils as individuals not as types. This contradiction has been brought about partly by labelling theory's origins in deviance theory which has often given rise to research which is disparaging of teachers and overtly focused on the negative effects of labels. Teachers are probably now more aware of the effects of expectations, self-fulfilling prophecies, labels, and the organizational policies of streaming, for example, and do not want to make themselves appear as 'villains', as some sociologists have described them. When teachers do label pupils, they evaluate and classify pupils' behaviour and act upon that information, and this process, clearly, is not confined merely to the classroom, it is part of an everyday way of making sense of the world (Schutz, 1964). By doing so, pupils make names for themselves and, maybe, gain reputations (good or bad) which affect their educational 'career'. This chapter is an attempt to study that process by examining a particular label, namely, the 'troublemaker' in the specific context of physical education.

Labelling Theory and Typing

Labelling theory was popularized by the work of Becker (1963), who takes the view that,

> Social groups create deviance by making the rules whose infraction constitutes deviance, and by applying these rules to particular people, and labelling them as outsiders. From this point of view, deviance is not a quality of the act the person commits, but rather a consequence of the application by others of the rules and sanctions to the 'offender'. The deviant is one to whom that label has successfully been applied; the deviant behavior is behavior that people so label.

This approach opened up an analysis of deviant behaviour from the point of view of the labeller and rule maker, as well as the labelled and rule breaker, and also of the process of labelling.

Labelling theory can be applied easily to deviance where a criminal law has been breached, but it has been extensively used where social conventions rather than laws are broken, for example, in studies of homosexuality, or where abnormalities exist, as in the case of physical disability. People in these groups can become labelled and as stigmatized as others who have achieved a criminal identity.

The most direct application of labelling theory to the teaching situation is Hargreaves *et al*'s (1975) research. Their study, in the phenomenological tradition, attempts to explicate teachers' commonsense knowledge and interpretive work in relation to pupil deviance. They sought to answer the questions, 'how does a teacher come to define a given pupil act as deviant?' and, 'how does a teacher come to define a given pupil as deviant?'. They did this by examining in detail teachers' classroom rules, and how teachers fit the pupils' acts to the rules by use of evidential cues and strategies. Thus they were able to state how pupils become known as a given type, for example, a 'troublemaker'. Hargreaves *et al.* found that teachers' typing revolved around five main aspects — appearance, discipline, academic, likeability and peer group. Quite clearly, academic and behavioural constructs are common and important, because academic ability and behaviour are organizing concepts in schools.

Hargreaves *et al.* outline a theory of typing in three, though not discrete, stages. The first is the 'speculation' stage, where the teacher first comes to know the child, and it is clear that first impressions are important as it paves the way for possible future expectations. The second stage is the 'elaboration' stage, a kind of confirmation or non–confirmation phase, where clues are being sought and tested. The final stage is the 'stabilization' period, where there is a relatively clear and stable conception of the pupil's identity. Variations within types are noted by the teacher, which Hargreaves *et al.* refer to as 'idiosyncratized', that is, the pupil displays his or her own particular way of 'troublemaking'. What is perhaps most important from all this in the interaction process is that pupils become known as particular types, take on the characteristics of the type, and explanations for their behaviour are seen in the light of this identification.

It is clear that this theory of typing is not restricted to labelling theory in the narrower sense of Becker's definition, nor is its application confined only to schools. It is a theory of the categorization and labelling of people more generally, and it offers a way of making sense of people's behaviour and how they respond to a given label applied within a specific context. Labelling for Hargreaves is not only unavoidable but is in fact a positive way of responding in a more orderly fashion to the array of information which bombards the teacher, and assists the teacher in formulating his or her plans of action, or, in Schutz's terms, 'recipes for action' (Schutz, 1964).

However, what is clearly lacking in Hargreaves *et al*'s account is any reference to the pupil's perspective, although in a later work, Hargreaves (1976) discusses pupils' reactions but without any empirical support. By contrast, Bird's (1980) work takes the pupils' perspective and challenges some of Hargreaves' ideas. She suggests that pupils are able to differentiate between academic and behavioural labels, and that the academic labels are internalized by the pupils, whilst the behavioural ones are not. The latter ones tend to be inconsistently applied, and specifically related to context and time. This questions the 'use of labelling theory in the consideration of school deviance' (Bird, 1980), and certainly in the role that labelling plays in the amplification of deviance.

Other studies in recent years, although not so directly concerned with labelling theory, have been concerned with pupils' educational identities and the related teacher expectations. A gamut of educational and sociological research has suggested that teachers label pupils, usually to ill effect. The teacher expectation and self–fulfilling prophecy studies such as Rist (1970), Rosenthal and Jacobson (1968), and Nash (1973), revealed that the identity of the pupils emerged out of the teacher's beliefs and management of those beliefs, whilst Keddie (1971) amongst others showed that what a teacher knows about his/her pupils and how those pupils are treated in relation to curriculum knowledge is, at least, in part derived from organizational grouping policies, for example, streaming. These organizational structures provide an institutionalized polarization of identifiable cultures from which distinct educational identities emerge. Pupils are launched on an educational 'career' from which it is extremely difficult to escape, and which provides teachers with a basis for evaluating and labelling pupils (see, Hargreaves, 1967; Lacey, 1970; Ball, 1981). Abolishing streaming does not appear to be the total answer as Nash and others have shown, for even in mixed ability groups, the pupils still recognize their hierarchical levels of ability as ranked by the teacher. In Mapledene, too, a primary school where a child centred philosophy predominated, Sharp and Green showed that the hierarchical nature of identities was transmitted as readily as in more traditionally orientated schools streamed by ability (Sharp and Green, 1975).

Although these studies are concerned with teachers and schools generally, physical education is not mentioned as the context of teacher labelling. However, there is evidence to suggest that physical education activities do form the basis of friendship groups and do provide the basis for the emergence of a type and a label. For example, Meyenn (1980) found that the 'PE girls' were a very distinct group of girls who were 'good at and interested in PE and games' and this grouping was accepted and acknowledged by themselves and the teachers, and in another study, Pollard (1984) noted the existence of the 'netball group of jokers' and the 'football group' of boys, and both groups consisted of pupils good at sport. Woods also provides limited evidence of labelling in physical education from the pupil's perspective (Woods, 1981).

A Study of a Label

The aim of my study is to examine teachers' labels in the context of physical education. It is not a study of labelling theory or deviance theory in the way Becker proposed, as this would necessitate limiting it to a focus on pupils breaking 'rules'. It is a study of teachers' labels, that is, their categorization of typing of pupils. Like Hargreaves *et al*, it was carried out within the phenomenological tradition, by using in depth semistructured interviews to probe secondary school teachers' taken for granted conceptions of their pupils. The sample consisted of thirty men and women teachers of physical education from towns in North West England. The study sought to answer the following questions from the teachers' perspective: Do PE teachers label pupils? If so, what labels do they use? When are they used? What does the pupil do to receive the label? What are the consequences for the pupil of receiving the label? How is the label used? The analysis used what the author has termed the 'Five C's' (Carroll, 1976), but extended it to include six other categories. These eleven categories cover the sociological questions of importance in the area.

1	Constructs	What are the labels/categories/tags used by the teacher?
2	Context	When is the label used? What is the relationship between labels?
3	Criteria	What is the criteria for the label?
4	Cues	What does the pupil actually do to receive the label? Evidential cues.
5	Causes	What does the teacher feel are the causes for the pupil doing what s/he does or being like s/he is?
6	Consequences	What are the consequences for the pupil of receiving the label? Treatment.
7	Changes	Does the teacher change the label of the pupil? If so, when and why?
8	Career	Is there a typical career for pupils with this label?
9	Comparison	How do other teachers label this pupil?
10	Child's Consciousness	Is the pupil aware of the label?
11	Uses	How does the teacher use the label? Function. Purpose.

The categories are not necessarily discrete, and in the following analysis are not presented in this order. One way of presenting the data would be in the form of individual case studies of pupils, as Hargreaves *et al.* have done. However, it was soon obvious that different teachers, both men and women, talked about the same types of pupils, and, perhaps surprisingly, there were many common elements. This makes it possible to cut across the interviews and present selected types of pupils. This raises the problem of the relationship between the teachers' constructs (first order) and the researcher's constructs (second order), and the researcher's interpretations (see Schutz, 1964). I am in fact presenting the second order construct of 'troublemaker', although that construct is used frequently by the teachers as well, and, an amalgam of evidence of teachers' perceptions about different pupils (mostly boys but often girls) under that label. They may therefore be regarded as ideal-typical instances of that type. The advantage is that I am not presenting just case studies of individual pupils which are limited to those pupils and contexts, but showing types of pupils which may be found in many physical education lessons in many schools.

There were in fact many different labels used by the PE teachers. Common ones were concerned with the dimension of physical ability, for example, the 'Athletes', 'The natural sportsman', and at the opposite end, 'the spassies' and the 'motor morons', whilst others revolved around attitude, such as, 'the sporting gent', and 'the temperamental sportsman'. Common too, were those based on the criteria of academic ability, for example, 'the intelligent', 'quick learner' at one end of the spectrum with 'the thickies' and 'slow learners' at the other. But, perhaps, the most common was 'the troublemaker'. To discuss only a few of these labels would take up a lot of space and perhaps lend itself to superficiality and triviality, so I have decided to concentrate on just the 'troublemaker'. This focus will enable me to cover the eleven categories detailed earlier, and will show how complex the process of labelling is in teacher-pupil interaction.

'The Troublemaker'

When teachers were asked to talk about their pupils, very often they first spoke about a 'troublemaker'. It was not that there were many troublemakers in each school, in fact just the opposite in some cases, but the 'troublemaker' stood out. The main criteria for 'troublemaker' was of course bad behaviour by the pupil, which was at the very least a nuisance to the teacher. It was seen as intentional provoking behaviour, which broke the teachers' or school's unwritten but not unspoken, rules. Many constructs were used by both men and women teachers which show the range of troublemaking; cheeky, mischievous, fool, silly, stupid, boisterous, bad, evil, pest, nuisance, bolshi, berk, disruptor, troublemaker, problem kids. These constructs were used on a dimension of troublemaking which appears to have something to do with a combination of, the pupil's intentions, the way the pupil commits his or her act, the degree of unpleasantness, and the degree of acceptability on the teacher's part. The dimension goes from mildly mischievous, at one end, for example 'the class clown', to very malicious, such as 'the class nasty', at the other. The way the pupil commits his or her acts is very important in giving evidential cues to the teacher who is continually making subtle interpretations and distinctions of the pupil's behaviour in terms of motives and intentions, for example, '... I don't mean he was just being lazy, but he was deliberately aiming to sabotage the whole exercise ...'

There is in fact a very thin line drawn between behaviours and between labels, and the teacher has to draw upon his or her knowledge of the pupil to make those distinctions. This quote from a Head of Department illustrates this.

> 'As a "berk", that would be said in a light-hearted manner. If he were to tangle the rope on the trapeze in the gym which means that it flies up to the ceiling and you have to climb up the wall to untangle it, something like this, then I would say he was a "berk"... If he repeated the action you might realize he was doing it because he

enjoyed it the first time, causing the inconvenience. If he did it again then he wouldn't be a "berk"... well troublesome, he would obviously be trying to cause trouble.'

The behaviour is the same but the teacher interprets different intentions the second time. This is a good example of Lemert's secondary deviance, where the original motives have given way to those centring on the deviant behaviour (see Hargreaves, 1975). A teacher might find some disruptive behaviour more acceptable than other similar acts by different pupils, because of the way it is carried out, for example 'the class clown's' behaviour as in this instance.

'... There's certainly no animosity between us. I often end up laughing at his antics myself, ... even though he may disrupt the smooth running of a lesson, it's normally in a comical fashion which ends in chaos as a result ... He is known as the "class clown" and seems to enjoy the tag ...'

The 'troublemaker' may operate within three distinct patterns of behaviour according to the direction of the pupil's actions. Firstly, it may be directed at the teacher and directly affects the teacher–pupil relationship, for example one teacher tells us of 'a lad who has caused me a lot of trouble ... who is disturbing me and disrupting the lesson'. And again, another teacher talks of the insolent pupil, 'did not actually turn round and laugh in your face but that's what was going off inside him', whilst another teacher tells us about aggressive pupils, 'they are aggressive towards me'.

Secondly, it may be directed at other pupils and directly affects pupil-pupil relations. One teacher gives an example of a bully, '... to me he seems to be a bully, more of the lads will stand up to him.' Other teachers talk of ringleaders and those who follow, 'He's a ringleader of about five or six lads, when he's not doing games, the others buckle under...' '... because she was a good leader' 'He is usually led ...'

Thirdly, it may be directed at neither teachers nor pupils but at objects in the classroom or gymnasium or Sports hall, for example, teachers talk of pupils interfering with and damaging equipment and school property.

Although most teachers reported that 'the troublemaker' came from the lower streams, was a 'thickie' or in 'the remedial group', it should be noted that not all troublemakers in physical education were 'anti academic' or 'unintelligent'. Many of the troublemakers in this study were perceived as 'intelligent' or 'clever children'. However, in addition to intelligence, physical ability is seen as being very important in physical education, but, troublemakers do not come from only one group of physical ability pupils. In this study many of them were seen as 'no good at games', 'lacking in physical ability' or, as some teachers stated, were 'spassies'. It was suggested that many of these pupils become 'skivers' and cause particular problems for the PE teacher. However, other troublemakers are perceived to have ability, for example, 'As

I said, he's a good gymnast', and in another instance, 'and in fact is a member of the school swimming team', and again 'big lad, very good rugby player'. Some of these become 'show offs', and caused a different type of problem to the PE teacher, as in the case of 'the temperamental sportsman'. This latter type was particularly galling to some of the PE teachers because they felt these pupils were wasting their ability, and very often, would not perform for the school team. This type set a bad example to the 'triers' who see them reaching a higher standard with little effort, and whilst 'messing about'.

But Look What S/He's Done

There are a wide range of pupil behaviours and evidential cues to warrant the teachers using the label 'troublemakers', from, merely chattering and shouting out, which is a nuisance to the teacher, to the fooling about, which can be dangerous, or to the downright objectionable and malicious attack on the teacher or another pupil. The following are just a few of the examples given by different teachers:

'by pestering and drawing attention to themselves, they tend to be disruptive, and it does annoy me.'

'Well, the way they run into the gym, run in and sort of start fooling about . . . er get a basketball and slam it against something, instead of getting the stuff out . . .'

'You sometimes get a nucleus who fool around and waste time and then just do silly things . . . as far as I can see one is trying to compete with the other as to who can be the biggest fool.'

'She tells her to "F off", and she says she's bloody well not going to do this work.'

'. . . regard them as undisciplined children . . . they are insolent children about half of them . . . no control, they'll just go beserk.' (referring to backward remedial group)

'. . . you know, back chat, answering back, this sort of thing . . . they are aggressive towards me.'

'they are objectionable in their attitude towards work. They're disruptive in class . . .'

'. . . usurp his leadership — he turns round and thumps them.'
'They tend to fight . . . usually led.'

Perhaps the most important feature of 'the troublemakers behaviour is the frequency with which it occurs in spite of the teachers' attempts to stop it. This is the main factor which leads the teacher to believe it is intentional, and this leads to the 'elaboration' and 'stabilization' of the label. There are numerous quotes to illustrate the frequency: '. . . they are constantly seeking attention . . .' 'He's always disrupting the class . . .' 'Usually he does it by . . .' '. . . nine times out of ten, it would be him messing about.' This does not mean to say there are not any periods when the troublesome behaviour fades away or the pupil is not co-operative, but this is usually 'when he is doing something he wants', as in this case, '. . . but if he's playing the game he's great, you never have any problem at all'. However, quite typically, when the mood takes the 'troublemaker' or interest is lost he or she begins to cause trouble again, as two teachers explain, '. . . if you're not doing something he likes, he goes off and sulks', and '. . . it's when he loses interest, the trouble starts'.

Most of these troublemakers are seen by the PE teachers as 'troublemakers in general'. They felt that these pupils were also difficult in other lessons and that other teachers also saw them as 'troublemakers'. However, some of the 'troublemakers' were considered to be better behaved in PE and were regarded as only 'mildly troublesome' compared to their behaviour in other lessons. As one teacher remarked '. . . I would suggest that other teachers have more trouble with him than I do'. Very few of the 'troublemakers' were seen to be only a trouble in PE, except possibly 'the skiver'. These pupils did not bring PE kit or tried to evade taking part in PE, and became troublesome on occasions and were seen to be difficult to supervise when not fully taking part.

S/He Knows You Know

Many teachers felt that the pupils must be left in no doubt what they thought of them. As one teacher stated, 'You've got to let them know what they are', and another teacher indicated when this often happened, 'There was once a confrontation and I told him exactly what I thought of him. I said, "You're a ringleader, there's no two ways about it, you're leading these lads astray".' In less serious cases many teachers stated that they were not so open as this, but, as far as they were concerned, the pupil knew that he or she was under close scrutiny from the teacher.

The pupil may well be aware of his or her label or the teacher's close scrutiny, but how much importance and meaning the pupil attaches to the label or his or her reputation is sometimes difficult for the teachers to say. But, clearly, some teachers felt that the reputation and labels did have some importance for some pupils when they suggested that they revelled in their reputation of 'troublemaker' as it gave the pupils status amongst their peer group, as this teacher indicated, 'He gains his friends from this reputation and he wants to keep it.'

Another teacher suggested that the importance and meaning depended on the pupil's age and consistency of behaviour,

'I think they have a greater meaning for the child at an early age. . . . descriptions of transitory behaviour, used to express disapproval at that moment in time are not likely to have a permanence. If however, a child's attitude, behaviour or what you will is consistent; then our descriptions are likely to have a permanence because the situations are recurring ones.'

This seems to support Bird's (1980) proposition regarding the pupils' acceptance of behavioural labels. In this study, however, there is evidence of consistent 'troublemakers in general' where the behavioural label has stuck, and 'pupils living up to their reputations' is another example of this.

Don't Blame the School

Teachers perceived 'the troublemaker' as deliberately seeking attention and causing disruption. It seems typical of the milder cases, that, 'they are constantly trying to draw attention to themselves' or 'always seeking attention and disrupting the class', and typical of the more serious cases, that, 'they deliberately aim to sabotage the whole exercise, which gives pleasure', or 'they are trying to maintain a reputation'. However, behind these 'in order to' motives are a wider range of predisposing factors, the teachers' perceived genuine 'because' motives (Schutz, 1964). The attention seeking behaviours are only symptoms of more basic 'causes', which the teachers feel they can do little or nothing about. The home background, parents, and neighbourhood bears the brunt of this blame, as in these cases;

> 'From what I've been told, or from what I've found out, he has a lot of problems at home, it stems from home . . . I don't think he gets a lot of attention at home.'

> 'Split family I think . . .'

> '. . . given a fair degree of autonomy at home . . . and this led to him (the father) backing the lad up in practically anything he didn't want to do.'

> 'Then his mother arrived and you could understand his behaviour . . . His mother was very neurotic and that makes him a bit dizzier than he should be . . .'

> '. . . Well you know, it's a bit like history repeating itself, generally because you sort of see a small model of the father coming through . . . he was a similar bolshie, agin the government . . .'

Sometimes the family background as a cause was ruled out on the evidence of meeting the parents, and this allowed the teachers to make suppositions and judgments. '. . . yet I've met his parents at a parents' evening, and they seemed quite pleasant . . . there didn't seem any problems there.' In these cases the child's personality or immaturity, or outside school interests are blamed.

'... when I see them doing things which I feel are childish, then I think he is immature ... He hasn't reached the stage of maturity when he can see reason.'

'Well I know for a fact that he's not very intelligent, that is compared to the rest of the class. He is certainly an extrovert and likes to be the centre of attraction ... this might be the reason for his extraordinary behaviour.'

'... but by the third year he'd got a paper round and I think he has many outside interests ...'

This latter case is generalized to the 'anti school' group,

'... if they are poorly behaved in the school and they have trouble with other teachers, become anti school, and because they are anti school, no matter what it is, they are anti everything in the school, whether they may like it or not. Because of their attitude they decide they are not going to co-operate with anything in the school, and that includes PE, even if it is cutting their noses off to spite their face.'

The influence of the peer group is implicated explicitly in many other instances, '... his friends in his class encourage him to act the fool. He certainly seems to be easily led astray according to reports I've heard from colleagues and of course from my own experience with him.' The peer group then, in the teachers' view, is instrumental in maintaining the image or reputation of a 'troublemaker' but it is not only the peer group which is influential in this way. The origins of a label sometimes lie in broader community or familial contexts, as these cases suggest,

'He's got a reputation in the locality with most people, police included, and although he is not a violent lad, he has got this reputation and he wants to keep it.'

'I think he did it to maintain his reputation and the reputation of his family name ... He is mischievous because he has got to keep this thing up.'

Occasionally the teacher knows there is a medical reason for non-participation in physical education activities, which, in turn, results in frustration and difficult behaviour, for example,

'He has had heart trouble and has had an operation, and for one year he was out of PE completely, standing on the sidelines ... so to some extent I can see him as a lad with potential who was not able to realize this.... I think it was just pent-up frustration that he had to stand on the sidelines ...'

The medical reason may be seen by the teacher to be the direct cause of troublemaking in the case of the maladjusted or remedial children, as another teacher explained, 'There was the problem, that they were, in fact, brain damaged children.'

It was somewhat rare for the teacher to blame him or her self or the school for the troublesome behaviour of the pupils. However, one young teacher took some of the blame and saw the teacher-pupil relationship as a common problem for new teachers,

> 'I think I fell into the trap that many teachers do in their first year of talking to children, particularly the older ones as equals which doesn't work and makes it difficult for you to then impose discipline if you need to. He was taking advantage of the situation where we had been reasonable friendly.'

In another case, a teacher generalized the problem of pupil's behaviour and did not see it as a personal or age problem, when he attributed a cause to the way in which teachers dealt with pupils, suggesting teachers may lack understanding and flexibility. 'Well perhaps it's lack of understanding on our behalf. It could be us. It could be our problem perhaps we are not flexible enough. I'm not saying we are perfect; not by any means.'

For most teachers then, the origins of the troublesome behaviour were to be found in the pupils themselves or in a context beyond the school itself. Rarely was the problem associated with the staff, curriculum or school organization, which they might have been able to have done something about. The fact that most of the 'troublemakers' were seen as 'troublemakers in general' was evidence to the teachers that they themselves were not to blame. In this study they do not seem to have thought of analyzing the school curriculum and the part this may have to play in 'troublemaking'. Obviously, where the fault may be thought to lie in the curriculum as a whole then the PE teacher alone could do very little. However, the case of the 'skiver' may well emphasize the point that an examination of the PE curriculum would be very worthwhile. Certainly Casper could well have benefitted from such an action!

Give a Dog a Bad Name Then Beat Him/Her

The teachers suggested that one of the most obvious consequences for 'the troublemaker' is that he is 'constantly being watched' by the teacher. They report that it is likely that many actions, even innocent ones are seen as the first signs of stepping out of line and so the pupil is 'jumped on immediately' and ulterior motives are read into the pupil's behaviour. This may be a case of 'give a dog a bad name', but it is something which the teacher found necessary to do in order to control the situation. However, this sometimes had unfortunate consequences for the pupil because the behaviour itself was regarded or treated as deviant purely on the basis of how the pupil had been identified, as the teacher imputed motives based on typical expectations of that identity. Thus there were examples of a 'troublemaker' who kept quiet, who found the teacher treated him with suspicion as he thought, 'Now, what's he up to, being so quiet'. Teachers admitted that it was possible for a 'good pupil' to exploit the situation and 'get away with murder', whilst 'the troublemaker' took the blame.

The interview data clearly revealed that the way to treat 'the trouble-maker' was often a problem for the teacher. Teachers often tried to prevent discipline problems by reacting immediately to any misdemeanours, as in this case, '. . . particularly in the gym, so the first time anybody steps out of line, I am down on them like a ton of bricks, with the verbal retorts, make a show of them in front of the class, make them feel small.' Sometimes every form of treatment was tried, and, usually, not with much success. Here is an example from one frustrated teacher.

> 'The first few weeks I was trying to talk him round, but that was no good. He did not actually turn round and laugh in your face but that's what was going off inside him. The next time he misbehaved I gave him a good hiding and that was of no value either, so I went to the Head of the second year and explained the problem. He said, 'Well, hitting him will be of no good, no good at all, for the simple reason that from what they've found out he gets clobbered at home, you know, so he's expecting it, he's used to being clobbered, so it's doing no good at all' . . . so I thought we'll give him a few responsibilities and see if that'll bring him round. I was trying various things to get him on my side, instead of always battling and fighting against him.'

It is not only the pupil's response to the treatment, or whether it is judged to be effective or not, which influenced the teacher's treatment, but also the teacher's imputation of the causes of the pupil's conduct and the pupil's intentions. If the pupil was seen to be deliberately provocative he was dealt with more severely, or if the causes of the action was seen not to be the pupil's fault, then he or she received a different form of treatment.

There were also suggestions of what Stebbins has called the'avoidance of provocation' reaction to the pupil's behaviour, as in the case of the teacher who admitted that he 'turns a blind eye' because he does not 'want the aggro — it's uncomfortable' (Stebbins, 1970).

Troublemaking is a Career

According to the teachers, 'once a troublemaker, always a troublemaker' seems to be a motto applicable to many 'troublemakers'. As we have already seen, some gained their reputation and status through making trouble or causing a nuisance of themselves, and they did not want to lose it. They made a 'career' of it, and many become part of an 'anti school', delinquent group, (*cf.* Hargreaves, 1967). However, some teachers explained this behaviour in terms of pupils' immaturity and so it was something which they could grow out of. On the other hand, there were another group of pupils who were seen to grow into 'troublemaking', particularly in the middle years of secondary schooling which the teachers suggested could turn out to be 'an adolescent or an awkward phase' in some instances, but more permanent in others.

Evidently, it is not always easy for the teacher to re-type pupils once the 'stabilization' phase has been reached, because as we have already seen, the teacher sees the pupils' behaviour in the light of their identities or labels. The pupils must offer proof, over a period of time, to show that they have reformed. Many pupils who have attempted a transformation find that they are 'under scrutiny', and still get accused of 'causing trouble' so they revert to type, merely confirming the teacher's original categorization. Most of the teachers feel that the 'genuine' 'because motives' are the cause of the behaviour, and as these lie in the home, or are part of a permanent quality of the person, then the pupils have little chance of reforming. The exception is when the cause is put down to the influence of a special group of friends, then if the pupil could be removed from their influence, then there would be a change of behaviour, '... change ... for the better ... I've seen them change by virtue of the fact that when they came up to the upper school they find themselves in a different group ...' Very often, though, these type of pupils are seen as being 'easily led' and 'very weak' and may fall under the influence of other equally 'bad' friends.

It is because the causes are perceived to be located in factors which the teacher feels are beyond his or her control that the teacher often feels the treatment has temporary controlling effects only. 'I wouldn't have thought that I was in any way changing him' seems to be typical of many of the teachers' views.

Did I Really Label?

Perhaps one of the most interesting questions is, 'how is the label used?'. This question examines the function of the label. The most important function appears to be that it is a way of differentiating between pupils' behaviour on different criteria and dimensions. It is used as a basis for identification and action. But, it is not merely a blanket term which neglects individuality; for instance, we have seen 'the troublemaker' is a complex character, for he or she may be 'intelligent' or a 'thickie', 'devious' or 'a fool', 'malicious' or a 'clown', 'the big headed rugby captain' or 'a skiver'. The teacher interprets all the subtle nuances of meaning and behaviour in the interaction sequence. This is a process of perception, interpretation, and evaluation which allows for 'idiosyncratization'. It is also a form of assessment of pupils in the dynamic teaching situation based on all the ephemeral fleeting signs in interaction. In this case, it is a 'natural' and necessary phenomena, and teachers often categorize without explicitly or directly labelling the pupil. Nevertheless, this process is a basis for teacher action and has consequences for a pupil's developing identity.

When the label 'troublemaker', or similar construct is used directly in interaction, it is often used as a controlling device. Sometimes these labels are used in the 'heat of the moment', sometimes with sarcasm, maybe with wit, but they portray 'the emotion' that is felt at that time. The teachers want to get a message across to a particular pupil and all the other pupils, and to show them that they cannot get away with causing trouble. The act of labelling publicly announces the teacher's authority. The fact that the label is used publicly and to a desired effect means that it may well be used in, or as part of, a 'public degradation' ceremony (Garfinkel, 1967), even though the teacher does not like to think there will be a permanent stigma for the pupil. However, as many teachers admit, once the pupil has been placed in a category it is hard for them to revise the label, because any further pupil misdemeanours merely confirm the original label. Whilst this may not lead to the amplification of 'trouble' by the pupil as such, it does lead to the teachers' confirmation of the identity, and the teachers' perceived increase in pupil misbehaviour. Whilst Bird (1980) dismisses the general acceptance of behavioural labels by the pupils and therefore the possible amplification of deviance arising from this acceptance, the evidence from this study suggests that teachers themselves not only use the label but accept the consistency of the application in the school generally. Consequently they act in accordance with that general application. Moreover, they see the pupils accepting the label, as in the cases of those pupils who try to 'maintain a reputation' of 'troublemaker'. Therefore it may or may not result in amplification, but the teacher cannot know this at the time. As far as the teacher is concerned, he or she 'needs' to use the labels as a discipline or controlling measure, it is expedient to do so. The present situation is given priority and the longer term consequences of a label cannot always be considered. The teacher would like to feel his or her actions do not lead to an increase in troublesome behaviour, but cannot always be sure.

Labelling then, is a complex process which deserves understanding from the teacher's point of view. The use of the label 'troublemaker' has significance for the teacher in a discipline dimension, it is functionally related to the problems of managing large groups of children in organizations which demand and expect that the teacher can control. Making a name is the other side of the coin, where the pupil is managing the knowledge and belief about his or her identity. That process too needs to be explored in much greater depth.

Acknowledgements

I am grateful to all those teachers who have taken part in interviews and discussions on this topic.

References

BALL, S. (1981) *Beachside Comprehensive*, Cambridge University Press.

BECKER, H.S. (1963) *Outsiders: Studies in the Sociology of Deviance*, Free Press.

BIRD, C. (1980) 'Deviant labelling in school: the pupils' perspective' in WOODS, P. (Ed.) *Pupil Strategies*, Croom Helm, pp. 94–108.

CARROLL, R. (1976) 'PE teachers' own evaluations of their lessons'. *Journal of Psycho-Social Aspects of Human Movement* 2.1.

GARFINKEL, H. (1967) *Studies in Ethnomethodology*, Prentice-Hall.

HARGREAVES, D.H. (1967) *Social Relations in a Secondary School*, London, Routledge and Kegan Paul.

HARGREAVES, D.H., HESTER, S.K., MELLOR, F.J. (1975) *Deviance in Classrooms*, London, Routledge and Kegan Paul.

HARGREAVES, D.H. (1976) 'Reactions to labelling', in HAMMERSLEY, M. and WOODS, P. (Eds.) *The Process of Schooling*, London, Routledge and Kegan Paul.

HINES, B. (1968) *Kes (A Kestrel for a Knave)*, London, Michael Joseph.

KEDDIE, N. (1971) 'Classroom knowledge' in YOUNG, M.F.D. (Ed.) *Knowledge and Control*, Collier-Macmillan, pp. 133–61.

LACEY, C. (1970) *Hightown Grammar*, Manchester, Manchester University Press.

MEYENN, R.J. (1980) 'School girl's peer groups' in WOODS, P. (Ed.), *Pupil Strategies* London Croom Helm, pp. 108–43.

NASH, R. (1973) *Classrooms Observed*, London, Routledge Kegan Paul.

POLLARD, A. (1984) 'Goodies, jokers and gangs' in HAMMERSLEY, M. and WOODS, P. (Eds.) *Life in School* Open University Press, pp. 238–55.

RIST, R. (1970) 'Student social class and teachers expectations: the self-fulfilling prophecy in ghetto education', *Harvard Educational Review* 40, 30, pp. 411–51.

ROSENTHAL, R. and JACOBSON, L. (1968) *Pygmalion in the Classroom*, Holt, Rinehart and Winston.

SCHUTZ, A. (1964) *Collected Papers I*, Martinus Nijhoff.

SHARP, R. and GREEN, A.G. (1975) *Education and Social Control*, London, Routledge and Kegan Paul

STEBBINS, R. (1970) 'The meaning of disorderly conduct: teacher definitions of a classroom situation', *Sociology of Education*, 44, pp. 217–36.

WOODS, J.S. (1981) 'PE teachers labelling from the pupils perspective'. Unpublished dissertation, Manchester University.

7   The Nature of Dissent: A Study of School and Junior Club Soccer

Colin Embrey

In 1975 Orlick and Botterill observed that:

> fights and brawls at organized kids games are no longer uncommon. There are confirmed reports of officials being assaulted by youngsters and fans; teams are refusing to shake hands with opponents; attempts to hurt or injure opponents physically are becoming too prevalent; lack of respect for opponents or officials is commonplace; and acceptance of overt aggression seems to be spreading.[1]

This highly overdramatic comment related to the junior sporting context in the USA and for many it may seem rather far removed from the British junior sporting scene. However, in 1980, at a meeting of physical education teachers in South Courtney, many of those present expressed their deepest concern that in schoolboy and junior club soccer 'dissent' was on the increase. Most of the PE teachers at this meeting seemed to share a common understanding of the term 'dissent'. It seemed to imply a range of player behaviours, including arguing with officials (teachers, team managers, referees) regarding the control of the game and an overly aggressive and competitive attitude towards the opposition and the 'game' generally. There was little doubt in most teachers' minds that the source of this problem lay in the junior club football played by pupils outside of school and in the clubs to which they belonged.

In 1983, as a teacher and player involved in both school and club soccer I set out to investigate this 'problem'. I wanted to consider more exactly what was meant by dissent, to explore its origins in the school and junior club situations and to see if there was any substance to these teachers' fears. Little research has been undertaken in this area. Research in the sociology of education has concentrated largely on dissent (deviancy) in classrooms, largely ignoring the PE and sporting scene, while research into football hooliganism has for the most part focused on behaviour on the terraces of professional club soccer. Only Pickering's (1976) research was focused generally on dissent in soccer, inside and outside school, of all age groups, amateur and professional.

Pickering's method was to impose, at the outset of his research his own definition of dissent. This included deliberate fouls, verbal abuse to officials and opponents, time-wasting and disagreement with decisions. Then, while watching games and using an observational schedule, he attempted to register the amount of dissent in evidence in football at one level or another. In this way he felt able to conclude that there is a 'significant increase in dissent from the age of thirteen onwards, with the greatest amount of it being displayed in the 'open-age', men's soccer games.[2] In this research however it was largely assumed that all those involved with the game of football (players, officials, researcher, etc.) perceived and defined dissent in the same way. The research methods used were unable to determine if there were differences in the perceptions or definitions between the various age groups and within the different social settings in which the game took place.

By contrast, in my investigation of soccer in the school and club situation, I took the view that dissent may be differently defined and sanctioned according to the context in which it occurs and the term dissent was itself taken to be problematic. Because my concern was to explore the nature of dissent in school and junior club football and to find out how and why it occurred in each of these situations, rather than merely to record its incidence, I adopted an ethnographic approach to the research, an approach which places great emphasis on the participants' perspectives and how they define their own and others' behaviour. (see Embrey, 1985)

The study revolved around a group of nine fifteen-year-old boys and their experiences of soccer both inside Longbush School (a large co-educational comprehensive) and as members of an 'outside school' junior club. Each was a member of the Longbush Comprehensive school football team and each played for Waverley Wanderers, the village football team, in the South Courtney Minor League.[3] As a PE teacher at this school I was able to follow and observe these pupils in both the school and club situation. All of the boys lived either in Waverley or within three miles of the village which has a predominantly middle-class population. The group were observed in fourteen school matches and twenty-five minor league and cup matches between September 1983 and February 1985. Extensive field notes were made at the matches, and unstructured interviews were also carried out with the pupils, parents, teachers, club managers and spectators.[4] I also consulted documentary source material supplied by the South Courtney Minor League and the Oxfordshire School Football Association. These included organizational directives, player misconduct reports and records of fines and sanctions. Club information documents, press cuttings and membership and club rules also acted as useful sources of data, while school records provided insight into the study group's social and family environments.

The Contexts of Dissent: 'Conflict'

As the study progressed it became very clear that no single party or person could be blamed for the difficult behaviour of players shown on the field of play. Both club and school were responsible for fostering dissent among young players and this had much to do with the nature of the relationships between teachers and club managers. Essentially, this relationship was one of conflict, arising out of a mutual suspicion and jealousy, a deep disagreement over the aims and values of soccer and a fundamental lack of communication between school and club. There was a great deal of evidence to suggest that PE teachers in the schools were deeply 'jealous' of the influence of junior clubs exerted over their young players. Certainly all the boys interviewed in the study said that they would rather play for their junior club if a choice had to be made between club and school teams. This view was endorsed by parents and club managers, as these comments indicate:

> Trevor W. (father)　'He never talks about it or tells you when he's playing' (for the school)
> Mick T. (father)　'He doesn't seem to like playing at school . . . he says they're not so friendly' (meaning the other boys at the school).

The boys also reinforced this view: Ian McT. (player) 'School is only for one term, at club it's a season so you can really get a feeling going.'

School soccer did not inspire the boys to participate, they felt that the one term of soccer, rugby and cricket organized by the PE department did not demand a serious involvement. Many boys opted out of team membership, often feigning injuries for Saturday school matches yet being 'fit' and available to play club soccer on Sunday. Another source of conflict centred on the FA Rule 30 which states that: 'Whilst a boy is receiving full-time education in accordance with the Education Acts, priority must at all times be given to school or school organized activities.'[5]

Many club organizers, managers, and parents felt that this ruling was an unjust restriction on their access to good players. The players, too, saw the ruling as an invasion of their privacy and felt the weekends and evenings should be theirs to do whatever they wished, including playing a sport of their own choice, for a team of their own choosing. As one player noted: 'Well, there's that FA law isn't there? . . . says the school comes first. I don't think that's right 'cos it's our time.' And another player Vic. O'M: 'Yeah! . . . s'right, we want to go down Reading on Saturdays.' Geoff B: 'It should be the other way round . . . we should choose.'

However, the origins of the conflict between school and club went a lot deeper than this formal FA ruling. Many PE teachers believed that they had a greater commitment to children and to the wider game of soccer than did their counterparts in the junior clubs. They saw club managers as only interested so long as their own children were playing. One PE teacher, involved in organizing area soccer for ten years as well as his own school teams stated:

> 'There's an enormous difference between the standards and aspirations of the different parent managers involved. There's those people (managers and teachers) who do the job with youth football because

they love the game and they do it right across the board ... a classic case is M — C — who has been involved with the county schools team ... he's totally dedicated to the game. Then you get the opposite of that, the parent who has great aspirations for his own kid, he becomes very much involved ... if his youngster was to leave the team then he would offer no more support to the game.' (Derek N.)

Conversely, the club managers viewed the teachers very much as 'new boys' to the game. Many managers saw themselves as having taught and trained their teams from an early age, often nine years old and they saw the secondary school teacher as someone who had no such depth of knowledge of the game or the boys playing it. To the club manager the secondary school PE teacher is one who only takes teams because 'he is paid to do it'; someone who arrives on the scene late in the boys' soccer 'career' and attempts to start laying down rules and regulations concerning when the boys will and will not play. There was then, much evidence to suggest that teachers and club managers held conflicting views as to each other's level of commitment to soccer in general and the players in particular. Both teachers and club managers each saw themselves as more dedicated and committed to the game and the players.

Schools also viewed the clubs as being overly concerned with competition, with the business of playing for some extrinsic reward, league or cup medal, at the expense of 'enjoyment'. When interviewed, teachers were typically at pains to stress that clubs: 'Ape the behaviour and organization of professional clubs ... they are too serious.' Or that in club matches: R.B.: 'There is very little humour in the games.' (P.W.)

There was, however, very little evidence to confirm that the amount of competition, if defined in terms of playing for cups and medals, had anything to do with displays of dissent on or off the field of play. Indeed, in five of the potentially most highly competitive games, (two school and three club) where a great deal was at stake in terms of cups and medals, there were no observable displays of dissent, as defined and sanctioned by officials. Neither could it be said that the players enjoyed these competitive games any less than others.

The term enjoyment is of course quite problematic and the views of the teachers often contrasted markedly with those of the boys, who clearly enjoyed their junior club football and its competitive edge.

C.E.: 'What would you say is different about playing for the school and playing for your club?'

Geoff B: 'Well ... you're always playing for something.'

Larry P: 'The league ... there's four teams can win it.'

Geoff B: And there's the cups ... at school you only play a team once as well.'

Vic O'M: 'Yeah, if you miss a game (at school) it isn't replayed so you don't get to play them that year.'

One of the parents succinctly summarized the boys' view of enjoyment in competitive junior club games: 'The boys don't half enjoy a real hard game ... afterwards they tell you.' (M.W.)

Much of the conflict between club and school had then to do with the way that 'competition' had been translated by the clubs into heavy league and cup programmes. However, there was no evidence to suggest that the number of competitive games, or the level of competition for medals within a game, in any way encouraged dissent on or off the field of play. However, there was evidence that these conflicting views regarding the significance and nature of competition and enjoyment were detrimental to a positive relationship between school and club and that this in turn had implications for how pupils behaved in the school soccer and club situations.

A further source of conflict between school, players and officials of junior clubs lay with the school's attitude which, from the managers' viewpoint seemed unfairly over-protective. When the subject of access to school facilities arose club officials remarked that:

Stuart B. (Manager): 'Well ... we use the sports hall on Tuesdays for training ... we have to pay a lot though. It's stupid really 'cos all the boys go to that school anyway.'

Trevor W. (Manager): 'No ... we tried to get the school pitch, but they said we'd damage it too much. Anyway, we had to clear it with "the County" and pay a lot more for it than the one we use.'

Players responded in a similar derogatory fashion:

Jim A: 'We wanted to use our (school) sports hall but it's used all the time ... so they said ... we know it's not though.'

Pete T: 'Anyway they said we'd have to pay ... quite a lot ... or get in with the senior team.'

Vic O'M: 'If we play for the school we can use it ... but it's ... you can't use it when you want to. Most of us got jobs straight after school so we could play later, but then the school's closed up.'

These comments emphasize how limited was the communication between school teachers and club officials, and this had created an 'us and them' situation. Of the eighty-four teams playing in the South Courtney Minor League 1984/85, only six teams played on school pitches, all but one had to pay for their usage. Although some clubs involved over two hundred boys from the local school they continued to be charged (very highly in the perspectives of officials) for the use of facilities.

There was then, a deep rift between school and club which had developed over a number of years (most respondents indicate ten to fifteen years). This was the setting of soccer that young players experienced. School and club had together constructed a social setting for junior soccer in which conflict between teachers and managers was both prevalent and inherent. It was a setting fraught with partial knowledge, half-truths, petty jealousies and mutual exclusiveness. Not surprisingly, players often experienced split loyalties and dual standards both on and off the field of play. Far from helping each other to provide the young soccer player with an homogenous experience of soccer, the school and club seemed intent on competing with each other to impress their own standards and values to the exclusion of others. Indeed the analysis that follows suggests that both the school and the club, because they have specific, and at present insurmountable problems, cannot alone be seen as ideal situations through which young players can be introduced to and encouraged to participate in the game of soccer.

The Origins of Dissent: 'Control'

Players, teachers, managers and spectators involved in this study all talked of dissent in youth soccer as a form of deviance. The belief was expressed that each situation, school and club, had its own interpretation of rules and standards and that this interpretation differed quite markedly between the two. Any attempt (*cf.* Pickering, 1976) to place some all-embracing definition of dissent on both situations thus seemed impossible. Dissent, or deviance, as we see below and as Haralambos (1980) reminds us, is relative. It varies from place to place and from time to time. In any given society and sub-grouping within that society, an act which is considered deviant today may be defined as normal in the future.[6] Dissent, as it was referred to in this study, had all these qualities. The official laws of the game, for example, were interpreted in very different ways by the school and club, and such interpretations had much to do with the relationships within the social setting of the game and the different authority structures inherent in the school and club situation.

In recent years debate in the sociology of education has made much of the school as a middle class institution and as a purveyor of middle class cultural values often to unwilling, working class children. Within school PE teachers have often been characterized as bastions of this system, middle class and conservative in outlook if not in background. By contrast, football has been described as 'the people's game', a context for the 'macho' expressions of the male working class.[7] Clark (1978) for example states that the crowd always were an integral feature of soccer, that they traditionally demanded to be accepted as participants in the primarily working class organizational structure of soccer.[8] Violence, or deviancy, in this perspective is often located in the culture of working class communities. However, in this study there is no clear overlap between the school and the club and middle or working class values. Waverley is essentially a middle class village and many of the boys/players were from middle class backgrounds. The major differences between school and club have to be characterized in terms of their authority structures. Longbush was essentially a middle class school, populated largely by middle class teachers and pupils. It was a school in which the relationships between teacher and pupils were clearly and hierarchically defined.[9] Little, if any, room seemed to be given for negotiation over the boundaries of acceptable pupil behaviour. By contrast, the club social structure was far less rigid. As we see, the rule system had to develop within the 'group' of players and managers as well as spectators. The establishment of order and control was the outcome of a complex negotiation process rather than the imposition of any single standpoint.

Spectators and 'Trouble'

Throughout the period of observation, it became increasingly apparent that spectators could have important influence on the behaviour of players. Indeed, spectators often seemed to be making a direct contribution to deviancy (dissent) on the field and this could occur through two main channels of communication. Firstly, the spectators' influence could be communicated directly to the player (see figure 3) or alternatively, the process could be transmitted through one or other of the game officials (referee or linesman) present (figure 4).

Figure 3   Spectator Initiated Dissent

Figure 4   Spectator/Official Initiated Dissent

The first type involved the spectator in a direct verbal or physical interchange with the player. This was the least subtle and also the fastest way of provoking a player into deviant behaviour. The study provides many instances of this type of spectator initiated dissent.

In one game for example, Waverley were playing Polbatch Wood. There had been no observable displays of dissent by players of either side. Waverley were leading 4–1. Larry Peters, the Waverley outside left finished an 'offside' run by shooting the ball into the opponent's net, at which point a Polbatch supporter shouted at him, 'You'd be made to fetch that ball yourself if I was refereeing.' Larry noted the remark by telling two of his team mates and waving his thumb in the supporter's direction. A little later the same supporter, now joined vociferously by two friends, shouted, 'He's offside! Anyone can see that, he's offside, the linesman flagged!' These remarks, combined with the earlier one, had an obvious effect on Larry who shouted back 'get knotted.' In the interviews conducted with the players after the match Larry had clearly noted the remarks:

C.E.: 'Did you enjoy the game the Sunday?'
Larry: 'Always enjoy getting a "hat trick"... those old "mateys" had it in for me though.'
C.E.: 'How do you mean?'
Larry: 'Sayin' I was a fouler an' that. Didn't do anything. They don't half go on at yer.'

In Larry's 'view' he had harmlessly finished off a good, but offside run, by kicking the ball into the net. He thus had interpreted the supporters' actions as being 'against him', they had made him out to be a deviant, a 'cheat' in some way. The effect on the field of play was to push the player 'directly' into dissent. Larry not only reacted verbally with spectators, but later in the game he was cautioned by the referee for swearing at the Polbatch linesman.

The second route to dissent tended to begin with an interchange between spectators and officials but almost inevitably led to dissent by a player. An incident from the Waverley v Catersfield United game serves as a good example. Waverley trailed two goals to nil at half time and up to that point the game had been an even, keenly yet fairly contested game. In the second half the 'trouble' started. An appeal for offside by the Waverley linesman was overruled by the referee (who later stated in interview that he believed the ball to be running safely to the Waverley goalkeeper). Minutes later the referee judged another 'flag' for offside by the same linesman to be incorrect. After this second 'no offside' decision both the linesman and some Waverley supporters began to make verbal comments to the referee. 'Are you trying to give 'em the game?' 'You must be blind if you didn't see that one' and 'We're never going to win this one with him reffing' were recorded as spectator-referee comment. They were issued very loudly, so that players and the official could hear, and in an aggressive rather than humourous fashion.

Directly following these remarks, the Catersfield right back brought down the Waverley 'winger' in what looked (to the researcher) to be more of a clumsy than intentional foul. The 'foul' was given but the spectators kept on at the referee about 'losing control' and 'ought to have booked that one.' The reaction to this situation by players of both sides was plainly noticeable. In the fifteen minutes from the first 'anti-referee' comment there were four free kicks for fouls, three caustic remarks made by players about decisions by the referee, two incidents of aggressive verbal exchange between opposing players and a penalty for the goalkeeper attempting to strike an opponent.

These forms of dissent were undoubtedly more prevalent in the junior club situation. Because these games were played at week-ends, rather than in mid-week (when the school games were played) they received by far the greater number of supporters. At fifteen of the club games observed over forty supporters were present and at eight of the club games over sixty were present.

Club managers were more than aware of the spectator 'problem'. Indeed, when questioned directly about dissent at matches many offered the view that supporters, rather than players, were by far the greater problem and the main culprits!

> Trevor W. (Manager) 'Gawd some of them (parents). . . . I just wish they wouldn't bother ... they're more trouble than they are worth.'
>
> C.E. 'Have you had any trouble of any kind in matches?'
>
> Stuart B (Manager) 'Not much, no ... not with the boys ... we've only had one player sent off in eight years and that was for a foul. The spectators though! ... we had a 'bust up' at Tipford. Dave, you know, 'Jock' always mouthing. Well, him and some of our supporters had a go a couple of weeks back. Not all his fault though, we've got some trouble causers.'

However, the problems junior clubs face with this form of player dissent cannot only be explained with reference to the presence of larger numbers of spectators. It also had to do with the clubs' restricted capacity to police matches and to exercise control over their crowds.

Unlike the school situation, where teachers, having 'ownership' of the pitch and the broader school context, were able to exercise considerable control over the crowd, in the club situation with games being played largely on public spaces, the behaviour of spectators could at best only be negotiated. Rarely was it in the power of the managers or any other club member to contain or curtail the actions of their own or others' supporters. Teachers and managers were clearly aware of their respective abilities and power to effect control over their 'spaces' and the people within them. As one teacher remarked, for example, when reflecting on his actions towards a group of parents who were giving verbal abuse to players during a game: 'Well, they were Lord Harry's supporters, not ours — but I just went over and told them to keep quiet or leave the school grounds.' (Roland B.) And on another occasion a different teacher remarked: 'I blew the whistle, stopped the game, walked over and said 'I've had enough of this, leave' ... and they did ... after some gesticulations and comments.' (Chris F.)

The club managers did not work under this umbrella of ownership and control. They had to negotiate order with spectators. Consider, for example, the following typical incident recounted from field notes. One spectator, identified as 'Glasses' had been positioned on the far side of the pitch in a relatively secluded spot. I had noted some earlier loud comments about Waverley 'fouls' on his son's team (Castle). The notes continue: — 'moves over to Castle supporters and begins to make audible comments to both the referee and other supporters. A woman agrees with him and herself makes a first audible comment: 'That was "dirty", come on ref.' (Five minutes later) 'Glasses' starts to make more and more comments. He shouts that the referee is 'allowing the Waverley lads to get away with it' (foul play). The Castle linesman flags for offside, the referee acknowledges, but allows play to continue. 'Glasses' remarks: 'You won't get anywhere with this ref.' The linesman (agitated) agrees with 'Glasses'. 'Glasses' and the linesman make audible comments to the referee: 'That was offside' (linesman) 'You can only see one side' ('Glasses'). The referee comes near to the Castle manager and says 'Tell your supporters to shut up'. The Castle manager slowly moves up the touchline to 'Glasses' and says 'Come on lads, don't give the ref any stick'. Holds 'Glasses' arm and reasons 'Yes, I know, but it only makes matters worse.' The Castle manager then changes his approach and talks about 'Glasses' dog, which he apparently brings to all games, but keeps emphasizing that 'it's wrong to get at the ref.'

While managers and officials used a variety of strategies to 'cool supporters down' during games, they also resorted to placing written requests that players and supporters avoid confrontation with known trouble causing opponents. The Waverley manager, for example, took advantage of the weekly team sheet-cum-newsletter, which he knew the parents would also read, to ask that supporters refrain from getting involved with the notorious 'Blue Rinse Brigade', a group of vociferous women supporters who followed Castle FC.

It could be inferred from all this that because of the school's greater power to control spectator dissent, school football would feature far less dissent than in the junior club situation. However, the situation is not quite so straightforward. Some forms of dissent, often more subtle than in the club situation such as the 'goading' of officials, for example, by moving the ball deliberately at free kicks, trying to look 'hard' at an official so that he speaks to you about it or backs down, moving corner flags out of the way at corner kicks and appealing for a decision, throw in, corner, penalty etc., when it was obviously not theirs, were much more prevalent and apparent in school games than club games. Dissent in school soccer could not be traced to the influence of spectators. It has to be located in the nature of the relationship between schools, teachers and players and the compulsory and ritualistic nature of school soccer.

School Football and Dissent: 'Compulsion'

The Waverley players from Longbush Comprehensive and many of their opponents from a number of other schools in the area, all preferred to play for their club rather than their school. This was so even when school football offered a high standard of prestige and competition, such as in 'area' team representation. Neither players nor their parents viewed representing schools football as of any significance, as this conversation (with a parent of a boy whom I knew to be a member of his area schools team) reveals:

> C.E.: 'I heard you say . . . last Sunday at the Tileham game . . . Jake had been ill . . . he played though?'
> G.C.: 'Yeah, . . . I told him to stay off school . . . not that he needed

any telling (laughs) . . . . I told him to stay off so's he'd be fit for the Tileham game.' (Jake had been selected for the area team in an important 'English Schools' Cup' game the day before the Tileham game, on the Saturday morning).

C.E.: 'Jake was off school all week?'

G.C.: 'Yeah ... did his ankle the week before against Castle.

C.E.: 'He didn't play in the area game then?'

G.C.: 'Nah ... no point in making the ankle worse. Proved right too . . . . he scored three against Tileham!'

On another occasion a manager recounted that he once had three of his players in the Newbury area schools' team, but that the boys had told him they 'didn't turn up so's the bloke would drop them.' Many more examples of boys 'voting with their feet' and opting out of school organized soccer could be presented.

The reasons for this apparent distaste for school football are complex. Firstly, it had much to do with the boys' opposition to the ritualistic nature of school based sport. It has been argued that there are two distinguishable forms of ritual in school, consensual rituals and differentiating rituals (Bernstein, Elvin and Peters, 1966). Hargreaves (1972) has suggested that school sport combines both these forms of ritual. School teams may function to both bind together members of the school, inculcating 'shared' values and a feeling of unity, while also encouraging attachment to specific group identities and legitimating the authority of schools and teachers.[10] At Longbush school, team organization was steeped in ritual. The team members were generally expected to meet at school and to travel together to the game. Uniform was compulsory since it was a 'school' activity. The teacher rigorously policed the players' activity and defined acceptable 'behaviour' (there would be no smoking and no ebullient behaviour). After the game had been played the results would be mentioned in assembly if the players' conduct and the score warranted it. All this emphasized that the game and the school team was an inseparable part of the school curriculum; they belonged to the school and were but one part of all else it had to offer. The boys clearly disliked these ritualistic elements of school team membership:

C.E.: 'You say you like playing for the club more, but what is it ... what is it you like about playing for a club rather than school?'

Ian McT: 'Well, you don't have to go to a match or anything in school uniform.'

Vic O'M: 'Sundays ... that's your free time, nothing to do ... nothing else better or anything, but weekdays you've had enough of school, just want to get home and relax, watch "telly" and that.'

As Vic's comment indicates, the boys felt that the club matches had a recreational quality because they were played on Sundays. Club soccer was synonymous with leisure time, it was up to them whether they chose to take part in it; whereas school soccer, organized and policed by teachers, was an intrusion into valuable, private, free time (evenings and Saturdays). School football was an occasion for just a little bit more of the same type of control that teachers imposed on them at other times. It was seen simply as a compulsory extension to the rest of school life. The boys felt that they were 'being watched' in school matches just as they sometimes were in school lessons. They disliked this aspect of school football as much as the element of compulsion.[11]

School soccer at Longbush was thus 'a game' over which pupils had little control. As pupils (and players) they took little part in the selection of the team, in the organization of the fixtures, administration, or the day to day running of the team. The school simply presented the game to them defined in the school's terms, with little room for negotiation. It was a context of organizational and formal powerlessness. By contrast the club situation represented to the players the opportunity for routine but often subtle forms of negotiation with the manager over selection, tactical considerations, and acceptable modes of behaviour (of both player and manager) off and on the field of play. As players, they could even influence who was to be an acceptable team member. If players did not agree with another's selection then the manager was informed either directly or via involved strategies aimed at isolating the unwanted player. This often carried over to tactics on the field where the players themselves often reorganized positions and systems of play. Team managers were very aware of their precarious position in the hierarchy of team organization, and their dependence upon a relationship and status negotiated with the players on and off the field of play. As one manager explained: 'I look on them (the boys) as friends and I think they look on me the same. You can't lay down the law with them, treat them like kids ... play the 'high and mighty' cos they won't have it ... they'll pack in.' (Stuart B.)

The authority of managers was thus curtailed by the ultimate sanction that the players might leave the club if he 'went too far'. The players in turn were restrained by their desire to stay with the club. Both parties had to negotiate their relative positions of security.

The relationship with the school and the sense of powerlessness which pupils felt, in turn had implications for how as players they behaved in the game situation. In much recent literature (Werthman, 1963; Nash, 1974; Gannaway, 1976), it has been suggested that pupils categorize teachers as 'good' if they are (a) able to keep order, (b) able to teach them something, (c) fair and impartial and (d) if they possess a good sense of humour. Following this it could be assumed that some teacher-referees would be better accepted than others. However, this was rarely the case. Pupils in the study perceived the teachers as a homogeneous social group, very much constrained by their designated role irrespective of their qualities as referees. In the following discussion, for example, the pupils were considering an incident where a player was not sent off in a club game after striking an opponent in full view of a parent referee:

> C.E.: 'I remember you telling me 'Sheersy' had punched an opponent and the 'ref' saw it but didn't send him off ... do you think he'd have been sent off in a school game?'
> Geoff B: 'Yeah ... I think so.'
> Ian McT: 'Wouldn't have played again.'
> C.E.: 'Why do you think he'd get sent off?'
> Vic O'M: 'Well, it's like school ... teachers have got to prove, show more discipline ... because they see them five days a week where Tom (manager) ... you know, don't. I think it's an out of school thing so they're (club managers/referees) not so strict.'

On another occasion a group of Waverley players commented on the Longbush PE department's policy of not taking boys on trips organized by the department if they had misbehaved in matches and drew attention to the case of a boy who had been dropped from a skiing trip because he had been in trouble in school and sent off in a soccer match.

> Jim A: 'There was M ... a couple of years back, he got stopped going skiing and things 'cos he got sent off.'
> C.E.: 'Just for being sent off?'
> Jim A: 'Yeah'
> G.H.: 'Well, he was in other trouble, with the Head once.'
> C.E.: 'Do you think it was right to stop him going?'
> Jim A: 'I think so ... yes!'
> C.E.: 'Mmm?'
> Jim A: 'Well he'd ... you'd have been responsible for him and that when he was away. Got to know you can trust him.'

In the boys' perspective teachers have no choice but to impose an excessive discipline, both on and off the field of play, because of their responsibilities as teachers within a school system which expected them to achieve control. By contrast, the club managers, who also often refereed the games in the junior league, were seen not to be subject to these external pressures. Their authority over them as we have seen had to be negotiated; these two managers emphasize the point;

> Trevor W.: 'We ain't got no rules as such, we all muck in together. When we go on tour I buy them a drink, we have a laugh, joke about, play cards, go to watch a match. It's a sort of mutual respect thing ... I don't order them about and they don't take the "mickey" out of me so to speak.'
> Don C.: 'These lads, outside school, away from the club ... they're

a bit naughty round town you know. There's some real characters among them. You got to treat 'em as adults, they respond to that and work with you. They come down here training Tuesday, most of them, without fail. They always let you know if they can't play in good time. Always somebody willing to help with the nets and so on ... good lads.'

Player-manager negotiation was thus the very essence of relationships within junior soccer clubs. Unless both participants could co-exist within this relationship then there was a break-down and either the player or the manager parted company. This negotiation extended from the selection and organization of the team and into the game situation. For example, during a game negotiation between two players and their manager after their team had conceded a fifth goal:–

Centre Half: (Calling to the sideline) 'We've got to do something about the fullback Jim, he's getting "skinned" every time.'
Jim (manager):   'Don't blame him Mick, it's not only him.'
Centre Back: 'Oh come on Jim you can see it is, change him over with Paul.'
Jim: 'You OK to change with Paul?'
Full Back: 'Yeah, I don't mind.'
Jim: 'OK Change then.'

This form of negotiation was accepted by both parties, players and manager, as a valid way to put things right.

When observing club games it was thus often easy to make the incorrect assumption that players were engaging in a form of dissenting behaviour as they entered into verbal disagreements about the game situation with club officials. In the setting of the club game this type of interchange was accepted by the participants as part and parcel of the junior soccer scene. However, similar behaviour almost invariably tended to be treated quite differently and harshly in school matches. Longbush were playing Deangate when one of the latter's players, a midfielder and one of their stronger team members, shouted at his full back for not marking the 'winger' closely enough. He was immediately reprimanded by his teacher: Teacher: 'Oates, get on with the game.' Oates: 'Well, look, if he can't do it why not put me or Jake there?' Teacher: 'I said get on with the game and don't whine.' Within five minutes of this interchange the midfield player was substituted. After the game, the teacher commenting on this incident remarked that the boy was a 'hot-head' and that he 'only played him because he was a bit short that day through illness.'

Dissent, then, was dependent upon the social setting and the participants' interpretation of the norms and rules of behaviour prevailing within it. Achieving deviant status on the field of play in school soccer also seemed inextricably wound up with a teacher referee's knowledge of the player, as a pupil in the broader school context. The teacher above, for example, clearly had prior knowledge of Oates as a pupil, which influenced his interpretation of his behaviour in the game situation. Oates was labelled a 'hot-head' in school and so as a 'hot-head' in soccer. It is perhaps for this reason that players were more likely to be defined as 'deviant' in school soccer than in the club situation. Labelling operates by teachers ascribing certain characteristics to pupils (Hargreaves, Hester and Mellor, 1975; Hargreaves, 1976; Bird; 1980). Pupils are discussed by teachers and the label becomes set or stigmatized. Teachers define certain acts as deviant and the perpetrators of those acts as deviants.

There were many instances, during the study, of pupil-players being negatively labelled by teachers. Some, as in the example above, led the teacher officials to define acts on the field of play which in the club's situation would seem pretty normal, as deviant. The teacher above regarded the player's actions as a further expression of the pupil's deviant identity, it was typical of that type of 'hot-head'. There were also general labels which influenced the teacher referee's decisions and which led teachers to enforce more vigorously the laws of the game than did officials in the club scene. Very frequently pupils were defined as 'typical soccer types', this characterization seemed to have evolved out of the PE teacher's conception of the image of soccer players portrayed by the media. Many made remarks condemning the image of players as cynical, verbose on the field, humourless and too concerned with extrinsic rewards, and blamed the media for the 'soccer type' qualities which they ascribed to some of the boys.

> Roland B: 'You can tell if a boy plays soccer, even if he's playing rugby!'
> C.E.: 'How to you mean?'
> Roland B: 'Questioning decisions, not accepting decisions ... that sort ... appealing for the ball when it's not his.'
> Gordon R: 'Soccer makes kids more verbal, you see them everywhere ... they can't keep quiet ... questioning decisions.'
> Derek N: 'They have this superior attitude, more often than not they come from a football background.'

It was not possible to investigate to any depth how deeply these labels were felt and taken on by the players, though the following remarks suggest that they had their impact:

> Player: 'Mr. B. (Roland above) ... gave that free kick (my school had scored off it) ... just for me shouting "goal kick". The ball was over the line, your 'keeper said so as well. He's always doing that ... it's stupid.'

It was also apparent that teachers connected dissent on the field by these 'soccer types' and their behaviour around school generally:

Chris F.: 'You're talking about an individual type really, the 'Prima Donna' the one who's likely to have other adolescent problems as well.'

Don C.: 'They're usually of a rebellious mould ... you see them around school ... don't wear uniform ... you have to ask yourself sometimes are these the type of people who really ought to be working on a school football pitch?'

The boys themselves made reference to this problem of being labelled a number of times:

Larry P.: 'Old Simmonds, he's got it in for me anyway (discussing a caution a staff member had given him during a school match). Doesn't like me, always calls me the 'Wally' ... just 'cos I play him up in Chemistry ... it's boring though.' (meaning the Chemistry lesson.)

Labels ascribed to pupils elsewhere in their schooling thus clearly affected the way in which teachers, as officials, defined behaviour as 'deviant' on the field of play and the media or the 'club' provide an available explanation. From the pupils/players perspective, the punishment afforded to such behaviour by teachers was thus very often considered harsh and unfair.

The Interpretation of Dissent: Authority

Teachers in the study placed 'arguing with officials' and 'questioning officials' decisions' as the most prevalent forms of dissent in their teams. This was in contrast to the clubs where dissent, as it was alluded to by club managers, had more to do with the behaviour and talk of spectators rather than of the players themselves.

Teachers viewed their position as referees in school matches as one of absolute authority. They alone were in control of the game. By contrast, the club referee (whether manager or other parent etc.) always had his power tempered by other adult linesmen, one from each club, whereas the school referee generally had only school children to help. These were expected only to indicate when the ball was in or out of play and whose 'ball' it was. As one teacher respondent put it: 'After all ... you can't expect a kid to be responsible for offsides, fouls, etc.'

Teacher officials were at pains to stress the letter of the law and the enforcement of ESFA rules and guidelines. For example, rule five of the ESFA Code of Conduct for players states that players should not appeal for throw-ins, off-sides, free kicks, etc.[11] The clubs, however, stressed a 'working rules' approach and saw no problem with such issues. Indeed the following managers argued that:

Trevor W.: 'It's OK claiming a throw-in and so on if it's a fifty-fifty. Well, that's normal isn't it?'

Stuart B.: 'Well, they got to do that or they'd never get the ball given to them.'

Some teachers, in an attempt to impose their authority, also introduced 'new rules' such as the 'ten yard rule' from rugby, or being much stricter on one team than the other to 'even the game up'. These strategies, not surprisingly, were found entirely in school games and never in club matches where it was generally accepted that if one's team were not strong enough then (as one manager commented) 'you expect to get hammered'. Teachers often employed such tactics for educational reasons, but whatever the motivation, they proved highly problematic for many young players and often resulted in antagonism, conflict and dissent on the field of play. As one pupil remarked when questioned after a game about the 'ten yard rule': 'Yeah, he always does something like that ... (meaning the teacher referee) ... it's daft'. (Player)

The authority structure of school games made teachers appear to the players as both less competent and more inflexible in their thinking and actions than officials in the club situation.

C.E.: 'Do you think there is any difference between club referees and school referees?'

Jim A.: 'Yeah ... people ... like Mark's dad (parent who referees regularly) and Tom (manager) they're doing it every week so they're used to it, don't make mistakes ... so many mistakes.'

Vic O'M: 'Mr. Simmonds and Mr. Peters they wouldn't, they'd say "I've given in now" and carry on.'

The way that order and authority was established on the field in both school and club games thus presented the young players with a differentiated, complex and often quite contradictory soccer experience. The upshot of this was often confusion in the players' minds and dissent, contingent upon the differentiated rule systems and sanctions imposed by officials within school and club.

Conclusion

There is not, then, one identifiable, homogeneous game that we can recognize and label 'youth soccer' or any single 'cause' of dissent. For many reasons, which have to do with the nature of control, authority and relationships, soccer within school and the junior club is often a quite different game. Clearly, it is only possible to understand the game in terms of the context within which it is played and the participants' interpretation of that game. It follows that dissent also needs to be understood in terms of the social and cultural context in which it occurs. Studies such as Pickerings', which ignores context and the meanings attached to it, and which attempts to impose an all-embracing definition of dissent for all game situations, will inevitably be limited and provide only partial insights into the origins and nature of a problem which is often uppermost in the minds of teachers and club officials.

There are various forms of dissent in youth soccer, both in school and the club situation, and this study has only just begun to explore them. Yet the data do suggest that competition has little, if anything to do with the genesis of dissent. It is not inherent in the competitive game of football nor, I would suggest, in any other such game. But neither school nor club can, on their own, reduce or remove dissent from youth soccer. The young player's experience of soccer is far from homogeneous, it differs inside and outside of the school. Community based soccer may offer one 'solution' as far as it may help utilize the strengths of both the schools and the clubs and break down the barriers between them. But there are substantial problems with this solution. Schools would have to adopt a completely different role and rule system. It would of necessity be required to surrender much of what it has traditionally held on to as its right; compulsion, control of facilities and its authority structures. Teacher, managers, players, parents, spectators and officials would need to communicate, to meet regularly to negotiate the very nature of the game and how and why it is to be played. The major aim might be to present a consensual experience to the young player, one which has educational merit as well as recreational value. Immediately this raises questions of economics and politics. It may be naive in the current financial climate, to expect that support in the form of money would be made available from central government to fund such schemes. Such a solution would also mean attempting to change deeply entrenched attitudes. All this would inevitably take time, a willingness to co-operate, and to at least entertain the possibility that the different behaviours shown by players and pupils lie less with the qualities of the game itself than with the social settings in which it is inextricably located.

Notes

1. ORLICH, T. and BOTTERILL, C. (1975, p. 5).
2. PICKERING, K. (1976).
3. All are pseudonyms.
4. This approach to interviews was adopted for the reasons suggested by BURGESS, (1982) that if one attempts to structure interviews too rigidly one runs the risk that talk, conversation and elements of everyday life go un-recorded and with them valuable research data is overlooked or ignored. It should also be noted that the role of teacher/researcher is highly problematic and the influence of teacher 'status' has to be acknowledged when consideration is given to the players' and the teachers' comments.
5. English Schools Football Association Handbook (1984–5, p. 102).
6. HARALAMBOS, M. (1980, p. 407).
7. See for example the work of WHITEHEAD, N. and HENDRY, L. (1976) and INGHAM, R. (1978).
8. CLARKE, J. in INGHAM, *op cit* p. 55
9. At Longbush pupils were left in no doubt as to their position as subordinate to the staff in the formal social structure. They were 'role bound' in PE classrooms and the broader school context.

10 HARGREAVES, D. (1972, p. 197)
11 Elsewhere CORRIGAN (1979) found a similar distaste for compulsion among
    secondary school pupils. In his study pupils felt that school would be 'OK so long
    as you didn't have to go'. Corrigan also observed that 'the simple concomitant of
    this experience of compulsion (is) the fact that they (have) a feeling of formal
    powerlessness' (p. 28).
12 See ESFA Handbook *op cit.*

Bibliography

BERNSTEIN, B., ELVIN H.L. and PETERS R.S. (1966) 'Ritual in education' in COSIN, B. *et
    al* (1971) *School and Society* London, Routledge and Kegan Paul.
BIRD, C. (1980) 'Deviant labelling in schools: The pupils' perspective' in WOODS, P.
    (Ed.) *Pupil Strategies*, London, Croom Helm, pp. 94–108.
BURGESS, R.G. (Ed.) (1982) *Field Research: A Sourcebook and Field Manual* Allen and
    Unwin.
CORRIGAN, P. (1979) *Schooling and the Smash Street Kids*, Macmillan.
EMBREY, C. (1985) 'The nature and incidence of dissent in youth soccer: A comparative
    study of a team in school and junior club soccer'. MA (Ed.) dissertation,
    University of Southampton.
ESFA, (1984–85) *Handbook*, available from A. Rice (Sec.) 4a Eastgate Street, Stafford
    ST16 2NQ
GRANNAWAY, H. (1976) 'Making sense of school', in STUBBS and DELAMONT *Explora-
    tions in Classroom Observation*, New York, Wiley.
HARALAMBOS, M. (1980) *Sociology: Themes and Perspectives*, University Tutorial Press.
HARGREAVES, D. (1972) *Interpersonal Relations and Education*, London, Routledge and
    Kegan Paul
HARGREAVES, D. (1976) 'Reactions to labelling' in HAMMERSLEY, M. and WOODS, P.
    The Process of Schooling, London, Routledge and Kegan Paul, pp. 201–8.
HARGREAVES, D., HESTOR, and MELLOR, (1975) *Deviancy in Classrooms* Routledge and
    Kegan Paul.
INGHAM, R. (Ed.) (1978) *Soccer Hooliganism: the Wider Context*, Inter-Action Print.
NASH, P. (1974) *Classrooms Observed*, London, Routledge and Kegan Paul.
ORLICK, T. and BOTTERILL, C. (1975) *Every Kid can Win*, Chicago, Nelson-Hall.
PICKERING, K. (1976) 'Dissent in soccer', unpublished thesis, Madeley College of
    Education.
REID, I. (1978) *Sociological Perspectives on School and Education* Open Books.
WERTHMAN C. (1963) 'Delinquents in school', *Berkeley Journal of Sociology*, 8, 1 pp.
    39–60.
WHITEHEAD N. and HENDRY, L. (1976) *Teaching Physical Education in England*, Lepus
    Books.

PART II
Innovation and Alternatives

8   *Research-Based Teaching in Games*

Len Almond

In this chapter I will attempt to integrate two ideas: the idea of 'teaching for understanding' as an educational innovation in games teaching and a concern to involve teachers in reflection about their practice of teaching. I shall provide a background to these ideas and then illustrate how a research project involved teachers in the monitoring of their practice through the teaching of a changing focus in games. Finally, I shall explore some of the implications of this project for teachers, teacher educators, and those who support teachers in their endeavour to translate complex ideas into reality and make learning come alive for young people.

Background to the Project

Games Teaching

In the last decade a number of lecturers, advisors and teachers in Britain have become increasingly concerned about the way in which organized games (football, hockey, tennis, for example) have been taught in schools. As a result, a change of focus has begun to emerge which places greater emphasis on the strategic features of games, and on the principles which underpin them, and less on the technical requirements of games. The advocates of this changing focus have not neglected these requirements, instead they argue that in order to learn to play games it is necessary to reduce the technically limiting factors within games. They propose that games with the minimum of techniques should be devised which represent the adult versions of games and that these should form the basis for a child's learning. The focus for these game forms should be the strategic features or principles of play which are common to all games.

In order to learn a game, children need to be exposed to games which illustrate the major principles of play. These enabling games represent the key principles of play in a form which is intended to allow all children to play at their level and feel that they are playing an actual game. The thinking behind this point of view has been developed by Bunker and Thorpe (1982) and has been clearly expressed in their writings. They call this approach, 'teaching for understanding'.

Research by Teachers

During the past few years there has been a growing concern about the role teachers play in research in educational settings. All too often teachers have been seen simply as the consumers of research and rarely as the producers of research (Nixon, 1981). This has led a number of researchers (Burgess, 1980; Smetherham, 1979; Verma and Beard, 1981) to identify and stress the key role which teachers can play in practical research in the study of their own classroom problems.

It is interesting to speculate why teachers have not been involved in educational research. Some (Elliott, 1975; Nixon, 1981) have claimed that much of the research in education has not been applicable to the teacher in the classroom. Teachers have had problems defined for them by people who are outside of and remote from the classroom situation. Questions have been posed which are of little concern to the classroom teacher and which show little sensitivity to their local institutional circumstances. Bartholomew, (1972); Burgess, (1980); Cosgrove, (1981); McCutcheon, (1981); Nixon, (1981); Verma and Beard, (1981) all claim that most educational research is an activity indulged in by those outside the classroom for the benefit of those outside the classroom. Research reports are also frequently full of jargon and statistics and often written in a fashion not accessible to teachers (McCutcheon, 1981) and they appear in journals which are not readily available to the classroom teacher (Bartholomew, 1972; McCutcheon, 1981; Verma and Beard, 1981). Thus, teachers have been left out of the research process; research reports appear to be of little relevance and what is available is not easily accessible.

The idea of teachers undertaking research in their own classroom is not new but only a few researchers have actively encouraged it. The late Lawrence Stenhouse (1975) did much to introduce and legitimate the idea of the teacher as researcher in educational debate and research practice, while Gorbutt (1972) advocated a similar notion when speaking of teachers as 'self-critical problem solvers'. The work of Stenhouse at the Centre for Applied Research in Education has been developed further in Elliott's (1975) notion of the self-monitoring teacher in the Ford Teaching Project and the growth of the Classroom Action Research Network based at Cambridge which publishes its own Bulletin.

The Project

In 1982, teachers who were prepared to try out a new games teaching approach and monitor their own practice were invited to Loughborough University for an induction course lasting two days. A small project team (three staff, including myself) presented ideas in the form of practical workshops where teachers were exposed to ideas in an experiential form. It was assumed by the course organizers that it is only in the practical situation that ideas begin to come alive and teachers can recognize through the practical form how they can translate them into action.

The starting point for examining 'teaching for understanding' was through net games because they are recognized as being the most simple, tactically, and it is possible to expose teachers to key ideas from an early stage. The teachers took part also in invasion-type games (for example, soccer) and fielding/striking games (for example, cricket). After each session the teachers had an opportunity to discuss the ideas presented with their colleagues and the project team. Some resource documents were made available and these enabled the teachers to return to their school and consider the practical sessions in the light of the documentation.

After the teachers returned to their school from the induction course a further meeting was arranged in their local authority. This provided the opportunity to raise issues from their reading, their recollections of the induction course, and any discussions with other teachers. The purpose of this meeting was to provide opportunity for further discussion and debate but also to make available a booklet of research procedures appropriate for monitoring the teachers' practice. All the research procedures were outlined and advice was provided about how to conduct research into one's own practical situation. The teachers were asked to explore the use of the research techniques and attempt to monitor some of their teaching over a short period of time — about five weeks. The subject for their monitoring was their games teaching using the 'teaching for understanding' focus they had been exposed to during the first induction course. This phase was considered as an exploration and the teachers were asked to plan a small teaching unit of approximately six weeks for the second phase. The focus for their games teaching was to be their interpretation of 'teaching for understanding'. During the course of this teaching the teachers were expected to monitor their teaching and produce a case study of their work for discussion with colleagues in different schools. Guidance in how to write case studies was provided but not in written form. The teachers were asked to write a diary of any problems they faced in trying to incorporate a research task into their teaching. A number of research students and lecturers in Institutes of Higher Education were associated with the project and they played an important role. These associate members of the project contributed to the debate about the rationale for 'teaching for understanding' and they formed a forum which enabled ideas to be critically tested.

In addition to the research by the teachers, the project team conducted a form of second order research about the problems faced by teachers in attempting to engage in research-based teaching. This was supported by an attempt to examine the project team's support for the teachers. All meetings with teachers were recorded on audio tape and field notes were taken by at least two research students and the author. The research students made contact with individual teachers at these meetings and discussed their reactions to this work: these reactions were recorded after the discussions.

An Action Research Perspective

Instead of the project team monitoring the work of the teachers, an action research perspective was adopted because it attempts to involve teachers in developing an understanding of their own practice as a basis for improving it and creating change. This perspective rests on the assumption that a systematic and critical reflection on one's actions can help teachers to:

1   learn about teaching
2   become more aware of the consequences of their actions in teaching
3   learn about games teaching and the nature of games.

In the same way, it was felt that systematic and critical reflection on one's own actions with teachers could help researchers to:

1   learn about how to support teachers involved in action research
2   be more aware of the consequences of their actions
3   learn about research in schools.

Adopting an action research perspective called for research-based teaching which would submit the idea of 'teaching for understanding' to critical testing. In this perspective it is assumed that as no two classrooms are alike, the only person who is able to realize an idea in practice with children is the teacher. Consequently, if teachers are to make informed judgments about what they are doing then they must rely on careful and systematic observation of their practice and be inspired by some vision of what it should all add up to. Teachers are attempting to study practice with a view to improving the quality of action within it. In their teaching they are adopting a research stance which is concerned with strengthening and informing their professional judgments. This should enable teachers to establish greater control over translating ideas into practice and to achieve greater understanding of the variables involved in teaching and the process of learning. Through this research-based teaching, teachers can progressively deepen their understanding of their own work and make more informed practical judgments.

However, there is a limit to individual reflection upon practice and the opportunity to develop it. Adopting a research stance to one's teaching needs a support structure in which teachers can communicate with one another and report their investigations. This involves rendering an account of one's investigations and deliberations — in written, spoken, or visual form — for the purpose of discussion and critique. This makes the work of the group of teachers a democratic process because it makes the basis of one's practical judgments open to public scrutiny. They can be examined in order that contrary and alternative perspectives can be made and considered. It also enables the group to recognize similarities and differences between other cases and one's own. By taking steps to overcome the arbitrariness, impressionistic or whimsical way in which practical decisions and judgments are made, one is attempting to develop a sensitive and self-critical subjective perspective.

In this way, curriculum research and development belongs to the teacher because it provides the potential and capability for teachers to develop their own practices. It is grounded in a systematic and critical appraisal of alternatives available to teachers and it enables them to act intelligently because they have taken steps to overcome the barriers that create unconscious behaviour patterns and perpetuate untested assumptions. This then was the context of the innovation and the 'theory' which underpinned the actions of all those involved. However, as we see below, the process of realizing teaching for understanding and of research based teaching was fraught with difficulties and unforeseen problems.

Analysis of the Research

The Teachers' Monitoring of their Practice

As the innovation progressed, it soon became apparent that the teachers had great difficulty in breaking away from their conventional conception of teaching which emphasizes the technical requirements of games as the principal focus for learning games. In the induction course where the emphasis was upon the tactical features of games and the reduction of the technical limitations of some games, it was made clear that 'teaching for understanding' focuses on those features which make a game a 'game' and these are essentially tactical and decision-making. The translation of the idea was difficult to implement and this was particularly true in the case of the teachers' lesson plans which were dominated by the pattern:

a   introductory activity
b   technique practice
c   small-sided game
d   full game.

Teachers without much experience of alternative forms of teaching or of structuring their lessons were unable to lose the constraints of a technique-orientated lesson. This problem was complicated further by the impression that 'teaching for understanding' was not concerned with techniques. Bunker and Thorpe (1982) have since consistently pointed out that 'teaching for understanding' focuses on what makes a game a 'game' and these are essentially tactical and decision-making features. But, if a game breaks down one of the causes may lie in the lack of technical ability and intervention in the skills and abilities of the players may be required. However teachers clearly felt that teaching for understanding was at the expense of teaching techniques or skills. It is little wonder that the teachers experienced problems in translating ideas into practice. Their own understanding of the idea of 'teaching for understanding' was called into question. Moreover when the project team examined field notes and video recordings of induction courses it became obvious that some teachers did not understand the tactical and strategic features of the games they played. While the teachers displayed a wide range of knowledge about what games can offer most felt that a list of techniques to be taught offered the strongest framework for thinking about games teaching. It was evident then, that teachers had been deeply socialized into particular ways of thinking about the content of the PE curriculum and of teaching. Clearly this has implications for teacher training because if teachers have difficulty in understanding games there is a need to re-appraise the form in which prospective teachers are educated and initiated into games education. Most of the teachers found great difficulty with invasion games, which proved to be more complex for teachers to devise ways of representing game forms or devising 'enabling games' to illustrate principles of play. However net games, for example tennis and badminton, appeared to be less problematic. This type of game is more simple and straightforward tactically and the teachers had received more support in this area of games.

By the seventh lesson in schools teachers were beginning to report that they were having serious problems with the innovation. They had exhausted ideas which they had learned in the induction courses and drawn from the resource documents and they were unsure about which game forms were appropriate to develop their work. Teachers working alone felt isolated and unsure of what to do, especially if little support was forthcoming from colleagues or advisors. When teachers worked in a group, this stage could be overcome because ideas were generated by sharing and discussing possibilities. However, those PE teachers with little experience or knowledge of games did not make further progress and they reverted back to their traditional practices where the emphasis was on technique. This pattern served to emphasize how limited was the support for the innovation in some of the departments and institutions.

It was evident that most of the teachers felt more confident when they were asked to repeat or copy ideas presented to them, rather than when developing their own ideas. This was unsurprising given their limited knowledge of how to teach differently and the fact there there was so little support available to them once they were in schools and their training had encouraged them to be passive recipients of ideas and not creators of ideas.

However one of the most successful features of the teachers' work was the opportunity it provided for young people to devise their own games. All the teachers reported that they had not tried this approach before, but they were very pleased with the results and surprised how well the pupils were able to devise their own games. It was reported also that technically less able pupils responded better to this approach than their more able peers, a result which deserves a great deal more investigation.

Presentation of an Innovation

During the development of the work on 'teaching for understanding' it was apparent that a new terminology was emerging. This caused problems for the teachers who came to the induction courses without any prior reading. Words like 'game form' 'enabling games', 'representing games' were part of the everyday language of the project team and some teachers who had been involved in this changing focus. However, at the outset this 'jargon' created a barrier for some teachers and the project team were unaware that a new terminology was emerging and was having this effect. The language of an innovation can clearly be as alienating and as problematic for teachers as the jargon of research reports, when it is constructed *for them* by others, (researchers or innovators). The idea of a common-shared language is important in the evolution of an idea and its innovation in schools; without this a new terminology can create a gulf between adopters of an innovation and those involved in translating it into action in schools, at the expense of educational change.

The teachers' reactions to the innovation identified another gulf between the adopters and the project team because the needs of the teachers as perceived by the project team differed from the actual needs of the teachers. The teachers wanted ideas they could go away with and try out; consequently they compared the practical induction courses with their own classes and they questioned whether they would be able to teach in exactly the same way. The tutors on the induction course perceived the needs of teachers rather different-ly, as being 'what is this idea all about' and as a result the induction courses attempted to illustrate this. The teachers wanted class-organization tips to deal with small-group teaching and situations where different equipment could be used by different groups. When this didn't occur, they expressed concern about the lack of reality and knowledge of the 'real' world in which they taught. The project team had designed the induction courses as a result of working with teachers trying out 'teaching for understanding' and recognizing that one of the problems was the teachers' own understanding of games. Hence, a particular approach was adopted in order to overcome this problem.

Teachers also had great difficulty in monitoring their own practice, in short, in being and becoming a teacher/researcher. The writing of field notes or any kind of report proved to be difficult to fit into a normal teaching day — there simply wasn't the space for them to engage in this sort of activity, finding time was a problem. The writing of notes was also far more complex than the teachers expected and they needed more time to acquire the habit and the facility. Short questionnaires for pupils were found to be more suitable than other techniques and interviews proved to be difficult and the teachers felt uncomfortable in using them. The recording of dialogue on playing fields also presented special difficulties and any sophisticated equipment created problems unless there was strong support from an advisor or local Institute of Higher Education. The use of a contract with a colleague to observe a lesson was found to be more acceptable and easier to handle. For many teachers all this was a new and sometimes exciting experience; but while they expressed the view that this procedure had potential and should be developed further, they also felt that in their present conditions of work their opportunities to effect research for the purpose of evaluation, were very limited indeed.

The analysis of data caused considerable anxiety. Many of the teachers collected too much data and they found it difficult to handle and isolate what was really relevant to their developing innovation. Too much data was simply confusing and a clear direction did not emerge. In the booklet (prepared by University staff) outlining different research procedures for monitoring their teaching, how to analyze data was left out because the project team had planned to provide assistance. This proved to be far too difficult to handle and had to be abandoned. This lack of support in this crucial stage revealed clearly how important it is to provide training in research procedures to monitor teaching. Even though the teachers had received some training in research procedures during their College or University course it did not provide them with the expertise or knowledge to monitor their own teaching. The evidence of this project would suggest that the research training of teachers is badly in need of attention. Teachers are ill-equipped with the kind of skills required for monitoring teaching or for curriculum development.

In discussions with teachers before the project, they did not appear to experience problems in their teaching, and for many the teaching of games was not perceived as problematic. Teachers identified certain types of problems like poor facilities, lack of sufficient equipment, and poor staffing ratios which they complained about. Their curriculum was not their first concern. Another type of problem was the timetabling arrangements or the kind of classes they received, along with the poor motivation of pupils and their reluctance to enter enthusiastically into what the teacher was offering. Rarely did teachers seem able or willing to consider that their teaching and work with young people could be open to many different interpretations or that their own actions might be at the root of the behaviours of their pupils.

However, by asking teachers to reflect on their practice and discuss it with colleagues, they became more conscious of their teaching and aware that how they taught was open to some question. All the teachers expressed the view that monitoring had enabled them to learn more about themselves, their teaching, their pupils, and the games they thought they understood. This in itself is a strong claim for encouraging teachers to engage in monitoring their practice, even if it is only of a limited kind and for a short period of time.

During the course of the project and in subsequent courses with teachers it became apparent that the presentation of an innovatory idea challenged a teacher's existing framework for conceptualizing games. Consequently, there was a need to demonstrate why a different framework was necessary and to show that problems existed within the current view of how games should be taught. This produced problems for some teachers and a certain amount of conflict. New ideas in the context of 'teaching for understanding' challenged the way the teacher worked with pupils and the kind of tasks that they set. Teachers had to abandon their existing frame of reference and explore practices which required new skills and in some cases a different working relationship with pupils. This conflict situation exposed teachers' values and provoked reaction. In order to help teachers reconstruct a new framework it was thus necessary to present ideas in a medium they understood and were familiar with. Thus in the induction courses a familiar game was chosen and key features were exaggerated to illustrate new ideas.

Ultimately, however, the adequacy of the new framework needed to be tested in the teacher's own setting and opportunity for further practical work and discussion had to be available. It is here in the practical situation that the teacher needed the real support in the form of guidelines about:

1   exactly what is involved in the new idea;
2   the progression of the ideas presented in the practical session with a clear identification of what is being attempted;
3   exactly what can be taught to young people over a clear time span;
4   alternative ways of developing the work further.

This support needed to be available in both written form and audio tapes with video recordings of work with children where possible. Innovators are asking too much of teachers in terms of translating an idea into practice unless they make these resources available. Once the teacher is in the practical situation they need opportunities to discuss their work with colleagues and wherever possible provide opportunity for observation of their teaching. In addition, the time scale for change must be seen in terms of years and not a few months. Changes do occur in the short term but they can be an illusion and real change is slow. The effect on pupils may not be seen for a long time.

Research-Based Teaching

Teachers who examined their practice critically and engaged in research-based teaching all claimed that it enabled them to learn more about themselves, their pupils, their teaching, and games. This is significant because it clearly demonstrates the value of asking teachers to scrutinize their teaching and take time to reflect about their work. However, it is time-consuming and we need further information about how teachers can incorporate research-based teaching into their teaching routines and the school calendar. This project has shown that this kind of work is only in the early stages of development. The teachers in the project were volunteers and perhaps are atypical of most in the PE profession. Questions need to be posed about the practicality of the 'average' teacher setting time aside to engage in research about his or her practice. For some teachers the will and motivation to question their practice and consider critically untested assumptions and habitual teaching behaviour may not be there. For others the 'will' is not supported by the opportunities to do otherwise. Experience with this project would suggest that the problem is not to persuade all teachers to engage in self-monitoring but to make teaching an absorbing area of interest that arouses curiosity. This is what happened with the teachers in the project: they found a new interest in their teaching providing a stimulus which was rewarding in its own right. However, so deeply are teachers rooted in the conventions and routines of their own practice that they also may need an outside source to show them that their content could be considered in a different light. The teachers' interest in the *content* of the curriculum rather than any consideration of different teaching styles, or evaluation of practice, was the starting point for discussion. These other factors were not strong motivators for reflection, whereas content and interest in content formed the basis for a reflective attitude.

The literature on action research and the teacher as researcher provides a picture of groups of teachers engaged in rigorous research. This may be because many of the teachers are involved in studying for higher degrees and further advanced study. In the games project nobody was involved in such studies and consequently there was no accountability involved and no requirement to complete an assignment. As a result the quality of the investigations in terms of research rigour was often lower than was anticipated or desired.

Teachers lacked research skills; they also worked within severe time constraints and they could not be given enough support at the right time. Meetings of teachers to discuss their work were invariably and understandably used as social occasions and not opportunities to discuss teaching or learning. The idea of emancipatory action research (Kemmis, 1980) in which teachers learn from each other and generate a commitment to change the constraints that inhibit their implementation of ideas is a worthy ideal but it is far from a reality with the teachers in this project. Research-based teaching may have the potential to stimulate such theory but teachers in the current climate and conditions of practice do not appear to perceive this as being an important priority, if they consider it at all. For teachers, research-based teaching can stimulate an interest in children and learning and in how they see physical education. It can awaken ideas about teaching and how content can be presented in a different way. Research-based teaching at present is all about stimulating interest and curiosity in what one teaches. Potentially it can aspire to informing teachers about the improvement of their practice and contribute to a teacher's understanding of teaching. However, teachers need a support structure of time and opportunity. At the moment it seems that time for research-based teaching can only come from one source — the PE curriculum and perhaps in particular the teachers' commitment to inter-school fixtures. Here lies the major problem, because inter-school teams and a commitment to practice places heavy demands on the teachers. To reduce this time commitment would require a major re-orientation of their values and a challenge to tradition. This may occur 'unintentionally' as teachers' strike action and economic climate provoke a challenge to traditional thinking and as further challenges are made within the profession (Almond, 1983; Glew, 1983). These factors may ultimately combine to produce a climate in which the thinking of the profession is again stimulated and new practices can flourish.

References

ALMOND, L. (1983), 'Away games', *Times Educational Supplement*, 20 May.

BARTHOLOMEW, J. (1972), 'The teacher as researcher: a key to innovation and change', Paper presented at the Nuffield Teacher Enquiry Conference at the University of York, April.

BUNKER, D. and THORPE, R. (1982), 'Teaching games in schools', *Bulletin of Physical Education*, 18, 1.

BURGESS, J. (1980), 'Some reflections on teacher-based research', *Insight*, 3, 2, pp. 20–23.

COSGROVE, S. (1981), 'Using action research in the classroom and schools: a teacher's view', Paper presented at the Annual Meeting of the Australian Association for Research in Education, Adelaide, 12–15 November.

ELLIOTT, J. (1975), *Developing Hypotheses about Classrooms from Teachers' Practical Constructs* (mimeo), Cambridge Institute of Education.

GLEW, P. (1983), 'Are your fixtures really necessary?', *British Journal of Physical Education*, 14, 4, p. 100.

GORBUTT, D. (1972), 'The new society of education', *Education for Teaching*, 89, 3.

KEMMIS, S. (1980), 'Action research in retrospect and prospect', Paper presented at the Annual Meeting of the Australian Association for Research in Education, Sydney, 6–9 November.

McCUTCHEON, C. (1981), 'The impact of the insider', in NIXON, J. (Ed.), *A Teacher's Guide to Action Research*, London, Grant McIntyre.

NIXON, J. (1981), 'Development through research', *Secondary Education*, 11, 1.

SMETHERHAM, D. (1979), 'Forward' to NIXON, J. (Ed.), *A Teacher's Guide to Action Research*, London, Grant McIntyre.

STENHOUSE, L. (1975), *An Introduction to Curriculum Research and Development*, London, Heinemann.

VERMA, G.K. and BEARD, R.M. (1981), *What is Educational Research?*, Aldershot, Gower Publishing Company.

9 Health Related Fitness as an Innovation in the Physical Education Curriculum

David Kirk

Physical Education has long been associated with the development and maintenance of the health of school children. The 1902 Royal Commission on Physical Training (Scotland) was set up as a government response to public concern over the state of the health of large sections of the population at that time. On the basis of the Commission's recommendations, physical education was established as a subject in the Elementary School curriculum, with the express purpose of improving the medical and nutritional provision for children in schools. By 1905, the Board of Education had provided the first National (British) Syllabus for Physical Education stating that,

> The primary objective of any course of physical exercises in schools is to maintain, and if possible, improve, the health and physique of the children. This may be described as the *physical effect*. (Board of Education, 1905, 9)

Thus, physical education was established as a school subject, primarily on the basis of its contribution to children's health. However, it was not long before the curriculum began to expand from its narrow focus on 'drill' and Swedish gymnastics to include dancing, games, athletics and swimming and with this expansion came claims for a broadening of the aims of physical education to incorporate the educational benefits to be derived from participation in organized physical activity.[1]

Over the years and until the present time, the link between school physical education and health has remained, but has tended to be obscured by attempts by physical educators to stress the educational, and more recently, the recreational aspects of physical education[2]. The contribution of physical education to children's health has, until recently, tended to exist only implicitly in the physical education curriculum, more often considered by teachers to be a by-product of participation in physical activity rather than a directly planned for and intended outcome.

However, we have witnessed within the last three to five years an increasing interest among members of the physical education profession in links between physical education and health. Courses in Health Education, serviced by physical educators, have appeared in schools and education systems around the world[3]. The phenomenon of 'Daily Physical Education' has, likewise, had an international impact[4], and some derivative programmes, such as 'Fifteen/Thirty' in Queensland, Australia, have advocated a daily fifteen minutes of exercise for fitness for all primary school children[5]. In Britain, physical educationists like Almond (1983) have argued that health related fitness ought to form an important part of the physical education curriculum. However, Almond has also suggested that,

> ... the physical education profession does not possess a coherent rationale for health related fitness in schools. The evidence of curriculum surveys and practical exercises with a number of teaching groups suggests that there is a mismatch between our practices in schools and the aspirations that the physical education profession is supposed to value. (1983, p. 5)

Other writers, such as Thomas (1977) and Haydock (1979) have also suggested that current physical education programmes in schools are ineffective in combating health related problems like obesity and other conditions linked with sedentary lifestyles. The comments of these writers are, perhaps, surprising, given the historical links between physical education and the promotion of health. However, I will argue in this chapter that these comments are, to a large extent, justified, and that the place of health education in the physical education curriculum is problematic. The main theme of this discussion is that, despite historical links between physical education and health, and the influence of health education in an implicit form in the school curriculum, the notion of 'health related fitness' is for many physical education teachers, a new and problematic idea. The discussion draws on data derived from an ethnographic case study[6] of teachers' attempts to introduce and develop a health related fitness course as a part of the physical education curriculum at Forest School, a 14–18, co-educational Upper School and Community College in England.

At Forest School, the rationale behind the introduction of the new course was that health related fitness forms the core of the physical education curriculum. 'The whole of the PE curriculum in secondary schools should be *based* around the teaching of health related fitness'. For teachers in the Physical Education Department health related fitness was not just another idea to be tagged on to an already diverse curriculum. Rather, the whole curriculum, in their opinion, needed to be reshaped and relocated within the rationale of health related fitness. According to the formal account[7] of the developments in health related fitness at Forest, the traditional physical education curriculum was re-organized into 'theoretical' and 'practical' elements. Theory lessons were classroom-based and included units of work on 'Physical Fitness and Exercise', 'Accidents, First aid, and Safety'; and 'Life Style Management', involving sessions on preventative medicine, weight control, nutrition, diet, use of leisure time, and lifestyle problem-solving. Practical lessons presented 'Ways of Exercising', involving two compulsory components covering weight-training and jogging, flexibility, and circuit training: and optional 'Activities for Fitness and Leisure' (focusing on individual and non-competitive activities); and 'Sports for Fitness and Leisure' (focusing on individual and team sports with a competitive flavour).

This conception of health in the physical education curriculum represents a marked departure from the idea that health benefits derived from participation in physical activity are merely by-products of teaching. The introduction of health related fitness into the curriculum at Forest School was therefore, an innovation; it was a *new* idea. As such, this situation had important implications for the teachers' practices and for the pupils' learning experiences.

The chapter is organized around three problematics which arose due to the innovative nature of health related fitness.

The Problem of Aspirations in Health Related Fitness

In a fundamental sense, the idea of teaching presupposes a concept of achievement or success. In other words, to teach is to attempt to achieve some goal; to be ineffective is to fail to teach. There is, then, a logical connection between teaching, achievement, and aims or aspirations.[8] Teachers' aspirations, or what Lortie (1975, p. 109) calls their 'perspectives on purpose' provide an indication of the criteria teachers employ to measure the success of their teaching.

Conventionally, the physical education teacher's success has tended to be judged publicly on the basis of such criteria as First XI or XV results, interschool competition success, international representation among students, and to a lesser degree, general participation levels in extra curricular sport. An assumption which appears to underlie this set of criteria is that if a teacher can coach sport to a high level, then this is a good indicator of the quality of the physical education teaching during curriculum time.

However, the aspirations shared by teachers at Forest School were to a large extent couched in *anti*-traditional terms. For instance, there was a general agreement that the individual and not the group was the basic 'unit of teaching', and that teachers should be concerned with the development of positive attitudes in students towards their own health and fitness, not the development of motor skills. But, if conventional criteria of success are inappropriate in relation to teaching health related fitness at Forest School, then the problem the teachers faced was how to measure the achievement of their own aspirations. If the teachers were concerned only with the transmission of propositional knowledge[9], then the effectiveness of their teaching in this sense could be measured by written examinations. But if the criteria of success must reflect aspirations like 'enabling students to have enjoyable and meaningful experiences' and 'developing in students positive attitudes to health and fitness'[10], then it is clear that conventional criteria are inappropriate. A discussion of these two aspirations serves to illustrate the complex problems inherent in aspirations in health related fitness.

First, in attempting to measure their effectiveness in achieving the aspiration of 'enabling students to have enjoyable and meaningful experiences', the teachers relied heavily on the cues and messages picked up from students during lessons. If students appeared to be interested and involved in the lesson, then teachers assumed that they were, more or less, enjoying themselves. This aspiration, and this means of measuring its achievement, are not exclusive to teaching health related fitness at Forest School; indeed, 'student enjoyment' would appear to rank among the aspirations of many physical education teachers. However, in a conventional programme, teachers do not only have the responsiveness of students in lessons as an indicator of success; they can and do often judge the success of this aspiration by noting levels of student participation in extra-curricular sport. This is because the substance of what they teach during curriculum time *is* sport. Some of the teachers at Forest did, also, cite this criterion. But in so doing, they divorced the aspiration of 'student enjoyment' from the innovative idea. High levels of student participation in extra-curricular sport were not, necessarily, felt to be good indicators of the success of a health related fitness based physical education curriculum. The criteria for success in teaching the health related aspects of the curriculum were located primarily in student response during lessons and in other student behaviours and attitudes outside the classroom, for instance in relation to diet, or exercise during free time, to which the teachers had no direct access. Thus, it was primarily in the classroom context that teachers had to judge the meaningfulness of the information they were imparting, and the enjoyment the students derived from their teaching, through attempts to pick up cues from students' behaviour, gestures, talk, and so on. Clearly, there are important implications here for the development of teaching methods in relation to the health related aspects of the curriculum, and these I will discuss later in the chapter.

The measurement of teacher effectiveness in achieving this aspiration was further complicated because indicators of success or failure from cues picked up in the classroom could not be trusted as infallible guides. The case of 'Paula' illustrated this point. Paula was a fairly stout fifth year student who intended leaving school early. She was present in some of the lessons I observed at Forest, and her behaviour in these lessons could be described generally as 'mildly disruptive' and 'inattentive'. She appeared to be uninterested, and was easily distracted by other students. The cues available suggested that Paula was getting very little out of the lessons. However, as Kevin Edmonds, her teacher, later related

'At the end of the lesson, in fact, Paula saw me and is now monitoring her diet, and has arranged to come and see me once a week to be tested and measured. And this is as much by her own volition as prompting from me, so obviously something has gone in there. I think perhaps that the way she was diverting her attention might have been a bit of a defence on her part, because it is quite an embarrassing message to receive for the fattest girl in the class. In a way, she had to direct her attention from the embarrassing messages that were getting through.'

In assessing the effectiveness of his teaching towards this aspiration, Kevin Edmonds felt that he needed to take wider contextual factors into account. To this end, no one lesson was used to judge his effectiveness; his opinion was also influenced by his knowledge of the individual or group in question, of student sub-culture within the classroom, and of the state of mind of a fifth year early leaver in that last few weeks of compulsory schooling.

And so, additional factors such as the extent to which students exercised during free time out of school, and are conscious of their diets, were important indicators of the success or failure of teaching towards this aspiration. The problem for the teachers at Forest, however, was how to gain access to this sort of information. One way they attempted to overcome this difficulty was to administer a short questionnaire at the end of the fifth year to all students who had taken the course. But the limitations of this were obvious. This information could only at best be an indicator of teacher effectiveness, it was by no means direct evidence of the success of the teaching programme.

Indeed, a similar problem existed in relation to the second aspiration which was 'developing in students positive attitudes towards health and fitness'. Underlying this aspiration was the idea that, through the development of such an attitude, students would take steps to become fit, or else stay fit, now and on into adulthood. Again the problem arose of how to test the effectiveness of this aspiration, when the 'pay-off' occurs after the students have left school and the teacher's immediate sphere of influence. Without direct evidence of what the students think and do when they leave school, the teachers had no way of knowing how effective their teaching had been. Of course, they could have moved somewhere towards overcoming this difficulty by carrying out some sort of longitudinal survey of students at intervals after they had left school. However, this would have involved a number of difficulties relating to finance, time, consistency of staff, locating students, and access to relevant and mostly confidential information from, for example, doctors and employers. Perhaps in anticipation of these difficulties, such a survey had never been seriously contemplated, either by the physical education staff or the school administration. The teachers at Forest were themselves aware of these difficulties, and as one remarked

'It's one of those things where you hope you are doing a good job, but I suppose it's like any other subject in the school, you can't guarantee that anything kids do at school will be of any use to them when they leave. For the majority of kids, it's something you can only hope will happen.' (Steve Finney)

Without some feedback on the effectiveness of their teaching the best the teachers could do was *hope* they had some influence.

The problems which arose in judging teacher success in this case are due, to a large extent, to the nature and character of this aspiration itself. Its 'futuristic perspective' involved a concern for what students did once they left school, which made the monitoring of success an almost impossible task. Another problem, however, arose out of the ambiguity of the aspiration. There was no clear, precise statement of what student behaviour would be appropriate evidence of teachers' effectiveness in terms of having developed in students positive attitudes towards health and fitness. Even if support services had been available to allow a longitudinal survey to be carried out, a whole range of student behaviours might count as legitimate, from 'walking to work' to 'swimming five miles before breakfast' to 'drinking only five pints of beer instead of ten on a Saturday night'. The teachers could, of course, have stated the aspiration in more precise, behavioural terms; but whether this would have solved the problem is debatable. The choice of behaviours which indicate 'a positive attitude' is elusive and at best arbitrary, as the examples above suggest.

Without direct evidence of their success or failure at Forest School, the teachers were forced to argue the case for teaching the health related aspects of the curriculum entirely on the basis of the vital role this knowledge plays in students' lives. In other words, they had to argue that this knowledge is *so* important, that it is better that students are 'in the know', and then allowed to make decisions for themselves concerning whether or not they want to use this knowledge, than to be left in ignorance. This in turn created another difficulty for the teachers, because they were then in a position of making prior claims about what is and is not good for their students. Certainly, these claims were based on research information and other available knowledge on health and fitness, but such claims are nevertheless preconceived when they are couched in terms of students' needs. One of the major ideals within the rationale for teaching health related fitness at Forest was the notion of 'treating students as individuals'. However, without firm evidence of the influence that their teaching was having on individual students, the teachers could not consistently claim to be catering for individual students' needs by providing relevant knowledge and skills. Working with students on a one-to-one basis, as in the case of 'Paula', might help surmount this difficulty. But this could not be said to be true in relation to entire groups of students. Thus, the teachers at Forest were forced to make decisions about what health related matters to teach and what not to teach, not on the basis of their students' *actual* needs, but on the basis of their *apparent* needs as adjudged from the teachers' perspective.

The physical education staff at Forest School were faced, then, with a number of complex issues that arose as a result of a change in aspirations and a related change in the criteria for successful teaching. By evolving aspirations which were less tangible than those commonly held by more conventional colleagues, they were presented with the difficulty of judging their effectiveness on the basis of criteria quite different from those employed by other parts of the school system in which they operated. One expression of this was their enthusiasm for administering a questionnaire to the students at the end of their course. This at least provided them with some quantitative, if only limited, measure of their impact, which could be used, if necessary to help legitimize their practice and publicly inform their colleagues in the broader school community.

However, neither examination results nor student participation rates indicating levels of involvement in extra curricular sport are particularly good indicators of effective teaching of a health related fitness based physical education curriculum. This, as we will see has important implications for the reward and recognition which teachers can or may receive in the context of an innovation of this kind.

Recognition and Reward in an Innovative Situation

There is little doubt that teachers do seek rewards for successful teaching. Lortie (1975, pp. 101–3) suggests that reward can come in different forms for teachers, most obviously through increases in salary or status by promotion. However, both of these rewards are extrinsic to the activity of teaching. Lortie goes on to argue that there is a third kind of reward, which he terms 'psychic' rewards, which are intrinsic to teaching. Satisfaction, a sense of achievement and pleasure would each count as examples of this, and in Lortie's view, the occupational structure of teaching, which offers limited prospects for promotion, favours rewards of this kind.

'Recognition' represents a special kind of reward gained through 'public acclaim'. While intrinsic reward tends to be a private and personal affair for teachers, recognition is a corporate matter, achieved through a collective acknowledgement of a person's worth. As we have seen at Forest School, the criteria for successful teaching changed with the introduction of health related fitness. In the relative privacy of the classroom and gymnasium, these changes were accommodated, worked through, and rationalized by individual teachers. However, as recognition is a corporate matter[11], involving the judgments of people outside the teacher's immediate sphere of personal contact, problems arose through this change in criteria for successful teaching. For instance, in a conventional physical education programme, teachers seek recognition for themselves, their departments, and their schools by publicizing success in interschool sports competitions. However, the work associated with teaching health related fitness at Forest School could not be publicized in this way.

> 'It's much easier to publicise first XV and hockey XI results than it is to publicize "Fat Boy Makes Good" or "Recalcitrant Fifth Year Girls Enjoy PE". It just does not make headlines in the local paper, or get

the school governors or the local parents excited.' (Kevin Edmonds, Head of Boys PE)

This problem was compounded by an awareness among the teachers of what Hendry (1976) has referred to as the physical education teachers' 'marginality' in relation to the 'central purposes' of the school. Notwithstanding the existence of an innovation, the Physical Education Department had to fight in any case for survival on the timetable alongside traditionally more prestigious subjects.

> 'It's a political battle because we have to justify the worth of the course against courses in Maths and English, Humanities and so on. The problem is that because our subject is non-examinable, it is probably not seen to have great vocational or academic value, and therefore tends to get pushed to one side.' (Kevin Edmonds)

Thus, the teachers at Forest School had to operate within an educational system which imputed only low status to physical education teaching. These broader school expectations were important factors, defining professional activity worthy of recognition. Within this 'system' however, there are further factors, like public examinations, which have a momentum and prestige quite beyond the control of individual teachers and groups of teachers and schools. Michael Williams, the Principal at Forest, makes this point

> 'We're always going to have people saying "we mustn't forget the examination classes, they've got to pass the exams", and I say myself, with only five terms to push people through their O Levels and CSEs that's bound to loom large during much of the year. That's one of the problems we have as a fourteen to eighteen establishment, and that tends to lead people to take up what might generally be described as 'conservative' stances. But that's just part of our normal operation; we have to live in the "real world", where kids have to get "real" examination results.'

Public examinations, as key factors in the educational system, exert a powerful influence over the way in which schools operate. And because the health related fitness course at Forest was non-examinable in terms of O Levels and CSEs, the most apparently prestigious means of gaining recognition was denied the physical education teachers. Any recognition they gained, therefore, reflected the subject's marginal status in the school curriculum.

The conventional physical education programme has, in any case, as Hendry suggests, traditionally occupied a marginal role in relation to the school's central purposes, and so the criteria of success which have developed over time has tended to emphasize and reinforce physical education's contribution to the extra curricular life of the school, through recreative and sporting activity. However, with their focus on the individual student, and a relocation of sporting and recreative activity within the health related fitness framework, the teachers at Forest were obviously more concerned about the effectiveness of their teaching *during* curriculum time. We can see, then, that in terms of establishing criteria of success by which the teachers' effectiveness can be judged and so recognized, health related fitness as an innovation pulls against traditional and public criteria in two ways; in terms of the wider educational system, with its key feature of public examinations, and in relation to conventional orientations to teaching physical education. As a result, the teachers at Forest had to find new ways of publicizing their efforts. One method they employed was to provide a fitness evaluation and exercise prescription service for other teachers in the school. This brought 'outsiders' into the department and while providing a service of some benefit to them, also acquainted teachers with what was going on in the department. Another way was to talk to professional groups in seminars, workshops, and to write papers and articles for professional journals. Both of these approaches were on-going, over a period of time. In addition, the teachers staged some 'one-off' events in an attempt to attract attention. One of these events was 'Project '82'.

> 'We put on an exhibition of fitnesss activities, of information, and of demonstrations of activities. We had a group of celebrities help us do that, and they helped us show that even for superstars there is a fitness for health, and a fitness for recreation, as well as a fitness for serious competitive sport. We had a huge audience, we estimated that we had about two thousand kids through the morning session, and probably fifteen hundred adults came to the evening session. We had the local TV cameras along which certainly gave us some good publicity and the Headmaster was ecstatic about that!' (Kevin Edmonds)

Recognition gained through exercises like 'Project 82' provided the Physical Education Department with some credibility for the health related fitness course, and it also helped support the teachers' case for better equipment, more resources, and better timetable provision. However, while the achievement of greater bargaining power was a 'bonus', some teachers in the department sought reward at a more personal level.

> 'If this new course is going to be successful I want to be a part of it, because I've done so much to make it possible anyway, as far as I'm concerned. It's not as though I've picked up on this thing to try and make a name for myself, but if there are names to be made then I want to be involved in it. I'm not someone who goes out and aims for glory, I mean I'm not bothered about being famous particularly, but I would like to see credit where credit's due. Often with this kind of thing you see people get shoved into the background when they've really been the ones responsible for what's happening, and I'm not going to let that happen to me. I react quite strongly when people start to do this, because I think I have a right to be recognized, mainly

because I've put in so much work.' (Phil Bayle, Physical Education Teacher)

This comment provides us with an important insight into what being involved in innovation means to individual teachers. House (1974, p. 73) has suggested that 'people are often shocked that teachers should require tangible incentives to try a new innovation'. In this case, Phil Bayle was not asking for recognition for 'innovating', but rather for what innovating involves; extra work and an investment of energy and commitment above and beyond what is required contractually. But, because the teachers at Forest put this extra effort into a *new* idea, these rewards were slow to arrive. The change in criteria of successful teaching meant that a teacher's 'success' was not readily apparent to those in a position to offer reward. However, in addition to this, there was the further problem of lack of support services which allowed teachers to develop and disseminate their ideas. For instance, Phil Bayle remarked that 'The people who are regarded as being responsible for change, we expect to recognize and acknowledge what we're doing, and here I am referring to HMIs and PE Advisors'.

It was through an initiative taken quite independently of the Inspectorate and the Advisory Service by a lecturer in a nearby university that the teachers were provided initially with opportunities to disseminate their ideas, through talks and publications. From the teachers' point of view, the support structure which could and should have provided an input of guidance and fresh insight, and a vehicle for disseminating their work, was quite inadequate. The teachers of course may not have been sufficiently aware of the best way to use the support that was available. However, there is little or no organized support structure for innovation available to teachers in physical education, at Forest or elsewhere at this time. The agencies that do exist, and which *were* used by the teachers at Forest, like the Health Education Council, the Sports Council, and professional bodies like the PEA, are not designed specifically to support innovation in schools.

The fact that the teaching of health related fitness at Forest School has evolved and survived is, in some respects, surprising. On the one hand, various factors such as public examinations and the conventional expectations of parents and teachers create an unlikely environment for an innovation such as this to take root and flourish. The fact that it did so suggests that these factors alone are not, after all, overriding. Indeed, the apparent 'problem' of physical education's 'marginality' to some of the school's central purposes may have been a positive factor in this respect. It is perhaps unlikely that such developments would have been possible in more prestigious school subjects like Mathematics, or the Sciences. Physical education's marginality also permitted the development of alternative norms and a criteria for success, quite separate from those applied to teachers in other subjects[12], which worked to make the health related fitness innovation at Forest School possible.

Tailoring Means to Suit New Ends

The change in criteria for successful teaching which accompanied the introduction of health related fitness at Forest School, and the consequent difficulty teachers experienced in gaining rewards, caused the teachers to fall back on their interactions with students as the main measure of the success of their teaching. It was on the basis of cues picked up from students that the teachers were able to judge the level of student involvement in learning, and so their effectiveness as teachers. As such, the quality of interactions with students was for the teachers a major source of reward.

The teachers at Forest used a number of approaches to presenting and structuring students' learning experiences. Some of these means of designing students' learning experiences, like games and sports, are also used within conventional approaches to teaching physical education. However, the teachers were required to develop additional approaches, such as discussion, and dramatization[13], because some of their teaching was classroom-based. As the health related aspects of the curriculum involved teaching new concepts, information, and skills, there was a need for new means of structuring students' learning experiences. In addition, the development of these new approaches reflected the change in teachers' aspirations. Thus, much of the teaching was designed to 'create an environment', not only where information was passed on, but in which 'desirable attitudes occur'. The problem for the Forest School teachers was that their traditional teaching methods were, by and large, inappropriate for achieving this end. Formal lecturing may be a useful way of transmitting information and 'facts', and sports and games may provide an ideal environment in which the development of motor skills and competitive attitudes can be developed, but achieving the goal of 'developing in students positive attitudes to health and fitness' required, in the opinions of the Forest School teachers, something more and different. In their view, the development of attitudes towards health and fitness has an essential affective dimension. 'We hand out information to all the kids, and if one takes it in and it has some effect then that's great. But we can't *make* them listen, we can't *make* them believe' (Steve Finney, Physical Education Teacher).

The kind of interactive skill that achievement of this aspiration required goes beyond what one of the teachers, Phil Bayle, called the 'sheep-dog method'.

> 'The PE teacher is more like a sheep dog, where the real skill is how efficiently the dog herds the sheep around obstacles. It doesn't matter who the sheep are, as long as you can do it in the most efficient way, and you're back on time, that's how you score the highest points, and that's the skill a typical PE student comes out (of training) with. Damned good teachers, and damned good at herding people about in gymnasiums, and in sports halls, and on playing fields. But let's face it, these are the tools we've been using for the last fifty years, along

with the football and the rugby, we ought to be good at them by now.' (Phil Bayle)

In the 'sheep-dog method', the group is the basic teaching unit. However, in the health related fitness innovation the individual student was the focus of the teaching. Because of this, there was a greater emphasis placed on interactions with students on a personal level, and this change of focus required a consequent shift from the 'sheep-dog method' to methods which could cater for individuals.

The kinds of methods and approaches that the innovation required were in many respects quite different from those in which most of the teachers in the department were trained or had developed through their teaching experience.

Writers such as House (1974) have suggested that in innovative situations, where teachers are being asked to master new information and new practices, there is a high potential for stress. In this respect, the teachers at Forest not only had to master new practices, but they had to rely on these new approaches as an important measure of the success of their teaching. What was created, then, was a potentially stressful situation for the teachers. However, most of the physical education teachers already had some limited experience of classroom teaching and so had used some of these new methods. A CSE (mode 3) in Physical Education had operated in the department prior to the development of health related fitness. So they had already acquired some of the necessary skills to teach the classroom-based aspects of health related fitness. It was noticeable that some of the younger teachers who had not had the CSE experience, found the teaching more stressful than their colleagues. Certainly, they were less willing and able to deviate from the course syllabus than their more experienced counterparts, and less clear about what they were trying to achieve in their teaching. Indeed, they seemed more concerned with simply surviving[14], on mastering 'the subtle skills of getting through the school day', than achieving the course aims. Although as new but inexperienced teachers, they were in possession of up-to-date ideas and information fresh from teacher preparation courses, they were ill-prepared to be innovative in their own teaching and to teach the health related fitness course.

In general, though, the teachers at Forest School displayed a high degree of adaptability and flexibility in their teaching, particularly in their ability to change the format of their lessons in order to maintain student interest and attention, and to capitalize on incidents and comments which arose in the flow of discussions to exemplify particular ideas or concepts. Being 'cued in' to the classroom environment and to the interpersonal messages available in the teaching/learning situation, was clearly an important quality possessed by innovative teachers.

Conclusion

The teaching of health related fitness as part of the physical education curriculum is currently highly problematic. Perhaps Almond (1983) gets to the root of the problem in his claim that the physical education profession lacks a coherent rationale for teaching health related fitness in schools. The study at Forest School indicates in particular that the aspirations teachers have for teaching the health related aspects of the curriculum are not easily assimilated into conventional approaches to physical education, or into the prevailing climate in schools which is strongly influenced by public examinations. In addition, the teachers' struggles to gain recognition for their efforts are complicated by the fact that the criteria for judging the effectiveness of their teaching pulls against conventional criteria prevalent within physical education. On the one hand, the teachers at Forest were attempting to have some impact on students' values and attitudes towards health and fitness in the classroom environment, while on the other hand they were being judged publicly on their contribution to the pupils' school experience through extra curricular sport and recreation.

With current interest in health related fitness running high, a rationale which reflects criteria for effective teaching that is, in addition, coherent to a professional and lay public, is urgently needed. Otherwise, teachers will continue to be judged according to inappropriate standards.

If the idea of promoting individual health is to be anything more than rhetoric, then it has to be acknowledged, by teachers and administrators that a health related fitness based physical education curriculum is a new idea and as such must be supported with appropriate expertise and resources. Otherwise, the teaching of health and fitness in the Physical Education curriculum will remain only implicit in physical education programmes, and will continue to be regarded as a mere by-product of participation in physical activity. At a time when physical education's place on the timetable is increasingly under threat, many physical education teachers feel that they can no longer afford to only pay lip-service to the idea that physical education can play a major role in the development and maintenance of the health and fitness of children. However, without the kind of teaching qualities, including knowledge, skills, and expertise, required by innovations of this kind, we should not be surprised to find a widening divide between good intention and practice.

As we have seen, there are personal (psychological) and professional risks to teachers involved in innovation which are not inconsiderable. This will be especially true for teachers whose professional preparation has equipped them with teaching skills based on conventional methods which take the group as the basic teaching unit. These, I suggest in conclusion, involve the teaching of skills and drills within the context of sports and games and have more to do with group management, maintaining order and reinforcing routines than meeting or responding to the educational, health, and lifestyle needs of individual children.

Notes

1 In the 1933 Syllabus, Sɪʀ Gᴇᴏʀɢᴇ Nᴇᴡᴍᴀɴ claimed 'It is now recognised that an efficient system of education should encourage the concurrent development of a healthy physique, alert intelligence, and sound character. These qualities are to a high degree mutually interdependent, and it is beyond question that without healthy conditions of body, the development of mental and moral faculties is seriously retarded and in some cases precluded. In a word, healthy physical growth is essential to intellectual growth.' (Bᴏᴀʀᴅ ᴏғ Eᴅᴜᴄᴀᴛɪᴏɴ' (1933) 6)
2 Kᴀɴᴇ's (1974) study suggests that physical education teachers are most concerned with (1) the development of motor skills, and (2) the provision of leisure-time pursuits.
3 See for example, Cᴏᴏᴋ (1983, pp. 11–20), and more specifically, the Dᴇᴘᴀʀᴛᴍᴇɴᴛ ᴏғ Eᴅᴜᴄᴀᴛɪᴏɴ, (1984) Queensland, Australia publication.
4 See Pᴏʟʟᴀᴛsᴄʜᴇᴋ (1982).
5 See Dᴇᴘᴀʀᴛᴍᴇɴᴛ ᴏғ Eᴅᴜᴄᴀᴛɪᴏɴ, (1983) Physical Education Branch, Queensland, Australia.
6 The original study is reported in Kɪʀᴋ (1986). The names of the school and the teachers have been changed at their request to protect their identities.
7 This formal account, or what Sᴍɪᴛʜ and Kᴇɪᴛʜ (1971) have called the 'formal doctrine' of the innovation, consists of a number of published and unpublished documents produced by the teachers. These sources cannot be acknowledged in the normal fashion because of the need to preserve the confidentiality of the teachers involved in the original study.
8 See Hɪʀsᴛ (1974).
9 Asᴘɪɴ (1976) discusses the issue of 'knowing that' and 'knowing how' in relation to physical education.
10 The source of these 'aspirations' cannot be acknowledged in order to maintain confidentiality for the Forest School teachers.
11 See Dᴇɴsᴄᴏᴍʙᴇ (1980); and Hᴀʀʀᴇ́, (1979, 3).
12 Research indicating that professional sub-cultures do exist within teaching — like the 'PE profession' — lends support to this idea. See for example, Esʟᴀɴᴅ, pp. 83–104 in Yᴏᴜɴɢ (1971), (Ed.); and Bᴀʟʟ and Lᴀᴄᴇʏ, pp. 149–77 in Wᴏᴏᴅs (1980), (Ed.).
13 See Cᴏᴡʟᴇʏ *et al* (1981)
14 See Wᴏᴏᴅs (1979)

References

Aʟᴍᴏɴᴅ, L. (1983) 'A rationale for health related fitness in schools,' *Bulletin of Physical Education,* 19(2).
Asᴘɪɴ, D. (1976) 'Knowing how' and 'Knowing that' and 'Physical Education,' *Journal of Philosophy of Sport,* 3.
Bᴀʟʟ, S. and Lᴀᴄᴇʏ, C. (1980) 'Subject disciplines as the opportunity for group action: a measured critique of subject subcultures, in Wᴏᴏᴅs, P. (Ed.) *Teacher Strategies,* London, Croom Helm.
Bᴏᴀʀᴅ ᴏғ Eᴅᴜᴄᴀᴛɪᴏɴ/Sᴄᴏᴛᴛɪsʜ Eᴅᴜᴄᴀᴛɪᴏɴ Dᴇᴘᴀʀᴛᴍᴇɴᴛ (1903) *The Royal Commission on Physical Training,* (Scotland), HMSO.
Bᴏᴀʀᴅ ᴏғ Eᴅᴜᴄᴀᴛɪᴏɴ (1905) *Syllabus of Physical Exercises for Public Elementary Schools,* HMSO.
Bᴏᴀʀᴅ ᴏғ Eᴅᴜᴄᴀᴛɪᴏɴ (1933) *Syllabus of Physical Training for Schools,* HMSO.

COOK, S. (1983) 'A health education approach to physical education,' *Bulletin of Physical Education,* 19(2).

COWLEY, J. *et al* (Ed.) (1981) *Health Education in Schools,* London, Harper and Row.

DENSCOMBE, M. (1980) 'The work context of teaching: an analytic framework for the study of teachers in classrooms,' in *British Journal of Sociology of Education,* 1 (3), pp. 279–93

DEPARTMENT OF EDUCATION, PHYSICAL EDUCATION BRANCH, QUEENSLAND (1983) *Daily Fifteen/Thirty Physical Education, Guidelines for Primary schools,* Brisbane, Australia.

DEPARTMENT OF EDUCATION Queensland (1984) *Health and Physical Education, Guidelines for Secondary Schools, Years 8–10* Brisbane, Australia.

ESLAND, G.M. (1971) 'Teaching and learning as the organization of knowledge,' in YOUNG (Ed.) (1971) *Knowledge and Control,* London, Collier MacMillan.

HARRÉ, R. (1979) *Social Being,* Oxford, Basil Blackwell.

HAYDOCK, E. (1979) 'Catching the fat girls', *British Journal of Physical Education,* 10(5).

HENDRY, L. (1976) 'Survival in a marginal role. The professional identity of the PE teacher', in WHITEHEAD, N. and HENDRY, L. *Teaching Physical Education in England,* London, Lepus. pp. 89–102.

HIRST, P. (1974) 'The logical and psychological aspects of teaching a subject,' in *Knowledge and the Curriculum,* London, Routledge and Kegan Paul. pp. 116–31

HOUSE, E. (1974) *The Politics of Educational Innovation,* Berkeley, McCutchan.

KANE, J. (1974) *Physical Education in Secondary Schools,* Schools Council Research Studies, London, MacMillan.

KIRK, D. (1986) 'Researching the teacher's world: a case study of teacher-initiated innovation,' Unpublished PhD thesis, Loughborough University of Technology (in process).

LORTIE, D. (1975) *School Teacher: A Sociological Study,* University of Chicago Press.

POLLATSCHEK, J. (1982) 'Daily physical education. The result of the french concern,' *Bulletin of Physical Education,* 18 (2).

SMITH, L. and KEITH, P. (1971) *Anatomy of Educational Innovation: An Organizational Analysis of an Elementary School,* New York, Holt, Rinehart and Winston.

THOMAS, V. (1977) 'Physical education for life,' *British Journal of Physical Education,* 8 (4).

WOODS, P. (1979) *The Divided School,* London, Routledge and Kegan Paul.

10 Strangers and Structures in the Process of Innovation

Andrew Sparkes

This discussion is based upon a case study of teacher initiated curriculum innovation at an eleven to eighteen mixed comprehensive school of 2000 pupils on the outskirts of a large English industrial city. The fieldwork took place during the academic year 1983–4 and the methodology involved observation, unstructured and focused interviews, along with documentary analysis. The research paradigm adopted was one of naturalistic enquiry (see Lincoln and Guba, 1985) and was guided by the grounded theory approach of Glaser and Strauss (1967) and Glaser (1978).

In April 1983 Alex joined the physical education department at Branstown School as Head of Department (Scale Three). After an initial settling in period he realized that he wished to begin making changes in the curriculum and to change the philosophical direction of the department which up until his arrival had had a strong 'traditional' ethos *i.e.* a strong emphasis on team games within the curriculum, and a desire to produce 'winning' school teams. Within the department there were six other members of staff, ranging in experience from a probationer to a teacher with ten years' experience.

Innovator As Stranger

Phenomenologists propose that 'man' lives in a 'common-sense world', an 'everyday-world', which is intersubjectively experienced within what Husserl (1938) calls the 'natural attitude'. It is this common-sense world that provides the context for social action, and it is here that men come into relationships with each other and with themselves. The common everyday world is however, one that is typically taken for granted by the individuals that inhabit it, in that the structures of daily life are not always recognized or appreciated formally. Instead 'common-sense' sees and acts in the 'real' world via a set of implicit assumptions which are contained within a stock of recipe knowledge. This stock of knowledge need not be homogeneous, and it is often incoherent, only partially clear, and often contradictory. It *is* however sufficiently clear, coherent and consistent to allow those of the 'in-group' to have a reasonable chance of understanding and being understood in their world. As Schutz argues: 'It is a knowledge of trustworthy recipes for interpreting the social world and for handling things and men in order to obtain the best results in every situation with a minimum of effort by avoiding undesirable consequences' (1964, p. 95).

Such recipes are seen to act as a precept for action as well as serving as a scheme of interpretation. Hence the recipe knowledge of the staff at Branstown functioned to reduce troublesome enquiries by providing ready made recipes for action; for example, why is rugby played for the majority of time with boys in the first term? The reply being, 'in order to produce good school teams.' The half year games system with a 'top group' aids this process, it also replaces 'truth' or even approximations of it with comfortable truisms, for example, there is a large drop out from the physical education programme in the fourth and fifth years. This is rationalized and explained away by some teachers in the form of 'children today are soft and idle', which then becomes a self evident 'truth' which negates any consideration of other possible causes. They also substitute the self-explanatory for the questionable for example, with reference to the 'games for understanding' approach it is claimed 'we do that already', 'It's nothing new.'

The common-sense reality of the physical education department is the matrix within which social action occurs and within which each individual locates himself in a particular manner according to his 'biographical situation' (Schutz, 1962). The history and development of each individual is seen as unique, and this in turn affects the way in which each member of the staff at Branstown interprets what happens in their world. The 'sedimented' structure of the individual's experience is the condition for all the subsequent interpretations of all *new* events and activities, in that 'the' world is transposed into 'my' world in accordance with the relevant elements in 'my' biographical structure. As Schutz (1962) expresses it;

> . . . there is such a selection of things and aspects of things relevant to me at any given moment, whereas other things and other aspects are for the time being of no concern to me, or even out of view. All this is biographically determined, that is, the actor's actual situation has its history, it is the sedimentation of all his previous subjective experiences. They are not experienced by the actor as being anonymous, but as unique and subjectively given to him and to him alone. (p. 77)

Whilst each member of the department located themselves by their own biographical situation, it is on Alex that we will focus, since there are elements of his biography that place him in the position of the 'stranger'. '. . . the term "stranger" shall mean an adult individual of our times and civilization who tries to be permanently accepted or at least tolerated by the group which he approaches' (Schutz, 1964, p. 89).

Ethnographers along with social and cultural anthropologists have utilized the 'stranger' perspective to argue that the common sense and theoretical knowledge of the researcher should be suspended during the research act in order to minimize the dangers of taking on trust their own, perhaps misleading conceptions, about a given social setting, or of replacing those of the actors within it. By making the culture 'anthropologically strange' it is hoped to make explicit the assumptions that the actor takes for granted as a cultural member, as the ordinary becomes strange and the taken for granted becomes problematic. It is proposed that the researcher as 'stranger' acquires an objectivity not available to those within the culture and by using this induced 'intellectual marginality' the researcher can attempt to construct an account of the culture that is 'external' and 'independent' of the researcher.

In attempting to be like the stranger in an alien culture, there is often a sense of estrangement known as a 'culture shock', of which the description by Chagnon (1977) of his reactions as a Westerner coming into contact with the exotic culture of the Yanomamo, is a good example. Whilst it is not being claimed that the physical education department at Branstown is an 'exotic' culture, it is of course unique in terms of its location in time and space. Despite many similarities with other physical education departments there were differences which had come to be taken for granted by those who were there and only became 'problematic' when Alex, the stranger, arrived and questioned their way of doing things, which in turn questioned their implicit assumptions concerning their view of physical education within the department.

Besides coming from the 'outside', from another school and area, there were other aspects of Alex's biography which made him a stranger in this new context. The fact that he had experience of teaching at another school was important since within a department of seven only Monica (Head of Girls) had taught elsewhere, everyone else had started at Branstown as probationers and had remained. Alex like the rest in the department had attended a 'specialist' physical education college, which although it had a traditional outlook in terms of producing high quality teams, also had a very strong gymnastics bias, an area where Pete and Chris the other men in the department lacked experience and confidence. At his previous school Alex had been encouraged by his female Head of Department to attend a great many courses and to meet as often as possible with other physical education teachers and advisors. She herself constantly made him question his own values and attitudes towards his subject, hence during his five year period there he was subjected to a large input of diverse perspectives. This orientated him away from the traditional approach of his training college and led to a clarification for him of his educational philosophy. This Alex regards as child–centred, egalitarian and individualistic, with a scepticism concerning the 'traditional elitist' (his words) approach to physical education which he sees as failing to meet the needs of children or cater for *all* children.

Previous to Alex's arrival, Harry the Head of Physical Education had run a strong traditional department, with a heavy emphasis within the curriculum on the major team games. There were high standards of dress and discipline with the children and a great deal of the department's energies, particularly on the boys' side, was geared towards the production of school teams, for which they had gained a reputation in the area for their strength in rugby, football and cricket. This in fact had been the climate in the department since the school had become a comprehensive in the 1960s. Harry had come to Branstown as a probationer, gone up through the ranks and took charge when his Head of Department became a Head of Year *at* Branstown. Harry recruited those with similar backgrounds to himself, hence within the department there was an air of consensus concerning the direction and aims of physical education. In a sense, in terms of development the department had begun to ossify since there was no input of new ideas and little, if any, questioning of their physical education programme, the activities offered, and the rationales which under-pinned them.

On arriving Alex implicitly adopted a 'stranger' role in that he initially set himself a time schedule of one year to look at the department, in order to see what was 'good' and 'bad' about it before deciding if any changes needed to be made. During the Summer term that Alex took over he noticed little difference between Branstown and his previous school since both were involved in athletics and cricket during this period. He felt at home in this 'typical' summer programme. However, even then as a stranger he noticed that cricket dominated the time allocation, and that all individuals were not being catered for in athletics. When Alex had to organize the next year's timetable, he experienced what can only be described as a 'culture shock'. It was at this point he realized that the Autumn and Spring terms were dominated by the major team games at the expense of individual activities such as gymnastics, particularly on the boys' side. That the boys at Branstown spend up to eighty per cent of their time in the Autumn term playing Rugby, was simply taken for granted. However to Alex it was highly problematic.

As a stranger Alex was able to notice aspects of the curriculum which remained unquestioned by the others in the department. His 'culture shock' was linked to his awareness of his own (a) 'ideal' curriculum — in which there would be a total expression of his educational philosophy; (b) his previous school curriculum — which allowed a great deal of expression to his educational philosophy; and (c) the present Branstown curriculum — which he saw as elitist, and team orientated, denying expression of his educational philosophy. Of course Alex had a knowledge of (a), (b), and (c) with which to frame the present, whilst others in the department except Monica, (who had also taught in another school), only had (a) and (c). Interviews with Monica indicated that her views were similar to those of the rest of the staff.

Within the curriculum at Branstown on his arrival, Alex could not find self-expression. Woods (1985) has considered the extent to which a teacher finds self-expression within the curriculum, and how far the 'subject' as practiced in the classrooms is a realization of the individual teacher's self. He proposes that the self interacts with the prevailing social circumstances, sometimes borrowing from them, at other times contributing, and it is this dialectical interplay which prevails between teachers and subject specialisms. Therefore just as teachers 'make' rather than 'take' roles (Turner, 1962), so they make the curriculum.

> ... a curriculum area is a vibrant, human process lived out in the rough and tumble, give and take, joys and despairs, plots and counter plots of a teacher's life. It is not simply a result of group activity (Goodson 1983). Tom's case shows that to some extent at least, individuals can and do chart their own courses, and can engage with the curriculum at a deep personal level. (Woods, 1985, p. 260)

As an outsider coming in, Alex not only questioned and made problematic some areas of the taken for granted world at Branstown, but also, since this present state prevented him from expressing his self via the curriculum, he 'decided' that some form of change must occur. This initial change was to try and change the balance of the curriculum to bring in more individual activities, for example gymnastics and swimming. The situation may well have been very different if Alex had come from a traditional department into Branstown and found that he could find self expression within the existing curriculum.

Alex questioned his colleagues' practices, their organization of the curriculum, along with other matters for example, the high drop out rate in the fourth and fifth years, the time consuming administration with half year games, the amount of repetition in lessons of work already covered, and finally the inability of the department to argue the case for the inclusion of physical education on the school curriculum. All this created for members of the department areas of tension and uncertainty which they had not previously experienced. Their 'thinking as usual' or as Max Scheler (1962) called it 'the relatively natural conception of the world' was fragmented by the issues raised by Alex. Since their recipe knowledge could not answer away Alex's objections, for many in the department, a 'crisis' of varying intensity occurred. As W.I. Thomas notes a crisis; 'interrupts the flow of habit and gives rise to changed conditions of consciousness and practice.' (Schutz, 1964, p. 96). In such situations, as Schutz (1964) indicates; 'The cultural pattern no longer functions as a system of tested recipes at hand; it reveals that its applicability is restricted to a specific historical situation.' (p. 96).

The fragmenting of 'thinking as usual' is a major contribution of the stranger to the innovation process, in that it challenges people to question the taken for granted. As the term progressed however, Monica, the Head of Girls, also became in part a 'stranger' due to her attendance on several courses and her contact with Alex. Monica had attended a prestigious all women's physical education college, and spent four years in her first school which she described as 'an all girl grammar school, very traditional, with strong discipline'. Having arrived at Branstown three years ago Monica felt comfortable in the traditional department run by Harry. The arrival of Alex raised questions for her which were for the most part beyond her framework, and as Alex comments, 'early on, without wanting to be rude, most of what I was trying to say was over her head.'

It was in the summer holiday after Alex's arrival that Monica went on a curriculum course at Leeds. Here she was inundated with contrasting perspectives concerning the nature of physical education. 'It got me thinking, it got me worried because I was so out of touch. It got me thinking about different ways of teaching things, although I didn't really start properly until I'd been to Cheltenham.' (Interview transcript.) This exposure began a 'crisis' for Monica that was to take two and a half years to resolve. The Leeds course led to an expansion in her perspectives and to her questioning the taken for granted world of the department at Branstown. The questioning caused her to feel uneasy about her own teaching and the curriculum offered, it also allowed her to move closer to Alex's framework and support his idea for change. Following Leeds, Monica went on another course at Cheltenham during the Spring term. This was for a whole term, one day per week. Here again she was exposed to diverse perspectives (particularly the games for understanding approach) and made to question her own practice. The course here also consolidated many of the ideas put forward at Leeds, and presented them in a practical manner, which helped Monica clarify her thinking. After Cheltenham Monica still did not feel confident to pass on her ideas until she had tested them in the 'real' world and it is only now, two and a half years later, that she feels conversant and confident enough to try to change the practice of the others in her department in a significant way.

Structural Change and Conflict

During the case study of Branstown a number of significant phases relating to the process of innovation began to emerge. The first phase was that of 'Orientation'. Alex as a newcomer or 'stranger' in the taken for granted world of this well established department slowly recognized that there was a need for change in the curriculum. This need was not fixed on entry but arose gradually during the process of his orientation to the teachers within his department and school. Initially Alex was concerned with 'pulling the department together', since he was aware of conflicts arising previously between one of the males in the department and Harry, and there were other strong characters within the department with their own points of view and ways of doing things. As Alex says 'I found it a very difficult department to pull together to discuss things, and offer opinions of what they are doing and how they think other people should do things.' (Interview transcript.) To assist in pulling the department together Alex covered the physical education detentions held one day a week, releasing the other staff from this tiresome duty. He also reorganized the fifth form activities which reduced pressure on staff during these periods, plus he made each member of the department aware of his/her responsibilities for certain activities. Departmental meetings were held one lunchtime every week, where Alex aired his views and opinions and encouraged the others to do likewise in an attempt to create an 'open' atmosphere in the department.

During this orientation period Alex's main task was to facilitate social interaction and to open up communication within the department, and as a consequence he did not probe at a deeper level the underlying educational philosophies of those involved. As he came to realize that his own philosophy of teaching was in direct conflict with the existing physical education curriculum Alex started to intimate via departmental meetings and casual conversations during the school day that there may possibly be a need for changes to be made in the future. However, the ideas that were voiced by Alex appeared to have little impact on the staff within his department. They appeared to be unaware and unable to conceptualize or relate to the different ideas which focused on a contrasting teaching philosophy. Three months after Alex's arrival Pete, for example, still saw the energies of the department being channelled into school teams;

> 'There is so much potential for PE in this place. I mean with the facilities we've got, Christ Almighty, we should be brilliant at everything ... We should have some bloody good teams in swimming, we should do men's hockey, we have got men on the staff who can play, they should be able to take it. We should have lads' tennis teams, which we haven't got.' (Interview Transcript.)

In the same period another teacher Chris also seemed unaware of Alex's views

> '... whereas here if you look at the schemes of work and the curriculum that's in there. It says third year basketball, badminton, hockey or whatever, and whoever's taking them does what they want to do with them I think ... I don't know if Alex is going to do anything extra on that. I don't know if he'd want to to some extent.' (Interview Transcript.)

During this phase it became clear that the members of the department were orientating themselves to Alex the Head of Department as a 'person', on a 'getting to know him' basis within the framework of the department as created by the previous Head of Department, Harry. This initial orientation phase meant that the staff did not probe at a deeper level the underlying educational philosophy of their new Head of Department or consider the implication of his tentative proposals for change.

Slowly, Phase Two, the 'Dawning' phase began to emerge. Members of the department had become orientated to the newcomer and were now starting to pick up on various cues which made them aware that a different teaching 'reality' was being proposed by Alex, that Alex was not happy with things as they were and wanted to change things. As Jamie the youngest male in the department points out in this phase;

> 'I must admit I admire Alex as a Head of Department. I think he is going to make changes, and I think they will be good changes.' (Interview Transcript.)

The 'Dawning' phase was relatively brief and led quickly into phase three, the 'Ambiguity' phase. This was characterized by a great deal of fuzziness and lack of clarity in terms of how the physical education staff attempted to interpret the incoming ideas which were being expounded by Alex in the departmental meetings and during informal conversations; they were having problems fitting Alex's views into their own cognitive framework.

Once individuals attempted to bring these unclear and ambiguous ideas into their own existing conceptual framework, a fourth phase, that of 'Translation' began to emerge. Distortion and intellectual manipulation were characteristics of this phase as novel ideas were processed and slotted into the dominant educational philosophy of each individual. This often led to the perception of 'change as no change', that is, there is nothing really new or different in what's being proposed. Peter comments on the 'games for understanding' approach, which was central to Alex's and now Monica's philosophy.

> 'You see this "teaching through understanding", it's been suggested that it's the new way of teaching. That's how Monica and Alex approach it, as a new way of teaching. But in fact it's not new at all. I've been talking to Philip (Head of Department before Alex and Harry), and they tried to bring it in twenty years ago, and it got pushed back out again. So all these ideas, none of them are new, they are just called different names, and they just go in and out of fashion as the decades change.' (Interview Transcript.)

By such manipulations there is less need for the individual to question their present practices and the taken for granted world once again become unproblematic and tension is reduced. It was not until a definite structural change in the curriculum was proposed that phase five, 'Conflict' emerged most dramatically, since this proposal produced a direct clash of the educational philosophies of those within the department. This phase was characterized by a form of conflict that was more concrete in its nature and therefore the resolution of this conflict became of paramount importance. It was more serious than the abstract conflict that had been quietly sedimenting to a greater or lesser degree in the earlier phases.

This 'overt' form of conflict became more evident at two departmental meetings at the end of the second summer term that Alex had been at Branstown. Here the thrust of the meeting for him was to get the department to agree to a change from a half year system (which was 'streamed' by having a 'top group' made up of the team players and the very able), to one where the children were taught in their tutor groups for all their physical education lessons *i.e.* a mixed ability grouping. This structural change with its obvious potential for affecting the way in which teachers teach, forced a realization and clarification in terms of relating to the implications of the change, and the risks inherent in the innovation. Any proposed change was assessed by the staff in terms of its positive or negative value for their own approach to teaching, for example, for some lack of contact with talented pupils and reducing the standards of school teams was classed as being of negative value, whilst increased contact with fewer pupils and reduction in competition were seen as of positive value by others. These structural changes involved personal 'risks' and direct conflict between teachers began to manifest itself.

In a study by Almond (1983) on the teaching of games, the structural change which brought about conflict was the point where teachers were asked to teach a particular unit of work, which required a different form of teaching to that which they were used to. Conflict became manifest as the teachers considered the risk value involved in changing their teaching style, which was forced upon them by the structural change. In both studies the structural change as part of the innovating process was crucial in making the innovation 'come alive'. It was this which began to create the notion that change could be a reality in the minds of those involved.

Policy Implications

The Branstown study has clearly emphasized the 'stranger' is more likely to raise questions concerning the taken for granted world of a department. These questions in turn start to fragment reality for those who may have become ossified in their thinking and leads to a crisis which needs to be solved by them. Indeed one might well argue that if a department is to affect changes in its practices then the innovator has to somehow produce the perspective of the 'stranger' for each individual in the department. Outside courses may help to achieve this since the individual is exposed to the ideas of other practising teachers, lecturers and advisors. This in itself may often be enough to initiate an expansion of consciousness and a fragmenting of a teacher's ossified world. The outside course also has the advantage of reducing the insecurity and threat factor caused by a member of one's own department questioning one's practice. Clearly the innovator as part of an overall strategy needs to be aware of the benefits of sending the members of his or her department on selected courses *before* he or she starts the process of instigating changes within their own department, since at least they will be aware of other perspectives and may possibly begin to integrate some of these into their own world views.

Having disrupted the everyday world and created a 'crisis' for the individual the innovative stranger has to then provide a framework within which the individual can feel safe and secure to adopt new ideas, and to clarify areas of confusion. This process cannot be rushed as each individual reacts to the crisis in their own way and in their own time, for example, Monica took two and a half years to adjust. Therefore without understanding and patience and a great deal of support (in the form of time and space to think) the resulting changes, if they occur, are likely to be only cosmetic.

Documentation is also an important feature of innovation. Unless teachers document their work, particularly in its early stages, then the innovation may be in danger of being left as an ambiguous idea in the minds of the staff involved. This can lead to and exacerbate conflict and antagonisms between teachers.

Furthermore, innovation requires a clear direction to be aimed at and there needs to be a structure to produce this change. Structural conditions for example, reduction in size of games groups, mixed classes etc., are crucial in influencing the way in which teachers teach, and need to be manipulated in order that the contextual conditions for teaching are changed. But once structural change is initiated or proposed there is likely to be conflict between the differing conceptualizations of the innovation and the various educational philosophies of the individuals involved. This then requires a departmental climate in which conflict can be resolved openly, where teachers can develop confidence, plus competence and feel in control of the new ideas. This is only likely to be achieved if the innovator tries to become aware of the underlying educational philosophies of those within his/her department as well as the potential risk factors involved for those who have to work with the innovation.

References

ALMOND, L. (1983) 'Teaching games through action research,' International AIESEP Conference, Teaching Team Sports, Rome.

BERGER, P.L. and LUCKMANN, T. (1971) *The Social Construction of Reality*, Harmondsworth, Penguin.

BLUMER, H. (1966) 'Sociological implications of the thought of G.H. Mead' *American Journal of Sociology*, 71, March, pp. 535–44.

CHAGNON, N.A. (1977) *Yanomamo. The Fierce People*, (2nd Ed.) New York, Holt, Reinhart and Winston.

GLASER, B.G. (1978) *Theoretical Sensitivity — Advances in the Methodology of Grounded Theory*, The Sociology Press, POB 143, Mill Valley, California 94941.

GLASER, B.G. and STRAUSS, A.L. (1967) *The Discovery of Grounded Theory — Strategies for Qualitative Research*, New York, Aldine Publishing Company.

GOODSON, I.F. (1983) *School Subjects and Curriculum Change*, London, Croom Helm.

HUSSERL, E. (1970) *The Crisis of European Sciences and Transcendental Phenomenology: An Introduction to Phenomenological Philosophy*, (Trans. DAVID CARR) Evanston, Illinois, North Western University Press, (Originally published 1938).

LINCOLN, Y.S. and GUBA, E.G. (1985) *Naturalistic Inquiry*, Sage Publications.

MEAD, G.H. (1934) *Mind, Self and Society*, Chicago, Illinois, University of Chicago.

SCHELER, M. (1926) in BECKER, H. and DAHLEE, H.O. (1942) 'Max Scheler's sociology of knowledge', *Philosophy and Phenomenological Research*, Vol. II, pp. 310–22.

SCHUTZ, A. (1962) *Collected Papers, Volume I* The Hague, Martinus Nijhoff.

SCHUTZ, A. (1964) *Collected Papers, Volume 2*, The Hague, Martinus Nijhoff.

SPARKES, A.C. (1986) 'The genesis of teacher initiated curriculum innovation' PhD dissertation in progress, Loughborough University of Technology, Loughborough, Leics.

TURNER, R.H. (1962) 'Role-taking: process versus conformity', in ROSE. A.M. (Ed.) *Human Behaviour and Social Processes*, London, Routledge and Kegan Paul.

WOODS, P. (1985) 'Teacher self and curriculum' in GOODSON, I.F. and BALL, S. (Eds.) *Defining the Curriculum*, Lewes, The Falmer Press.

11 'Learning for a Change': A Study of Gender and Schooling in Outdoor Education

Barbara Humberstone

'I think girls are as good . . . if you've been rock climbing before then it's OK for you, but girls and boys that haven't been rock climbing before must feel the same way, they can't feel differently can they? I think we are as good as the boys and they are as good as us.' (Debbie.)

The processes through which boys and girls come to believe that certain subjects are inappropriate for one or other sex, and girls in particular perceive themselves as unable or unwilling to participate in 'masculine' (often high status) activities, are complex indeed. At the most obvious level, within schools, divisions between boys and girls can be formally implemented through separate curricula. This practice (as Sheila Scraton argues in chapter 4) has conventionally featured in the physical education curriculum in secondary schools and may well have helped reinforce media (and family) representations of the exclusivity of sport to one or other sex and the superiority of male over female (Clarke and Clarke, 1983; Willis and Critcher, 1975). A policy of co-education in physical education has however, recently been initiated in a number of schools, in some cases because of practical exigencies, falling rolls etc., in others in an attempt to provide equal opportunities for both boys and girls (Bayliss, 1984; Duncan, 1985; Lopez, 1985;). However, studies have highlighted how, even within co-educational classrooms, boys and girls can come to think of girls as having 'different' abilities and inferior status in relation to boys. Wolpe (1977), Stanworth (1983) and Davies (1979) describe the ways in which the sex of the pupil influences the manner in which teachers relate to them. Not only do girls receive less of the teacher's time and attention in class, but also they generally experience different, less favourable treatment during those encounters. Teachers may thus assist in the formation of pupils' images of themselves and each other. This pattern of interaction often arises because boys tend to present teachers with their most serious problems of discipline and control (Sarah *et al*, 1980).

Teachers focus their attention upon boys' interests and needs (Scott, 1980, Lee, 1980) in order to maintain control and thereby provide instruction. As a result they may find themselves unable (rather than unwilling) to divide their time equally amongst male and female pupils. However, the patterns of interaction and different non-verbal and verbal cues, within the classroom, do not by themselves create particular pupil self images (or identities), rather it is the *interpretations* which pupils make of them which are paramount. We are, however, a long way from understanding how particular meanings are accomplished for different pupils within either the academic or PE 'classroom'. Nor do we know much about how situational features of a learning context (such as the organization of time and physical resource) when mediated by teachers, structure and shape the thinking and action of boys and girls (Denscombe, 1980a, Evans, 1985). It is these processes, in relation to co-educational practice within Shotmoor, an outdoor pursuits centre, which I wish to explore in this paper.

The discussion will focus on the teaching of climbing, the dilemmas which teachers experience in this setting and how they face them in lessons. I will show that features of this situation allow, and even demand that teachers give equal if not more attention to girls than boys. I will also examine the implicit and explicit messages received by the pupils and suggest that teaching at Shotmoor brings about a shift in pupils' understanding of what constitutes gender appropriate behaviour and gender related capabilities. Finally I will discuss these issues in relation to the practice and organization of the school physical education curriculum.

The discussion draws upon data which were collected during a ten weeks period of ethnographic research at Shotmoor, the focus of which was upon teaching and learning within outdoor activities curricula.[1] Each week one or more secondary schools sent from ten to sixty pupils to the centre. These were then usually organized into intra-school classes of between seven to ten pupils. Each week I identified one of these class groups and followed the pupils throughout their stay. These case study pupils were also informally interviewed and their accounts tape-recorded. Generally, these interviews took the form of small group discussions and consisted, usually, of same sex friendship pairs or groups.[2] Teachers' and pupils' views were also collected during the normal course of conversation.[3] Although in this discussion I will focus upon observations of two of these case study groups within two climbing lessons and the perspectives of the teachers and some of the pupils in them, the discussion will also draw upon the perspectives of many other pupils who visited Shotmoor during the period of research.

The Climbing Area

Physical features of any educational setting can shape the experience and actions of both teachers and pupils (Denscombe, 1980a; Pollard, 1980). Within the large undercover climbing area where a number of artificial climbing walls were located, the pupils could move freely over an unrestricted floor space with minimal teacher interference. Here, the teachers and pupils were highly visible to outsiders who could enter and leave the area to watch the activity largely without restriction. There was a degree of 'ecological open-ness' about the setting which might readily be found in games, PE and art lessons, and in some cases in 'progressive' primary or 'academic' innovatory secondary classrooms in mainstream schools.[4] The personal appearances of individuals at Shotmoor also presented a very different picture from that usually apparent in mainstream schools. Since both pupils and teachers tended to dress in either tracksuits or jeans, girls were frequently indistinguishable from boys and often, particularly when wearing climbing helmets, teachers from pupils. We have then, a situation in which, at least at the surface level of appearances, and to the adult observer, differences between boys and girls appeared to be obscured. As Margrain (1983) points out, sex related differences in dress at school are a possible source of discrimination, which may encourage teachers and pupils to perceive and treat boys and girls differently. At Shotmoor, not only were pupils less discernible in gender terms, but also the authority and status of teachers was less obvious than in schools. Evidence of this is presented later in the discussion. Here, Helen, one of the pupils points to the 'change' in her school teacher.

> 'She's just so different, she seems more our age here ... We were quite dreading coming... but she's really nice now, really different. I think she wants to see us enjoying ourselves ... I think it pleases her to see us doing different things'. (Helen)

The Shotmoor teachers also tended to encourage the development of informal relationships between themselves and pupils by introducing them-selves by their first names and generally expecting the pupils to use this form of address. The school teachers accompanying their pupils, often chose to participate and work alongside them. Although continuing to be called by their formal title, they appeared to be sharing in the pupils' new learning experience, as this comment suggests. 'Well, I suppose we are learning as well 'cause we want to help the kids and reinforce what is being taught to them. We aren't in charge ... The kids like you to do it, they think you bottle out if you don't' (Female school teacher).

A further integration between teachers and pupils occurred during breaktimes, when teachers and pupils came together in the same room for their drinks; an event which at least gave the appearance that privileges were being shared.

On the surface then, in terms of physical appearances and social relationships, there appeared to be a greater degree of informality than is generally found in mainstream schooling and indeed, judging by the pupils' comments, in many of the schools which they attended. However, it could not be assumed that changes in these surface features of interaction necessarily signified changes in the deep structures of communication between teachers and pupils and amongst pupils. Messages about what constitutes appropriate behaviour for girls and boys and those which contribute towards individual pupils' self concept, may be little different from those conveyed in school.

A wide variety of influences act within and on classrooms to create conflicting demands upon teachers (Berlak and Berlak, 1981). Tickle (1984) discusses the different ways art and craft teachers respond to the dilemmas present in their subject. In his study, the dilemma teachers faced was how to impose basic skills, while granting children freedom to make decisions. The particular dilemma for teachers at Shotmoor was how to ensure that pupils had acquired sufficient basic skills to enable them to cope safely with a task while, at the same time, giving individual pupils responsibility for, and control over decisions to accept a challenge. Shotmoor teachers handled this problem in a variety of ways, influenced not only by their personal assumptions about teaching and pupils but also by features of the organization in which they work.

One teacher, Eddy, for example, suggested that any teacher involved in teaching 'adventure' education responded to this dilemma according to their perceptions of their own and the pupil's capabilities and that this had implications for the manner in which they encounter pupils.

> 'Some staff are more concerned with the skill side as an end in itself. Some, with ... a more formal approach do this. They don't feel confident in themselves ... they feel that if they relaxed they may lose control. A member of staff in an outdoor pursuits situation should always be in control ... because of the safety aspect.' (Eddy.)

Most of the Shotmoor teachers observed however, laid emphasis upon the pupils' responsibility and upon their control over their own actions. Inevitably, in this context, the teacher's concern is directed towards the physical well-being of the pupils. Nevertheless, the motivations of teachers are more complex than this, as we see below, when we examine in greater detail the perspectives and actions of Doug and Eddy, two teachers who were responsible for teaching climbing to the case study class groups one and two. These case study groups came from a different school and consisted of ten and nine pupils whose average ages were fifteen years and one month and fourteen years three months respectively.

Both Eddy and Doug considered all pupils capable of achieving success in their lessons. In their view, it was fear alone which acted as a limit upon pupils' progress. This fear, either of hurting themselves or making a fool of themselves, Eddy perceived was a result of pupils' lack of confidence. Both he and Doug believed that helping pupils to overcome their nervousness was an important part of the teacher's task. However, Doug maintained it is 'mental attitude' rather than strength which inhibits pupils, particularly girls, participating in certain activities. He believed that girls are lacking in some way and so tended to 'treat them differently' because he suggested 'girls are different, they are not able to do some things'. In contrast, Eddy feels that boys and girls have similar talents and potential, as we see in this following interaction, in which he challenges a pupil's conception of gender appropriate behaviour.

> Pupil (boy): 'What will the girls be doing when the boys are climbing and skiing?'
>
> Eddy: 'I expect they will be leading you up the climbing wall and down the ski slope.'

In climbing lessons, both boys and girls were exposed to and experienced varying degrees of risk. However Eddy and Doug helped pupils to overcome their fear rather differently and the following accounts focus attention upon how they deal with pupils during the 'frightening' activity of abseiling.[5]

Both teachers considered that talking with individual pupils was an important influence on the ways in which pupils responded and participated in the lesson's activity. However, Doug, unlike Eddy, assumed responsibility for getting pupils to overcome their fear, 'If I had more time, I could talk to them . . . I gently push them because they think they cannot do it but once they are over the edge they think they have succeeded.' (Doug.) Eddy's approach was somewhat different.

> '. . . Abseiling, it's a large physical and psychological step . . to launch themselves off . . . If they are really, I mean really screwed up about it . . . I say . . . walk back again. Far better that they do that, than go down out of control, screaming their heads off, thereby losing more status with their peers.' (Eddy.)

Eddy assumed that the pupils should be in control and that they should take the decision when to carry out the activity. For him interpersonal relations between pupils were an important source of support and orientation for pupils. A point which he emphasized in this comment.

> 'Getting them to help each other, understand each other's problems . . . through trying to improve their skills, you try to foster a group awareness, develop their self confidence. Improving their skills is only a vehicle . . . if their skills improve their self confidence improves. Also by talking to them and encouraging them to talk to you, discussing the situation, again, will develop their self confidence.' (Eddy.)

The views of Doug and Eddy were not untypical of those expressed by most other teachers at Shotmoor. The syllabus was seen merely as a vehicle through which teachers enabled pupils to realize their potential and to experience achievement (see Humberstone, 1985). Indeed, the views expressed by teachers at Shotmoor were not unlike those often heard in the 'progressive' child-centred rhetoric of primary schooling and more recently promulgated in life skills programmes.[6] However, the connections between a teacher's philosophy and his or her classroom practice is often quite problematic. There can be a strong contrast between a teacher's child–centred progressive doctrine and the realities of both academic and PE classrooms.[7] Teachers can be constrained by a variety of factors, such as pupil numbers, material resources and the expectations of the school, colleagues and pupils' parents. These factors can influence the ways teachers go about organizing, managing and controlling their classrooms.

The discussion below is concerned, for the most part, with the introductory climbing lesson which Eddy and Doug taught on day one of the pupils visit to Shotmoor. It explores the nature of the constraints within which these teachers worked and how they practically accomplished their lessons with the pupils of class groups one and two. These practices were adopted by other teachers and could be observed on days one through to five. A marked similarity was also portrayed in the interaction patterns displayed by the majority of teachers and by the same teacher at different times.

The Organization of Lesson One of the Climbing Syllabus

Table 1 gives some indication of the way in which Eddy and Doug organized their lessons. The content of each phase of the lesson is represented in the left hand column and the amount of time, in minutes, each teacher gives to each phase is indicated in the column below that particular teacher. The timetabled time for each lesson was seventy-five minutes. However, within limits, teachers could and tended to use more or less of this time, depending upon their interpretation of the needs of pupils and the progress of the lesson.[8]

Table 1. The Organization and Use of Time by Teachers Eddy and Doug in Lesson 1 of the Climbing Syllabus with the pupils of Class Groups 1 and 2 respectively

Temporal structure and lesson content	Doug	Eddy
Phase	*Time, in minutes*	
1 Introduction to equipment	20	19
2 Practice climbing on small wall	4	–
3 Explaining and demonstrating climbing and belaying	12	15
4 Organization of pupils into pairs	2	3
5 Climbing in pairs	37	32
Time for phases 1 to 4	38	37
Total time	75	69

Revealed in Table 1 are a number of similarities and differences in the ways in which each teacher organized his lesson. The common syllabus followed by these teachers tended to impose limits upon what was to be taught. As a result, in terms of the formal curriculum content which teachers convey during each phase, and in the sequencing of these phases, teaching appeared to achieve a marked degree of similarity. Lessons tended to progress through the following phases:

Initially we have an introduction, phase 1, then generally a short phase 2, in which pupils practiced climbing on a low wall. Phase 3 was concerned with teaching skills of belaying and climbing. During phase 4 the pupils chose a partner with whom they wished to climb and in phase 5 the pupil pairs worked together climbing different walls. Although in phase 1 to 4 there was some interaction between boys and girls, in phase 5 pupils tended to work in single sex pairs. However, as the week progressed interactions between boys and girls became more common and prominent and the kind of grouping patterns displayed in these 'first' climbing lessons (described in Tables 2a and 2b) were rarely in evidence.

The syllabus also imposed constraints on the teachers' choice of teaching method. Both Eddy and Doug, like all the other Shotmoor teachers organized their teaching on a whole class basis during phases 1 to 4. This method of teaching, conventionally found within mainstream schools is not generally associated with a 'progressive' child centred teaching approach. At Shotmoor, however, it was adopted because of the pressures of time. Class teaching was assumed to be the most effective way of making available the basic skills and knowledge of climbing to all the pupils in the limited time available.

> 'One thing I've learnt (here) is that unless you're prepared to keep repeating yourself, you get them (the pupils) all together and quiet, and get the message over in one go. That way you spend less time giving instructions and they spend more time climbing.' (Eddy)

However, in the latter part of the lesson (phase 4 and 5), each pupils was placed in a situation in which, whilst working in pairs, he or she was relied upon to preserve their own and their partner's safety. They were expected to work largely independently of the teacher and they were given a great deal of control over the activity.

Teacher-Pupil Interaction During Phase 5, the Climbing Phase in the Lessons of Doug and Eddy Described in Table 1

In this phase pupils were climbing various walls. Attached to a rope, which ran through a Karabiner fixed at the top of the wall, was the pupil who was climbing. His/her partner was fixed to the ground by a short tape and this pupil controlled the other end of the rope. The belayer, as the latter person was called, concentrated intently on his/her partner, and was ready to hold him/her with the rope should he/she slip. The teacher moved rapidly around the class interacting with individual pupils, since the nature of the syllabus and its obvious potential for accidents required the teacher to continually monitor and assess individual pupil's progress. We see this highlighted in the following comment, in which Eddy likened his teaching, in this phase of the lesson, to the actions of a juggler who is 'trying to keep ten plates spinning on the top of poles'. He continued the comparison, 'You've got to keep an eye on all of them. You get to know who are likely to be the wobbly ones.'

It was this consideration for the safety of pupils, combined with Eddy and Doug's teaching philosophy which created considerable activity and busyness within their classes, as we see from Tables 2a and 2b. These tables show the incidence and distribution of interactions between Doug and Eddy and their pupils during 37 minute and 32 minute climbing phases respectively, of their lesson.

Table 2a. The Incidence and Distribution of Interactions in a 37-Minute Climbing Phase of One Climbing Lesson taught by Doug To Class Group 1

	Pair Composition	Number of teacher/pupil interactions
Pair 1	2 girls (Nicky and Tracey)	8
Pair 2	1 boy/girl (Dick and Glynis)	8
Pair 3	2 boys (Trevor and Ian)	8
Pair 4	2 boys (Keith and Stuart)	6
Pair 5	2 girls (Jackie and Debbie)	9
TOTAL	10	39

Table 2b. The Incidence and Distribution of Interactions in a 32-Minute Climbing Phase of One Climbing Lesson taught by Eddy to Class Group 2

	Pair Composition	Number of teacher/pupil interactions
Pair A	2 girls (Emma and Lyn)	13
Pair B	2 girls (Sue and Pat)	10
Pair C	1 boy/school teacher (Sam and Mr. Kip)	4
Pair D	2 boys (Tony and Clint)	7
Pair E	2 boys (Paul and Peter)	9
TOTAL	10	43

Each interaction recorded in the tables, represents a complete encounter between the teacher and a pupil of verbal and/or non-verbal type as adjudged by the researcher.[9] The majority of both teachers' interactions, although not evident from the table, were with individual pupils at a 'private' level, either with the belayer or the climber, rather than with the two pupils together. As we see from these tables, both teachers interacted frequently with all the pupils in the class. However, a significant feature of these interaction patterns is the way in which each teacher distributed his attention amongst the boys and girls. Tables 2a and 2b show that although there are differences between Doug and Eddy in their patterns of interaction, both teachers allocated their time marginally in favour of the girls. This contrasts markedly with the interaction pattern typically found in studies of mainstream academic mixed classrooms.[10]

All these studies reveal that boys receive more of the teacher's attention, in the form of instruction, praise and punishment, than do girls. In the climbing lessons described (as in many other lessons observed at Shotmoor), girls received equal if not more of the teacher's time than boys. Girls at Shotmoor, then, unlike in schools, were not peripheral to the central focus of classroom life; they were brought more actively into the learning experience. This pattern of interaction, as we see, has important consequences for the ways in which individual pupils perceived themselves, each other and their teachers.

How, then, is this interaction pattern to be explained? Shotmoor teachers could be no less sexist in their attitudes than teachers in mainstream schools. On comparing Tables 2a and 2b, we see that Doug distributed his attention more equally amongst the pupils than Eddy. The two boys of pair 4 in Doug's lesson, encountered him least frequently. Data from interviews, completed questionnaires, and observation of these boys in other lessons suggest they were highly committed to involvement in both school work and activities and to sport. These two pupils appeared self-motivated and as such Doug assessed them as confident and able to cope safely and independently with the skills of climbing. Similarly, in Eddy's lesson it is pair C, comprizing a male school teacher working with a boy, who received the least amount of teacher attention. Eddy, like Doug, expected the school teacher to have acquired the necessary skills and confidence to work safely and independently in this situation. As a result, he had more time available to spend amongst the remaining pairs, and he appears to have favoured the two girls' groups. Completed questionnaires from all the pupils in both lessons reveal that, with the exception of one girl in Eddy's class and one girl in Doug's class, pupils experienced climbing as the most frightening activity of the week. It is because Doug and Eddy adhered to a philosophy which placed the pupil central in the learning process and in which the pupils' interest is considered to be the primary motivation, that they concentrated their attention on those pupils who lacked confidence and therefore required more encouragement. At Shotmoor as in mainstream schools, these pupils tend to be girls. As Stanworth (1983) and others have pointed out, girls have lower self-expectations than boys and generally underrate their abilities, they are also less likely to perceive themselves coping in potentially dangerous situations (Davies, 1984a). Many of the girls saw the physical activities, offered at Shotmoor, as more appropriate for boys, as this comment, made by a girl to a teacher early on in her visit to the centre demonstrates, 'Why don't we do any girls' activities?' Girls at Shotmoor, as elsewhere, perceived themselves as less competent and were seen by the teacher as less confident than boys and, as a result, in need of more teacher attention.

However, it could also be argued that teachers were able to concentrate on the least confident pupils because there were few 'disruptive' pupils attending the centre. In the lessons observed there were very few occasions in which teachers had to discipline children. Nevertheless, not all the pupils attending Shotmoor were defined by their school teachers as 'good' pupils at school.

One visiting school teacher remarked, 'She's been suspended from school twice.' Another pupil was pointed out (to the researcher) as having spent the previous week in the school's 'sin-bin'. However, these pupils did not display difficult behaviour at Shotmoor. Their commitment to learning cannot, therefore, simply be explained with reference to the novelty of the task, but has much to do with the teachers' philosophy, their use of time and the nature of classroom talk. In the climbing lessons observed, teacher talk was different from that often found in conventional mainstream school classrooms, where much of the communication between teacher and pupil tends to be didactic in form and disciplinary in content.[11] The physical education lessons observed by Anderson (1979) for example portrayed an 'absence of teacher praise and acceptance'. By contrast, analyses of the content of communication between pupils and teachers at Shotmoor revealed that a considerable amount of praise and encouragement was routinely given to both boys and girls. There was a noticeable paucity of disciplinary communication.

The Pupils' Perceptions

The salient features of teaching at Shotmoor then, are the ways in which teachers use time, patterns of teacher–pupil interaction and the predominantly non-conflictual nature of these interactions. We can now consider how the pupils perceived and interpreted the style of teaching evident in this context and what conceptions of themselves and others were accomplished, reinforced or challenged by and through this learning experience.

I have chosen to present not only those accounts given to me by pupils who were taught by Eddy and Doug, both in the lessons described and elsewhere, but also of pupils who were taught by other teachers who portrayed similar styles and expressed similar philosophies to those of Eddy and Doug. Often, pupils were taught by two and occasionally three different teachers during the week. Each group of pupils referred to attended the centre at different times. Group 1 was the class taught by Doug, whose interactions with this teacher are displayed in Table 2a. Pupils in group 3 were taught by Eddy and other teachers. Accounts given by pupils in group 4, who were not taught by either Eddy or Doug, are included as they represent views of boys who, as members of an all boys group from one school, were mixed for their lessons with girls from an all girls school. Group 5 were mainly taught by an unqualified teacher, but did encounter other teachers.

The majority of the Shotmoor teachers were perceived by a high percentage of pupils as friendly and non–authoritarian, and it was felt that most of the teachers had given them encouragement and help. Bella for example, commented, 'They help you, if you can't do it they really help you do it . . . . like I done climbing. I couldn't go any further. I'm glad she made me go further, it was all right after that. She was trying to build your confidence, I think.' (Bella, Group 3) Gary interprets teachers' intentions in a similar way.

Gary. 'I thought they were good. They were trying to encourage you and trying to tell you not to be scared 'cause they know it's safe for you and try to get it into your head that you can do it. So if the girls think they can't do it, but they (the teachers) make sure they can in the end. Then they won't be scared.'

BH. 'Why do you think they are doing that?'

Gary. 'Just to — you believe in yourself really. Try to get you so that you can do things. You say you can't do it and you can if you really try.' (Group 4)

Gary was clearly aware of the ways in which girls underestimate their own abilities. Almost all the girls interviewed, and a high proportion of boys, expressed the opinion that they were being stretched beyond a level which they thought themselves capable. A few pupils, mainly fairly confident boys who participated in sports regularly, found the way in which they were taught particularly to their liking.[12] For Guy it was

'Pretty good. I think cause they teaches you what to do, then they lets you do what you want to. You don't 'ang about' doing the activities. They lets you get on with it when they've taught you what to do; the safety rules and that, there ain't no 'anging about'.' (Group 3)

In Guy's view a teaching approach which quickly enabled him to be involved and in which he perceived opportunities to make decisions, was very acceptable. Teaching at Shotmoor thus seemed capable of both motivating pupils' lacking in confidence and 'ability' to achieve more than they thought possible and sustaining the interests of the more confident pupils.

The pupils, however, explained their commitment to teaching and learning at Shotmoor in the following way. Shotmoor teachers would 'have a laugh' and 'help you'. Generally, the interviewed pupils' perceptions of the teachers' characteristics matched those attributed to 'good' school teachers by the pupils in Gannaway's (1976) study. Whereas Gannaway's pupils acknowledged strictness as an attribute of a 'good' teacher, the pupils at Shotmoor did not generally perceive this as a characteristic feature of the Shotmoor teachers. As we see from the following comment:

BH. 'What about your teachers. What are they trying to do?'

Keith 'Well, get us interested in it really and give us some know-ledge of it.'

BH. 'Do you think they managed it?'

Keith 'Yeh.'

BH. 'Is it what you thought it was going to be like?'

Keith 'It was better. I sort of imagined it would be more strict, not very easy going, but it's good.' (Group 1)

Moreover, some pupils felt that the relationship between themselves and the teachers was more personal. 'They (the teachers) seem to relate to you more.' The following discussion, amongst a group of fourteen year old girls, also aptly demonstrates this.

> Belinda   'We're really changed from school we are.'
>
> Carol   ''cause we haven't got no teachers and we haven't got to be quiet and all that lot.'
>
> Ann   'They treat us like normal people ..., we call each other — they don't call us girls.'
>
> BH.   'What have you been called then?'
>
> Ann   'Women, your names, sometimes Sunshine. You don't get treated like little kids like you do in school.'
>
> Belinda   'We goes, 'We're only kids,' and he goes, 'You're not kids'. If you do it wrong he treats us as though we're his age and he's our age ... you're treated like one of them ... If one of the teachers (schoolteachers) is with us they treat us exactly the same as the teachers. (Group 5)

These pupils were responsive to the forms of relationship which prevailed between pupils and teachers at Shotmoor, relationships which were more relaxed and symmetrical than those found in their mainstream schools. That girls did not receive less teacher attention than boys and that this attention was similar in type to that given to boys, indicated to the girls that their attributes were equally valued. Tracey, a pupil in Doug's climbing lesson, interpreted the teacher's actions like this,

> 'I think it was good that we weren't made to feel lower than the boys, that we was able to do exactly the same as the boys and we got the chance to do the same as them — 'cause sometimes you feel lower than them, that you can't do it. I don't think we was any better than the boys — maybe on a couple of things but everybody's got their weaknesses.' (Tracey, Group 1)

Some of the girls, then, saw themselves as more capable than they had supposed. It was immediately apparent to them that they could and did achieve as much as boys and that they were recognized for doing so in much the same ways as the boys. Glynis also takes this view,

> 'I like the climbing best, that was the most exciting and when you're at the top and looking down ... we did the abseil and I thought I'd never do that when you're going up but when you get to the top you see everyone else doing it. It's good when you're working with a lot of other people as a team, especially with boys as well 'cause they help out. Sometimes you see they're no good at something and you are so (laughter), boys aren't the best.' (Glynis Group 1)

Glynis, as the other girls in this setting, was motivated particularly by the boys, who she perceived as giving her support. This particular feature of relationships at Shotmoor, in which boys were seen to offer encouragement and support to girls to participate alongside them, and to become involved in a physical activity, is quite contrary to that revealed by Leoman (1984) in his study of girls' resistance to school PE. He points to various pressures on girls which tend to suggest to them, 'that sport is, in many ways, a masculine concept in which women can participate only peripherally.' Consequently girls tend to enter into a relationship with a man in a sporting context, either as a non–participant supporter or as the subordinate partner. These pressures, he suggests, militate against girls' involvement in sport. At Shotmoor receiving 'support' did not necessarily signify a subordinate role.

Pupils' behaviour observed in lessons, also suggested that the form of relationships between boys and girls was markedly different from that evidenced in main stream schools. Pupils seemed to be entering into relationships with each other in ways which were both collaborative and symmetrical. In so doing they were challenging conventional concepts of gender 'abilities' and what constitutes appropriate behaviour for boys and girls.

We see evidence of this reconceptualization in Debbie's remark. For her the machismo, stereotypical image of boys had been visibly challenged by the Shotmoor experience. 'They act so tough (the boys) but really they're not underneath' (Debbie, Group 1). The majority of boys and girls attending Shotmoor, preferred to work in mixed sex groups.[13] This contrasts with the attitudes evidenced in the work of Murdock and Phelps (1973), where the boys in their study favoured exclusively male groups. The boys at Shotmoor gave a number of reasons for preferring mixed groups. 'Well, I think it's better that way 'cause if you get a load of boys, they start mucking around . . . the girls, they don't want to bother. If you get a mixed group I think they (all) try equally well.' (Howard, Group 4)

For Howard, the presence of girls contributed towards a more committed involvement in the activities by both boys and girls than might otherwise be the case. The girls represented a form of control over potentially difficult or deviant behaviour of the boys and the boys' presence acted as an incentive for girls to participate.

Paul, whose class group was predominantly male in composition, had similar sentiments to those of Howard.

> Paul. 'I think it would have been better if we'd had more girls . . .
> it would have been a lot more fun with four girls and four boys.'
> BH. 'Why?'
> Paul. 'Well you would laugh at each other, with the boys they seem
> to do the same sort of thing but the girls do it differently. It would
> have been better, a lot of them are better than us at sport.'
> (Group 3)

Many of the pupils attending Shotmoor thus saw and felt that boys and girls motivated and supported each other and recognized each other as individuals. A more sensitive understanding between pupils appears to have been fostered. Again this contrasts markedly with the majority of studies in mixed sex classrooms in mainstream schools, which evidence that boys are reluctant to associate or identify with girls, and girls' abilities are often denigrated (Stanworth, 1983).[14]

The following remarks demonstrate how one boy's conception of girls had shifted as a result of his experience at Shotmoor.

John   'The girls got on quite well, some of them got on better than us.'

BH.   'Did they? How?'

John   'Ann.'

BH.   'She was good was she?'

John   'Yeh'.

BH.   As good?

John   'Yeh, better,'

BH.   'Why do you think she did better?'

John   'Don't know?'

BH.   'Would you expect that normally?'

John   No not really, we're supposed to be the stronger sex. (Laughter.)'

BH.   'Do you think the teacher treated them any differently, then?'

John   'No he treated them the same way.'

BH.   'Do you think that's got something to do with it?'

John   'No.'

BH.   'No? Just that she's ...'

John   'Well, if the girls wanted to back out he tried to push them. None of the boys backed out, we just went on with it.'

(Group 5)

The apparent contradiction in John's comments concerning his perception of the same but different treatment of boys and girls, may perhaps be explained in terms of his concepts of 'normal' behaviour of boys and girls. John perhaps took for granted that boys are expected to be adventurous and if they were to hesitate there would be an 'appropriate' response from the teacher. He assumed that girls are not expected to behave so. This apparent surface level contradiction may, therefore, be explained in terms of a 'taken for granted' deeper level of understanding of appropriate, expected behaviour of girls and boys. John's remarks along with those of the other pupils quoted earlier, indicate again a different form of relationship emerging between boys and girls than is reported in mainstream schools. Arguably, the behaviours expressed and the relations engendered within this context are concomitant upon and interrelate with not only surface features of the lesson, such as organizational procedures and situational factors, but also upon the relationships accomplished through the manner in which some Shotmoor teachers communicate; through the ways in which concepts such as safety, responsibility and order were made accessible and became meaningful to pupils.

Teaching at Shotmoor, then, appeared to foster amongst pupils a deeper understanding and awareness of each other as individuals, who needed encouragement and support. This is not to suggest that boys and girls do not hold certain stereotypical attitudes towards either sex. We see this in a number of the previous comments. However, the evidence presented here does suggest that many of the boys and girls see themselves and each other from a different angle; from a perspective which contradicts and challenges conventional concepts of appropriate gender behaviours and 'abilities'. Perceived images of what it is to be female or male are *visibly* challenged and redefined as pupils displayed their physical talent or emotional limitations. Such images became more diffuse and negotiable.

Concluding Remarks

Whichever mode of teaching (recitational, individualized or group) we choose or are forced to adopt, its effectiveness, in terms of the pupils' involvement and understanding is dependent upon the available resources, teacher/pupil ratios and so forth. However, data from this research demonstrate that it is possible in particular contexts, with certain resources and teacher predis-positions, for the majority of pupils to participate in collaboration with each other and the teacher and for there to be generated a greater degree of sociality amongst individuals. [15]

A one week stay at an outdoor pursuits centre (and we can only tentatively surmise that other centres evince similar teaching processes) may bring about a shift in how pupils perceive physical 'ability' and appropriate gender behaviour at least during that particular period of time.

There is no reason, however, to suppose that these new perspectives and attitudes will diffuse into their school or leisure time activities. We may advocate easier access for all pupils to centres of this nature, and resist endeavours to reduce the availability of this form of educational experience to pupils. But, unless these new perspectives are reinforced in the school situation, the 'realities' experienced by the pupils in that particular context will have little relevance to those which they experience in school and in the wider society.

We might suggest a greater drive towards co-educational PE within schools. Segregated PE, as Byrne (1978) rightly points out, may significantly consolidate the myths associated with gender stereotypes and we have shown that in particular contexts these can be visibly challenged. However, simply by changing the organizational form of PE lessons without a concomitant shift in both teaching approach and assumptions about gender may only reinforce girls' perceptions that physical activity is more appropriate for boys than girls (Evans, 1984). It may also, perhaps more importantly, strengthen in boys' eyes the notion that some girls are less capable than they themselves and thus consolidate the predominant concept that girls are unable to work on equal terms with boys.

Additionally, then, we need to consider the underlying structural properties of the physical activities we teach in schools, the perceived status given various activities and the ways in which these activities are made meaningful to pupils. We might consider fostering or introducing into the curriculum, forms of activities and ways of presenting them to pupils which counter the prevailing belief that it is competition which is the prerequisite to 'successful' learning and which is the prime motivator of our pupils. Certainly, we have seen in the context of this case study a challenge to this belief. Pupils are motivated when they see that their own capabilities are worthy of recognition regardless of their gender or 'ability'.

How difficult the task, remains to be seen. As we know, schools themselves are about winning and losing and not, for the most part, about collaboration and mutual support. Lynn Davies's penetrating comment on comprehensive schooling may be most pertinent in relation to an unconsidered and ill-informed practice of co-educational PE 'More girl winners may not only mean more boy losers, but also girls having to celebrate "masculine" attributes of ruthless competitive point scoring, of achieving success at the cost of another's failure' (Davies, 1984b, p. 64).

Forms of competition which have losers will engender antagonism between pupils, militating against a context which is conducive to mutual understanding. Most of the positive effects of competition, as Brown *et al* (1983) rightly propose, are in fact those which are generated from a challenge; the exciting experience of personal or group achievement against perceived difficult odds,

> 'Well, ... it's quite a challenge when you see other people doing it and you think, "Oh, I'll never do it", and you do. It's ... enjoyable to know that you've actually done it' (Nicky, Group 1).

Acknowledgements

I should like to express my sincere thanks to the teachers and pupils at Shotmoor who enabled me to share their experiences.

Notes

1   Outdoor Activities curriculum embraces such terms as outdoor pursuits, adventure education, outdoor education, outward bound experience. (*cf.* Schools Council Geography Committee 1980, Mortlock, 1984, Loynes, 1984, DES Survey, 1983). I shall refer to outdoor activities and outdoor pursuits as those physical activities which are potentially dangerous and in which safety is a prominent aspect. Such activities, for example, include ski-ing, climbing, archery, map work and sailing.

2   *cf.* SPRADLEY, J. (1979), BURGESS, R. (Ed.) (1982). pp. 107–22, SIMON, H. (1981), pp. 27–50.

3   The teacher's views or accounts were collected by the researcher during the normal course of conversation or during informal interviews. They were usually recorded immediately after the conversation or, on occasions during the informal interview using paper and pencil.

4   For a discussion of some of the problems experienced in the 'open' classroom in secondary school see DENSCOMBE, M. (1980b).

5   An abseil is a technique by which a climber slides down a rope using a device called a descender to control the speed of descent. A 'free' abseil is one in which the descending person's feet do not make contact with any physical object.

6   *cf.* THE PLOWDEN REPORT (1967) and HOPSON and SCALLY (1981).

7   In academic classrooms *cf.* SHARP and GREEN (1975), KEDDIE, N. (1971) and DENSCOMBE, M. (1982). In PE classrooms, *cf.* ANDERSON, H.G. (1979).

8   These findings will be reported at a later date (see HUMBERSTONE, B. 'The relationship between organizational factors, teachers' approach and pupil commitment in outdoor activity curricula,' research thesis in progress).

9   There are considerable problems associated with this form of data collection (*cf.* EVANS, 1985). These counts give only indications of an interaction pattern and should only be considered along with the more revealing interpretative data. Knowing when an interaction began or ended and what messages were conveyed in them, could only be achieved with further reference to the perspectives of teachers and pupils, and a 'shared' understanding of their actions.

10 *cf.* BROPHY, J. and GOOD, T. (1970), DEEM, R. (1980). DELAMONT, S. (1980), FRAZIER, N. and SADKER, M. (1973), LUNGREN, U. (1981), MARTIN, R. (1972), SPENDER, D. and SARAH, E. (1980). STANWORTH, M. (1983). FRENCH, E. (1986). More recently, it has been suggested that mixed PE 'classrooms' also exhibit similar interaction patterns to those found in academic classrooms. (*cf.* LEAMAN, O. 1984, p. 25)

11 *cf.* WALLER (1932), LORTIE (1975), WOODS (1979), who point to the apparently conflictual nature of schooling.

12 These pupils' degree of confidence was judged by the researcher from observations of their behaviour in lessons. Their amount of participation in sport was determined from their completed questionnaires.

13 385 questionnaires were completed by pupils. 165 were completed by girls, 219 by boys (1 did not indicate sex). 2 did not respond to this question. 352 pupils liked working in co-educational classes. 3 girls would have preferred working in an all-girls' class. 27 boys preferred an all-boys' class (18 of these boys were working in single sex classes). The classes referred to are those which the pupils were in during their stay at Shotmoor.

14 SALMON, P. and CLAIRE, H. (1984), in their study of collaborative classrooms do present evidence that in certain contexts there is greater understanding between boys and girls.

15 Sociality refers to the degree to which people understand each other's views, (SALMON, P. and CLAIRE, H. 1984, p. 5).

Bibliography

ANDERSON H.G. (1979) *Analysis of Teaching Physical Education*, The C.V. Mosby Company.

BAYLISS, T. (1984) *'Providing Equal Opportunities for Girls and Boys in Physical Education'* London, ILEA.

BERLAK and BERLAK (1981) *The Dilemmas of Schooling*, London, Methuen.

BROPHY, J. and GROOD, T. (1974) *Teacher-Student Relationships: Causes and Consequences*, New York, Holt, Rinehart and Winston.

BROWN, P. and MATZEN, L. (1983) 'Physical Education', in WHYLDE, J. (Ed.), *Sexism in the Secondary Curriculum*, London, Harper and Row, pp. 270–84.

BURGESS, R. (Ed.) (1982) *Field Research: A Source Book and Field Manual*, London, Allen and Unwin.

BYRNE, E. (1978) *Women and Education*, London, Tavistock.

CENTRAL ADVISORY COUNCIL FOR EDUCATION (1967) *Children and Their Primary Schools*, London, HMSO (The Plowden Report)

CLARKE, A and CLARKE, J. (1983) '"Highlights and action replays" — ideology, sport and the media' in HARGREAVES, J., *Sport, Culture and Ideology*, London, Routledge and Kegan Paul, pp. 62–87.

DAVIES, L. (1979) 'Deadlier than the male?' in BARTON, L. and MEIGHAN, R. *Schools, Pupils and Deviance*, Driffield, Nafferton, pp. 59–74.

DAVIES, L. (1984a) *Pupil Power, Deviance and Gender in School*, Lewes, Falmer Press.

DAVIES, L. (1984b) 'Gender and Comprehensive Schooling' in BALL, S., *Comprehensive Schooling: A Reader*, Lewes, Falmer Press, pp. 47–66.

DEEM, R. (1980) *Schooling for Womens Work*, London, Routledge and Kegan Paul.

DELAMONT, S. (1980) *Sex Roles and The School*, London, Methuen.

DENSCOMBE, M. (1980a) 'The work context of teaching: an analytic framework for the study of teachers in classrooms', in *British Journal of Sociology of Education*, 1, 3 pp. 279–92

DENSCOMBE, M. (1980b) 'Pupil strategies and the open classroom', in WOOD, P., *Pupil Strategies. Explorations in the Sociology of the School*, London, Croom Helm.

DENSCOMBE, M. (1982) 'The "Hidden Pedagogy" and its implications for teacher training', *British Journal of Sociology of Education*, 3, 3, pp. 249–65.

DEPARTMENT OF EDUCATION AND SCIENCE (1983) *Learning Out of Doors*, an HMI Survey of Outdoor Education, HMSO.

DUNCAN, M. (1985) *An Ethnographic Investigation of Curriculum Innovation Involving Mixed Physical Education within a Secondary School*, unpublished MA (Ed.) Thesis, University of Southampton.

EVANS, J. (1984) 'Muscle, sweat and showers. Girls' conceptions of physical education and sport: a challenge for research and curriculum reform,' in *Physical Education Review*, 7, 1 pp. 12–18.

EVANS J. (1985) *Teaching in Transition*, Milton Keynes, Open University Press.

FRAZIER, N. and SADKER, M. (1973) *Sexism in School and Society*, New York, Harper and Row.

FRENCH, J. (1986) 'Gender and the classroom', *New Society*, March, pp. 404–6.

GANNAWAY, H. (1976) 'Making sense of school' in STUBBS, M., and DELAMONT, S., (Eds.) *Exploration in Classroom Observation*, Chichester, Wiley.

HAMMERSLEY, M. and ATKINSON, P. (1983) *Ethnography, Principles in Practice*, London, Tavistock.

HOPSON, B. and SCALLY, M. (1981) *Life Skills Teaching*, London, McGraw-Hill.

HUMBERSTONE, B. (1985) *'Empowerment' and Gender in Outdoor Education? Teachers' and Pupils' Perspectives in one form of Co-educational Physical Education*, Paper presented to the XIIIth Workshop in the Sociology of PE and Sport, Manchester University.

KEDDIE, N. (1971) 'Classroom knowledge' in YOUNG, M.F.D., (Ed.) *Knowledge and Control*, London, Collier-Macmillan, pp. 138–60.

LEE (1980) 'Together we learn to read and write,' in SPENDER, D., and SARAH, E., (Eds.), *Learning to Lose*, The Womens Press, pp. 121–7.

LEAMAN, O. (1984) *'Sit on the Sidelines and Watch the Boys Play': Sex Differentiation in Physical Education*, Schools Council Programme 3, Longman.

LOYNE S.C. (Ed.) (1984) 'Editorial', *The Journal of the National Association for Outdoor*

Education, I. 3 pp. 2. 3

LOPEZ, S. (1985) *An Innovation in Mixed Gender PE — with Special Reference to Whether This Form of Grouping Can Undermine Gender Stereotypical Attitudes Towards PE* unpublished MA (Ed.) Thesis, University of Southampton.

LORTIE, D.C. (1975) *Schoolteacher,* University of Chicago Press.

LUNGREN, U. (1981) *Model Analysis of Pedagogical Processes,* Stockholm, CWK Gleerup.

MAIGRAIN, S. (1983) 'How skirts can discriminate against girls', *The Times Education Supplement,* 12 August.

MARLAND, M. (1983) *Sex Differentiation and Schooling,* London, Heinemann.

MARTIN, R. (1972) 'Students sex behaviour as determinants of the type and frequency of teacher-student contracts' in *School Psychology,* 10: 4, pp. 339–47.

MORTLOCK, C. (1984) *The Adventure Alternative,* Cumbria, Cicerone Press.

MURDOCK and PHELPS (1973) *Mass Media and the Secondary School,* Schools Council Publications, Macmillan.

POLLARD, A. (1980) 'Negotiating deviance and "getting done" in primary school classrooms', in BARTON L., and MEIGHAN, R., (Eds.) *Schools, Pupils and Deviance,* Driffield, Nafferton Books, pp. 75–94.

SALMON, P. and CLAIRE, H. (1984) *Classroom Collaboration,* London, Routledge and Kegan Paul.

SARAH, E. (1980) 'Teachers and students in the classroom: an examination of classroom interaction,' in SPENDER, D., and SARAH, E. (Eds.) *Learning to Lose,* The Womens Press, pp. 155–64.

SCHOOLS COUNCIL GEOGRAPHY COMMITTE (1980) *Outdoor Education in Secondary Schools,* Schools Council.

SCOTT, M. (1980) 'Teach her a lesson' in SPENDER, D. and SARAH, E., (Eds.) *ibid.*

SHARP, R and GREEN, A. (1975) *Education and Social Control. A Study in Progressive Primary Education,* London, Routledge and Kegan Paul.

SIMON, H. (1981) 'Conversation piece' in ADELMAN C., (Ed.) *Uttering, Muttering: Collecting and Reporting Talk for Social and Educational Research,* London, Grant McIntyre, pp. 27–50.

SPENDER, D. and SARAH, E. (1980) *Learning to Lose,* The Women's Press.

SPENDER, D. (1982) *Invisible Women: The Schooling Scandal,* Writers and Readers Publishing Cooperative.

SPRADLEY, J. (1979) *The Ethnographic Interview,* New York, Holt, Rinehart and Winston.

STANWORTH, M. (1983) *Gender and Schooling: A Study of Sexual Divisions in the Classroom,* London, Hutchinson.

TICKLE, L. (1984) 'One spell of ten minutes or five spells of two ...? Teacher-pupil encounters in art and design education,' in HAMMERSLEY, M., and HARGREAVES, A., (Eds.) *Curriculum Practice,* Lewes, Falmer Press.

WALLER, W. (1932) *The Sociology of Teaching,* New York, Wiley.

WHYLDE, J. (1983) *Sexism in the Secondary Curriculum,* London, Harper and Row.

WILLIS, P. and CRITCHER, C. (1975) *Women in Sport,* Working papers in Cultural Studies, No. 5 University of Birmingham.

WOLPE, A.M. (1977) *Some Processes in Sexist Education,* London, WRRC.

WOODS, P. (1979) *The Divided School,* London, Routledge and Kegan Paul.

12 Equal Opportunities and Physical Education

Bruce Carrington and Oliver Leaman

There would appear to be little problem in defining what equal opportunities represents in most areas of the curriculum. For example, there is evidence to suggest that young women in this country often fail to realize their full potential in subjects such as mathematics, physics, chemistry and engineering/technology, where they continue to be under-represented at all levels from CSE through to higher degree (Smail, 1984). It has been argued that this and similar differentiation is *in part* the outcome of social processes occurring *within* schools. Studies of classroom interaction (in primary, middle and secondary schools) have indicated that pedagogical practices frequently reinforce rather than undermine inequalities of gender: male pupils tend to receive more attention from teachers than females; teachers may be psychologically and socially predisposed to favour boys; and the organizational and management strategies employed by teachers in the classroom can often be premised upon the tacit acceptance of stereotyped conceptions of gender-appropriate behaviour (Clarricoates, 1980; Delamont, 1980; Galton, Simon and Croll, 1980; Stanworth, 1981; Spender, 1982). Although it is conceivable that some teachers would view differential achievement in mathematics and science as largely the outcome of immutable differences between the sexes in terms of visio-spatial and analytic abilities, few, if any, would advocate separate provision in these subjects if this entailed that girls were provided with a 'watered-down' curriculum and discouraged from pursuing more advanced courses of study. Yet (as Scraton and Humberstone have argued in this book) this is almost exactly the situation in PE in many British secondary schools where single-sex teaching remains the norm and continues to be legitimated both by appeal to tradition, and to sex differences in size and strength. Segregated PE can militate against equal opportunities. Netball, for example, provides girls with a poor substitute for soccer in that it is less complex, dynamic and aggressive. The split for PE not only results in differential provision (which can lead to girls having fewer opportunities than boys to develop their physical stamina and coordination) but also serves to reinforce the image of the 'exclusive masculinity of the prestige sports' (Byrne, 1978).

Some commentators have pointed to the narrowing *performance* gap between the sexes in some swimming and athletics events arguing that, in the not too distant future, these sports will be de-segregated enabling males and females to compete on equal terms (Ferris, 1979). Whatever the validity of this argument, it does not have any great relevance for practising teachers who are currently concerned to devise strategies to obviate the negative attitudes shown by many adolescent girls towards sport and physical recreation (Leaman, 1984a) and to increase *participation* amongst the sector of the school population. Notwithstanding this, however, teachers concerned to develop and implement an equal opportunities policy in PE should recognize that sex differences in both performance and participation are, in part, socially and historically conditioned and that the bodies of school children are no more *tabulae rasae* than their minds. To some degree, differential socialization from early childhood onwards, may help to ensure that male pupils are more confident, skilful and favourably disposed towards sporting activities than their female counterparts. For example, there is evidence to show that in seven year olds, boys receive more parental encouragement than girls to play outdoors (Newson and Newson, 1963, 1968, 1976). Similarly, in schools, from the infant stage onwards, sex-segregated play, with boys receiving the lion's share of facilities, is often sanctioned. Moreover, there is a tendency for teachers to encourage toughness, strength, assertiveness, aggression and boisterousness in boys rather than in girls (Clarricoates, *op cit*). Obviously, an equal opportunities policy in PE will need to take account of these and other sex differences in socialization.

Whereas withdrawal from or failure in mathematics, science and other curriculum areas can *directly* jeopardize pupils' future employability, career and life chances, this is not generally the case in PE. Yet despite its marginal status in schools, PE cannot be summarily dismissed as inconsequential, for it is an essential component in gender socialization, playing an important part in differentially shaping pupils' attitudes to their bodies, health, fitness and physical recreation. Of course, PE is also important in other ways. For example, both curricular and extra-curricular activities in this area can sometimes provide pupils with an alternative sphere for achievement and potential source of status, prestige and self-esteem. Furthermore, the cultural and ideological significance of PE has long been recognized by educationalists who, amongst other things, have depicted it as: a medium for 'character-building' and disseminating favourable attitudes to authority; an appropriate vehicle for enhancing the unity and solidarity of schools and channelling the interests and energies of 'problem' children; and a means of fostering a competitive ethic (Hargreaves, 1981).

Despite the strident efforts of the Sports Council over the years to implement its policy of 'Sports for All', increased public awareness of the importance of physical fitness to health and a growing recognition within the

Women's Movement that sport is a 'feminist issue', female participation levels have remained below those of males. In secondary schools, girls are more likely than boys to eschew involvement in both curricular and extra-curricular physical activities (Saunders, 1979, Moir, 1977 *et al*). Although there is evidence to show that women aged sixteen and over now make greater use of sports centres and swimming pools than men, men still 'greatly outnumber' women when the whole spectrum of recreational sport is examined (Sports Council, 1982). There are various reasons for these differences. For example, married women, constrained by domestic commitments, often have little time for leisure activities outside the home, sporting or otherwise (Deem, 1982, Hobson, 1981). The lives and lifestyles of unemployed adolescent girls can also be circumscribed in this way. As Hendry *et al* (1984) have shown, girls are frequently expected to do the family shopping and other household tasks, whereas their unemployed male peers have greater freedom to choose how that 'enforced leisure-time' is structured. Furthermore, although attitudes to women in sport may have shifted recently, there are indications that sport continues to be perceived in popular culture as a quintessentially male domain, and female participants regarded with a degree of ambivalence or, in some cases, ridicule and contempt. Commenting on this in 1974, Paul Willis remarked:

> There is an important element in the popular response to the female athlete, of uncertainty before the deviant, distrust of the strange, dislike of the marginal. As the athlete becomes more outstanding, she marks herself out even more as deviant. Instead of confirming her identity, success can threaten her with a foreign male identity. In so far as she is affected by popular consciousness — and she can hardly ignore it — the female athlete lives through a severe contradiction. To succeed as an athlete can be to fail as a woman, because she has, in certain profound symbolic ways, become a man. Indeed in certain areas it is not only symbolic power she faces. The demand for sex tests on female athletes shows us the power of the suspicion — 'if she's successful she's a man'. A moment's reflection that no male athlete lives this painful contradiction of success-being-failure-really, to say nothing of this failure being physically tested, throws up for us once again the severe interest which sport manifests in differentiating the sexes. (p. 49)

Other writers have also shown how top-level women athletes in Britain (and America) are not only characterized as 'unfeminine' but their achievements are often minimized, trivialized or ignored by the mass media. Moir (*op cit*) draws attention to the following observations made by Anita White (then Captain of England's Hockey team) and Gillian Gilks (a European women's badminton champion).

'We're still regarded as freaks. One is not expected to be competitive, aggressive or strong.' 'Our men are not as high standing in world competition as the girls are, but unless the men have done nothing at all, we will never get into the headlines.'

In a similar vein, Leaman (1984a) contends that the mass media continues to represent sport as a 'male domain into which women occasionally stray' and women athletes as 'peculiar', or as sex objects. He notes:

Women's pictures appear on the sports page in many cases only if there is something extraordinary about them, either in that they look peculiar (Russian shot putters), are doing something peculiar (bending down so that one can see their knickers) or are sexually attractive. There are also items on women involved in stereotypically masculine sports like wrestling and boxing, although not on the sports page, which fall into the 'what peculiar things some people get up to' category. (p. 17)

It could be argued that such imagery not only prompts the withdrawal of many girls and women from participation in sports, but also presents a number of dilemmas to those who retain their commitments to these activities. The female athlete, especially at the higher lever of competition, will have the problem of reconciling her sporting behaviour (with its accompanying characteristics of aggression, competitiveness, independence, physical stamina and strength) with prevailing conceptions of femininity stressing *inter alia* passivity, dependence, tenderness, sensitivity and fragility. David Triesman (1980), in his article 'Politics and sport', makes reference to this form of role conflict with the following anecdote about the Olympics:

An American woman silver medalist who lost to Kornelia Ender thought that East German women were unattractive, 'unfeminine', obsessed with their sport, and therefore, unlikely to win the ultimate of all competitions, finding a man. (p. 15)

Adolescent girls may also show an ambivalence towards sporting activities for similar reasons. Adolescence and early adulthood is a period for reflecting on one's attitudes, values and ideas and for re-examining one's relationship with members of the opposite sex. Girls, at this stage, are often strenuously involved in constructing their notions of femininity and, invariably, are preoccupied, with attracting and retaining a boyfriend. Many will identify with the lifestyles of the female characters in teenage magazines, who are frequently depicted as helpless, lethargic and dependent upon others, especially young men. In these magazines, serious involvement in sport and physical recreation tends to be portrayed as part of the naive world of childhood and at variance with an adult female persona (Dunne, 1982). It is not surprising that many girls, when confronted by these conventional conceptions of femininity during the latter years of secondary education, will come to view sporting activities (and their associated masculine images of muscle, sweat and showers) with increasing disdain, perhaps thereby establishing lifelong habits of physical inactivity.

Sport in our society is a symbol of self-transcendence, freedom, autonomy and effort, in other words, of activity. It could be argued, therefore, that by withdrawing from sporting activities in schools, girls may also be forging for themselves future roles of passivity, physical dependency, timidity and weakness. The crucial part played by sport in gender socialization is, of course, generally recognized by feminists in Britain and elsewhere who have taken various steps to cultivate a positive image of female physical strength, stamina and competitiveness, and thereby extend female participation in this sphere (Leaman, 1982, Talbot, 1981). Of course, not all the activities traditionally included in the PE curriculum for girls in secondary schools can be regarded as at variance with prevailing notions of femininity. For example, educational (rather than Olympic) gymnastics and dance have traditionally been 'reserved' for girls. Such differentiation, by giving credence to the stereotype that all girls are 'naturally' suited to activities involving grace, balance and aesthetic movement (as opposed to those involving strength, stamina and aggression), can be regarded as reinforcing relations based on patriarchy.

In analyzing the responses of girls to PE we are confronted with this apparent paradox: on the one hand, by rejecting and opting out of PE in schools many girls *indirectly* facilitate the reproduction of patriarchal relations, because they are not exposed to the major women's team sports which tend to emphasize the development of traditional 'masculine' attitudes, skills and dispositions; on the other, girls who find themselves able to accommodate to the PE curriculum are not only faced with the problem of being labelled by their peers as 'childish' or 'unfeminine' because of their involvement in, for example, team sports, but are also faced with exposure to other activities which can be seen as *directly* reflecting (and indeed celebrating) a division of labour in society founded upon the subordination of women by men.

Having suggested why an equal opportunities policy is as necessary in PE as in other, higher status curriculum areas, let us now attempt to evaluate strategies employed by teachers to obviate girls' resistance to PE indicating, where appropriate, alternative directions for curriculum policy and practice.

As Leaman has indicated in his Schools Council Report, the responses of teaching staff to girls' alienation from PE are highly differentiated. Some adopt a strategy of *confrontation*, making no attempt to understand the reasons for the girls' hostility to this area of school activity. Such teachers often find it difficult to empathize with pupils having never experienced any antipathy towards sport themselves, or role conflict arising from the perceived disjunction between the culture of sport and the culture of femininity.

In contrast, others will opt for a strategy of *compromise* in an attempt to assuage disaffected and potentially disaffected pupils. Concessions will be made to secure co-operation and compliance from the pupils. For example, some traditional curricular activities may be abandoned in favour of more 'feminine' activities such as keep-fit, pop-mobility and disco-dancing. Although this strategy may be more successful than the former in retaining the interest of adolescent girls in PE, some teachers may view it as unsatisfactory on technical and other grounds. By making the curriculum more relevant to the interests of girls, teachers may not only find themselves substituting recreational for educational activities, but may also be emphasizing stereotyped distinctions between the sexes.

A third strategy is to try to raise the pupils' aspirations by presenting them with role models of top-level female athletes who combine sporting achievement with conventional femininity. A problem with this approach is, that by defending the notion of women in sport as 'normal', it may serve to reinforce rather than negate any doubts which girls may already have about the compatibility of sport with femininity. Teachers employing this strategy may also suggest to pupils that sport and physical recreation can provide worthwhile and rewarding forms of leisure. It is unlikely that girls will be very receptive to this line of argument or regard it as realistic. Many will have seen how their father's leisure is often at the expense of their mother's. Furthermore, much of their spare time outside school will be taken up with domestic chores or, in many cases, will already be at the mercy of their boyfriends (Hobson, *op cit*).

A fourth strategy, often justified by appeal to the rhetoric of equal opportunities, is that of mixed PE. Before considering this strategy and its limitations in more detail, it might be useful first to address the question 'What is equal opportunities in PE?'

Do equal opportunities in PE mean adopting a strategy of 'non-discrimination', whereby *formal* restrictions limiting the participation of boys to one range of activities and girls to another are lifted? Thus, if female pupils wish to take part in a traditional male activity such as soccer or boys wish to participate in girls' games, then no obstacle will be placed in their way by PE staff. In other words, is equality of opportunity synonymous with boys and girls having equal access *de jure* to the same activites? Or does it mean that steps will be taken to *ensure* that boys and girls alike have *de facto* a balanced curriculum comprising a mixture of the activities currently reserved for one or other of the sexes? For example, boys as well as girls would be expected to take part in educational dance and modern educational gym. Similarly, girls would be required to participate in activities such as soccer or outdoor education, which, at present, are either restricted to or favoured by boys. Can equality of opportunity in PE be equated with equality of *outcome*? For example, are staff to aim for the same *overall rates of participation* by boys and girls in curricular and extra-curricular activities, yet not to insist that each group takes part in the same activities? By equal opportunities, do we mean a policy which aims to *equalize the performance* of the sexes in the same activities? For example, are staff to aim for the situation where boys and girls can not only participate but perform as equals on the track, in the swimming pool, dance theatre and gym? Or alternatively, does equal opportunities refer to a situation in which every pupil is provided with the chance to *realize his or her* full *potential* in a diverse range of physical activities?

If by equal opportunities in PE we mean a policy which aims to ensure that (1) there are no significant differences between the sexes in terms of overall participation and, (2) that all pupils irrespective of gender receive a balanced, broadly-based curriculum which affords every individual the same chance to realize their full potential, then we would argue that the strategy of non-discrimination is antithetical to this aim. It is unlikely that this strategy would result, for example, in any fundamental change in existing patterns of participation, since it takes no account of the physiological differences between adolescent boys and girls, or socially-conditioned differences between them in attitude, motivation and skill. By failing to take cognisance of such differences and by advocating, in effect, that unequals be treated as equals, the strategy of non-discrimination in PE merely serves to reinforce the *status quo* between the sexes.

As Baylis' (1984) survey of PE provision in London has shown, a growing number of secondary schools are now beginning to experiment with mixed PE lessons, and that this innovation is often justified by an appeal to the rhetoric of equal opportunities. It is held, amongst other things, that mixed PE can help boys and girls break out of stereotypically masculine or feminine movement patterns, enable them to work together and learn from each other, and allow their teachers to group them according to aptitude and skill rather than the seemingly spurious criterion of gender. Without wishing to impune the motives of those who advocate mixed PE, we would suggest that the initiative is neither practical (especially if based on traditional team games) nor likely to be conducive to the goal of equal opportunities. As we have already noted, in coeducational settings boys tend to receive a larger proportion of the teachers' time and attention than girls. It would seem likely that such 'gender imbalances' will be more pronounced in PE than in some other curriculum areas for the following reasons. Teachers faced with a class containing a greater number of boys than girls socialized to view PE in a positive manner and with the confidence, knowledge and skill to realize their physical potential, will invariably be more favourably disposed towards the former rather than the latter category. Moreover, the pressures on pupils to conform to traditional sex-roles may be greater in mixed than in single-sex lessons. In the presence of girls, adolescent boys will wish to be seen as 'manly', tough and assertive and will be more likely to eschew activities perceived as feminine. Similarly, adolescent girls, anxious not be viewed as childish, tomboys, or unattractive to the opposite sex, will be more likely to avoid activities perceived as threatening them with a 'foreign male identity'. Certainly, in the initial stages of an innovation involving mixed sex grouping, the curriculum change as Evans *et al* (1985) have elsewhere argued, may well announce rather than dissipate the conventional and stereotypical conceptions of gender held by both boys and girls and their teachers.

There are a number of related practical problems associated with mixed

PE. The sports that are available and, more importantly, acceptable to both sexes (for example, tennis, squash, badminton), are more expensive to mount than traditional male or female team sports; in individual and partner sports extensive facilities are required for a relatively modest number of players. Having said this, a case could be made for mounting mixed lessons to teach the basic skills and strategies common to both male and female team sports (for example, throwing, catching, bouncing, passing, attacking, defending, positioning). However, external constraints (perhaps coupled with resistance from pupils themselves) will often ensure that coeducational sport does extend beyond these skills-training sessions. The FA (Football Association), for example, has continued to oppose mixed football beyond the age of 11, even though there are no significant differences between boys and girls of this age in terms of physical stamina and strength.

In schools with a significant proportion of Muslim pupils, mixed PE will not be an option available to staff. As the Swann Report (DES 1985, pp. 341–2) has shown, Muslim parents frequently raise objections to it on both religious and moral grounds, arguing that mixed PE may bring their daughters into direct contact with males in what is regarded as a shameful and potentially compromising situation. Obviously, staff committed to the goal of equal opportunities will need to show sensitivity to this and related issues. For example, in schools with a significant Asian population, staff should take cognisance of the values and beliefs of Muslim girls and their parents when planning both curricular and extra-curricular activities. In the case of the latter, it may be necessary to arrange training sessions, inter-school competitions etc. at lunchtime (rather than after school or at the weekend) to accommodate the preferences of this sector of the population. More generally, PE staff in *all schools* (along with their colleagues in other specialisms) ought to consider the extent to which their teaching reflects in a positive manner the cultures and lifestyles of different ethnic groups. Various strategies can be adopted to obviate curricular ethnocentrism and incorporate a global perspective in PE. As Leaman (1984b, pp. 216–7) has noted elsewhere:

> The introduction of ethnic dance into the curriculum can be immensely rewarding in *any school*. For one thing, it provides an interesting link with different kinds of world music which can considerably broaden pupils' knowledge. Most significant, perhaps, is the fact that the basic principles of ethnic dance are so dissimilar that they lead to the exercise of a very varied series of movement skills. West African dance, for instance, emphasizes the use of the bulk of the body with a very low centre of gravity, while some kinds of Asian dance place a great deal of emphasis upon the hands and neck, with a staggering expressiveness based upon different symbols which these parts of the body can represent. Both forms of dance contrast sharply with aspects of most European dance, with its high centre of gravity, rigid body bulk and emphasis upon uprightness. It is not surprising that dissimi-

lar cultures should express themselves differently through the medium of dance, and this diversity can be used by the dance teacher to increase both pupils' movement vocabulary and their understanding of different lifestyles and countries. The teacher may be able to learn from ethnic minority pupils for whom traditional dance might still play an important part in recreational activities, and work with those pupils to develop movement phrases which can be shared with the whole class; the class could be led to discuss why ethnic dance forms have the form they do, how they are connected with religious and social attitudes and so on. This would be to use different dance forms not just to increase pupils' repertoire of movements but also to increase understanding of ethnic cultures in a valuable way. (emphasis added)

PE staff in multi-ethnic schools will need to give *particular* consideration to the hidden (as well as formal) curriculum when assessing their pedagogy. Certainly, staff ought to be aware of the dangers of racial stereotyping in this area of school activity. For example, account should be taken of anxieties voiced within the Afro-Caribbean community that teachers tend to view black pupils as having 'natural' athletic ability and, as a result, encourage them to concentrate on sport in school to the detriment of their academic studies (DES, 1981, Cashmore, 1982). When implementing an equal opportunities policy in PE, staff will need to respond to this and other related issues. As well as aiming to ensure that there are no significant differences between the sexes in overall rates of participation, staff should also make certain that pupils from different ethnic backgrounds are provided with the same chances of realizing their full potential in PE. In working towards this latter goal, staff will often need to take an active stance against sexism, racism and prejudice. As Carrington and Wood (1983) have shown, in their case study of ethnic differences in sports involvement in a Yorkshire Comprehensive School, inter-group hostilities and rivalries can be accentuated through sport. They found that the overrepresentation of Afro-Caribbean pupils in school teams was enhanced by the withdrawal of white pupils from these activities. Some whites were found to eschew sports because of their hostility and prejudice towards blacks. Equally, black pupils at the school seemed to perceive sports as their own 'ethnic territory' and deployed various strategies to control these activities and exclude white pupils from them.

Despite our reservations about mixed PE, the existence of separate and protected male and female enclaves in PE is far from desirable. As we indicated earlier, traditional female team sports are often not only less complex and demanding than corresponding male activities, but are generally accorded low-status and prestige and receive less media coverage. It would seem, therefore, that teachers committed to the goal of equal opportunities in PE are faced with the following dilemma. On the one hand, segregated provision can not only reinforce the so-called 'exclusive masculinity of the prestige sports', but can also result in girls receiving a relatively 'watered-down' curriculum comprising, amongst other things, traditional female team games and re-creational (rather than educational) activities such as pop-mobility, disco-dancing and keep-fit. On the other, mixed PE, as currently conceived and practiced, may do little to undermine differences between boys and girls in attitude, motivation and skill, or redress the 'gender imbalances' prevalent in pedagogical practice.

It is worth saying, though, that some approaches to physical education teaching (see Humberstone, chapter 11) make equal opportunities far more likely than others. Educational gymnastics and dance for example, seem (see Evans *et al*, 1985) to offer some potential for mixed sex grouping and for challenging stereotypical conceptions of gender held by both boys and girls and their teachers. However, whether some of the difficulties outlined above can be worked through in these curricula depends, it seems, on the nature of the innovation, on how and why mixed sex grouping is introduced, the degree of fore-planning and collaboration amongst staff and perhaps more crucially on the capacities of teachers to effect a pedagogy which is capable not only of reaching and teaching both boys and girls but the broad range of abilities, interests and predispositions which they together and invariably present to the teacher (see Evans, *et al*, 1985).

An ethic which emphasizes competition rather than general participation is a difficult one to reconcile with egalitarian concerns. A health-based fitness regime is far more likely to enthuse girls and persuade them that physical education is not a macho and 'unfeminine' activity, and from that starting point the teacher can expand gradually girls' feelings of physical well-being, power and confidence. There is obviously going to be no one approach which will be successful in all cases, and a variety of techniques should be tried and varied to take account of individual and class differences. One of the great difficulties in this area of curriculum innovation is the identification of criteria of success. How can we tell when boys and girls work together, that they have learnt from each other something of the differences in the ways in which they experience their bodies? How can we know that girls will be encouraged to regard their leisure as important, and refuse to have it coopted by the leisure interests of their husbands/boyfriends/children/parents as is so prevalent at the moment? One of the most valuable aspects of an equal opportunities policy in physical education is its ability to show girls how significant their leisure is, how they should carve out for themselves in their present and future lives a portion of time and space which is their own and inviolable. This would represent a powerful weapon in their struggle with men for increased resources, resources of time as well as money and status.

References

BAYLIS, T. (1984) *Providing Equal Opportunities for Boys and Girls in Physical Education*, Inner London Education Authority.

BYRNE, E. (1978) *Women and Education*, London, Tavistock.

CARRINGTON, B. and WOOD, E. (1983) 'Body talk: images of sport in a multi-racial school,' *Multi-Racial Education* 11, 2, pp. 29–38.

CASHMORE, E. (1982) *Black Sportsmen*, London, Routledge and Kegan Paul.

CLARRICOATES, K. (1980) 'The importance of being Ernest ... Tom ... Jane. The perception and characterisation of gender conformity and gender deviation in primary schools' in DEEM, R. (Ed.) *Schooling for Women's Work*, London Routledge and Kegan Paul, pp. 26–41.

DES (1981) *West Indian Children in Our Schools*, (Rampton Report), London, HMSO.

DES (1985) *Education for All* London, HMSO, (Swann Report)

DEEM, R. (1982) 'Work, leisure and inequality' *Leisure Studies* 1, pp. 29–42.

DELAMONT, S. (1980) *Sex Roles and the School*, London, Methuen.

DUNNE, M. (1982) 'An introduction to some of the images of sport in girls' comics and magazines' in JENKINS C. (Ed.) *Sporting Fictions*, Birmingham, CCCS.

EVANS, J., DUNCAN, M., LOPEZ, S., EVANS, M., (1985) *Innovation and Evaluation in the Physical Education Curriculum*, Paper Presented to ICPHER Conference, West London Institute of Higher Education, August.

FERRIS, E. (1979) 'The myths surrounding women's participation in sport and exercise' (I) and (II), *Olympic Review* 138/9, pp. 249–54 and 140, pp. 332–9.

GALTON, M. SIMON, B. and CROLL, S. (1980) *Inside the Primary Classroom* London, Routledge and Kegan Paul.

HARGREAVES, J. (1981) 'The political economy of mass sport, in DALE, R. *et al* (Eds.) *Education and the State Politics, Patriarchy and Practice*, Lewes, The Falmer Press, pp. 55–70.

HENDRY, L.B., RAYMOND, M. (1984) and STEWART, C. 'Unemployment, school and leisure: an adolescent study,' *Leisure Studies* 3, pp. 175–87.

HOBSON, D. (1981) 'Young women at home and leisure' in TOMLINSON, A. (Ed.) *Leisure and Social Control*, Brighton Polytechnic.

LEAMAN, O. (1984a) *Sit on the Sidelines and Watch the Boys Play: Sex Differentiation in Physical Education*, York, Longmans/Schools Council.

LEAMAN, O. (1984b) 'Physical education, dance and outdoor pursuits' in CRAFT, A. and BARDELL, G. (Eds.) *Curriculum Opportunities in a Multicultural Society*, London, Harper Row.

LEAMAN, O. (1982) 'Sport and the Feminist Novel' *Physical Education Review* 5, 2, pp. 100–6.

MOIR, E. (1977) *Female Participation in Physical Activities*, Dunfermline College of Physical Education.

NEWSON, J. and NEWSON, E. (1963) *Patterns of Infant Care in an Urban Community*, London, Allen and Unwin

NEWSON, J. and NEWSON, E. (1968) *Four Years Old in an Urban Community*, London, Allen and Unwin.

NEWSON, J. and NEWSON, E. (1976) *Seven Years Old in an Urban Community*, London, Allen and Unwin.

TALBOT, M. (1981) 'Women and sport: social aspects,' *Journal of Biological Social Sciences* 7, pp. 33–47

SAUNDERS, C. (1979) 'Pupil involvement in physical activities in comprehensive schools,' *Bulletin of Physical Education* 15, pp. 25–32.

SMAIL, B. (1984) *Girl-Friendly Science: Avoiding Sex Bias in the Curriculum*, York, Longmans/Schools Council.

Bruce Carrington and Oliver Leaman

SPENDER, D. (1982) *Invisible Women: the Schooling Scandal*, London, Readers and Writers Publishing Cooperative.

SPORTS COUNCIL (1982) *Sport in the Community: The Next Ten Years*, London, Sports Council.

STANWORTH, M. (1981) *Gender and Schooling A Study of Sex Divisions in the Classroom*, London, Women; Research and Resources Centre.

TRIESMAN, D. (1980) Politics and Sport, *Marxism Today*, June, pp. 12–17.

WILLIS, P. (1974) 'Performance and meaning — a sociocultural view of women in sport' in GLAISTER, I.K. (Ed.) *Physical Education — An Integrating Force*, London, ATCDE pp. 46–60.

Contributors

Len Almond lectures in the Department of Physical Education and Sports Science at the University of Technology, Loughborough and is Director of a two-year project funded by the Health Education Council on Health-based physical education. He has published widely on the Physical Education Curriculum and is author of a booklet on 'Evaluation in a PE department' and co-author of 'Rethinking Games Teaching'.

Les Bell is Senior Lecturer in Education at the University of Warwick. He taught in primary and secondary schools before joining the staff of Coventry College of Education which merged with the University of Warwick. He has particular interests in school organization and management and has published a number of articles in these fields.

Bruce Carrington is a Lecturer in the School of Education, University of Newcastle Upon Tyne. He has written articles on young people and leisure, ethnicity and education and child abuse. His current research interests include: sport and leisure in the Asian Community and the occupational culture of teachers.

Bob Carroll is a Lecturer in Physical Education at the University of Manchester. He has nine years' teaching experience in schools and has published articles on PE, Leisure, Tennis and Social Theory.

Brian Davies is Professor of Education in the Centre for Educational Studies, King's College Chelsea (KQC). He was formerly Senior Lecturer in Sociology at the University of London Institute of Education and lectured at Goldsmith's College, London, after a period as a school teacher. He has written widely on the sociology of education and is author of *Education and Social Control* (1976) and the editor of an issue of *Educational Analysis* which dealt with the *State of Schooling*.

Colin Embrey Following a period with Shrewsbury Town Football Club and working as an engineer, Colin taught Physical Education and was Head of Boys' PE for seven years. He is now Head of House at Longtree Comprehensive near Reading.

John Evans taught in comprehensive schools before embarking on research into mixed ability teaching methods at the London Institute of Education. He now teaches the Sociology of Education and Physical Education in the Faculty of Educational Studies, University of Southampton. He is author of *Teaching in Transition: The Challenge of Mixed Ability Grouping* (1985) and has published widely in the sociology of education.

Leo B. Hendry is Senior Lecturer in Education, Department of Physical Education, University of Aberdeen. He has been a school teacher in England and Scotland, a lecturer and Head of Department in Colleges of Education for seven years, and has worked within the University of Aberdeen since 1971. He has published over fifty research papers and his major book publications include: *Teaching Physical Education in England and Wales; Schooling Sport and Leisure: three dimensions of adolescence; Towards Community Education; Growing Up and Going Out.*

Barbara Humberstone teaches Physical Education and Outdoor Pursuits in the Department of Physical Education at the University of Southampton. She taught for nine years in secondary schools and was formerly responsible for the Outdoor Pursuits programme at a Sixth Form College. Her current research is into gender and schooling particularly in outdoor education and physical education.

David Kirk is a Lecturer in the Department of Human Movement Studies, University of Queensland. He taught Physical Education in a Scottish secondary school before studying at the University of Glasgow and Loughborough University. His main interests are in Curriculum Studies, and he has published papers in a number of curriculum and physical education journals.

Oliver Leaman is a Lecturer in Philosophy at the Department of Education, Liverpool Polytechnic. He is Author of *Sit on the Sidelines and Watch the Boys Play: Sex Differentiation in Physical Education* (1984); 'Physical Education, dance and outdoor pursuits', in Craft, A. and Bardell, G., (Eds.) *Curriculum Opportunities in a Multicultural Society*, (1984).

Sheila Scraton is a full time research student in the School of Education, Open University. She taught for eight years in secondary schools and was formerly Head of Physical Education and Leisure Activities at Widnes Sixth Form College. Her current research is into gender and physical education.

Andrew Sparkes has taught Physical Education in Comprehensive, Public and Special schools. He is currently Lecturer in Physical Education in the Department of Physical Education and Sports Science, University of Technology, Loughborough. His special interests are the sociology of innovation and qualitative research methods.

Index